Making Money With
Option Strategies

Making Money With Option Strategies

Powerful Hedging Ideas for the
Serious Investor to Reduce Portfolio Risks

By Michael C. Thomsett

THE CAREER PRESS, INC.

This edition first published in 2016 by Career Press, an imprint of
Red Wheel/Weiser, LLC
With offices at:
65 Parker Street, Suite 7
Newburyport, MA 01950
www.redwheelweiser.com
www.careerpress.com

ISBN: 978-1-63265-046-7
Library of Congress Cataloging-in-Publication Data available upon request.

Cover design by Rob Johnson/Toprotype
Cover photograph © Nick M. Do/istock
Interior by Diana Ghazzawi

Printed in the United States of America
IBI
10 9 8 7 6 5 4 3 2 1

Contents

Introduction | Solving the Time and Proximity Issues

Options trading is a paradox.

It can be highly speculative or highly conservative, or both, depending on when and how it is used. This paradox can be employed to respond to the unceasing symptom of investing in the stock market: Those who buy shares of stock worry, no matter how price moves. If price moves up, should you take profits now? If price moves down, should you cut your losses or buy more shares? Owning stock is a troubling activity because of the uncertainties it involves. Options—with the paradox they bring to the picture—can solve some of the risk issues for you.

A lot of focus in the market is on short-term trading opportunities, and these exist without any doubt. However, the more permanent value of options trading is not in short-term profit potential, but in how options can reduce risk in your portfolio. At the same time, reducing risk and generating income is an elegant combination of features. The flexibility of options is the great advantage; as a hedge against risk, an options position can also generate income and enable you to take profits without needing to sell shares. For most traders, identifying high-risk versus low-risk strategies is where emphasis is placed. This is not a simple matter, because the rapidly changing stock and options markets define emerging risks and opportunities that change from day to day and even from minute to minute. Within this ever-changing situation, today's high-risk option can be tomorrow's low-risk solution.

This suggestion—that "risk" is situational and not position-specific—is one way to look at options. In this book, the idea is demonstrated through examination of strategies designed to hedge positions, reduce risk, and generate income.

The distinction between speculative and conservative is not merely an issue of which strategy you employ, but when and in what proximity a price is found. "Proximity" in this sense refers to how close the strike of an option (the price at which it can be bought or sold) is to the current price of the underlying stock. It also

7

refers to how close price is to the top (resistance) or bottom (support) of the trading range.

Reversal is most likely to occur when price is close to resistance or support, especially when price moves through these range borders. Reversal back into range is very likely; the trading range brings structure to the price chart, and significant events such as breakout above resistance or below support point the way to trading opportunities.

This is where options play a role.

Chapter 1 of this book begins with a summary of the basics: terminology, terms of each option, and how trading works. For many traders, this is familiar ground, but for many more it is new and perhaps even mysterious. The purpose of this chapter is to set the foundation for understanding options. Because these are complex trading devices with exotic jargon and rules, many traders just stay away. But this means they miss opportunities to reduce risk and manage portfolio exposure in all types of markets.

Throughout the book, as terms are introduced for the first time, they are shown in boldface and italics. Every term is also defined in the glossary at the end of the book.

The next topic is hedging, covered in Chapter 2. A hedge is nothing more than a method for offsetting risk, consisting of a limitation or even elimination of exposure. Following this is an explanation of how option valuation works in Chapter 3. The "moneyness" of options (referring to the fixed strike price versus ever-changing value of the underlying stock) is one element in valuation. The other element is time remaining until the expiration of the option.

Chapter 4 offers an examination of the differences between speculation with options and conservative application of options. Unlike most products, options cover the entire risk range and can be tailored to fit any risk profile. In this book, the assumed profile is that of an investor with a portfolio of stocks, whose interest is in developing conservative hedging strategies.

Following this, Chapter 5 explains charting and trade timing. Though this topic is usually of interest only to day traders and swing traders, even a buy-and-hold investor benefits by being able to recognize the exaggerated price movement of a stock in specific circumstances; for example, after an earnings surprise, price tends to overreact, only to correct itself within two to three sessions. Knowing this, a conservative investor can use options to create short-term income and even out the momentary price movements—all with little risk.

Chapter 6 begins with what has become the favorite options strategy among traders: the covered call. This is a strategy combining capital gains on stock, dividend income, and premium from selling a call. The risks are low, explaining the popularity of the strategy. However, there is a lot to say about covered call. Not only should they be opened on carefully selected stocks; there are very real risks as well. With any strategy, including covered calls, knowing the risks before entering the strategy is essential as part of a conservative strategy.

An interesting twist on covered calls is introduced in Chapter 7. The uncovered put seems at first glance to be the opposite of a covered call. In fact, it is in many ways an identical strategy with the same market risks. This chapter explains the risks of uncovered puts and compares them to the covered call.

In Chapter 8, the discussion is expanded with introduction of the spread. This is the simultaneous opening of two different options with dissimilar strikes, expiration dates, or both. The risk levels vary considerably, so the full range of spread types is explained here with careful attention paid to the risk level and where spreads help you to manage your portfolio positions.

Chapter 9 expands on the basic spread with an examination of two types: the butterfly and the condor. Both are described in this section as 1-2-3, a reference to opening of three different positions with different expiration dates. This is an advanced set of strategies, but for those willing to monitor positions, they can offer a variation on the portfolio that introduces some interesting cash-generation possibilities.

Chapter 10 introduces more variations: collars and synthetic stock hedges. These present opportunities to cap risks when stock prices turn volatile.

Chapter 11 explains how straddles work. These are viewed by many investors as overly risky, but they do not have to be. These devices—opening two options with the same strike and expiration date—can be designed to provide potential profits with minimum risks.

Chapter 12 explains the "roll," a technique in which one option is closed and another opened with a later expiration date. This is done to avoid exercise. The roll is appropriate in many circumstances, but not in all.

Chapter 13 moves into new territory by explaining how to recover once the underlying price declines.

Following this, Chapter 14 covers collateral and tax rules for options trading.

Chapter 15 discusses importance of proximity between price and technical signals, and how this affects timing of options trades.

The whole range of options trading is complex, but only because so many investors have not learned the rules, terminology, and risks involved. Once these are mastered, options trading is more easily understood and mastered. None of the aspects for options trading is beyond your abilities, even though the complexity often is what gets emphasized. This book remains basic and non-technical in how the issues of this topic are explained. The purpose is to introduce a range of hedging methods and to demonstrate how everyone can learn options and apply them with full awareness of—and management over—the risks.

1 | The Basics of Options

The options market is characterized by specialized jargon and terminology. This chapter explains all of the terms used and places them in context for you, as an investor. Beyond definitions, you also need to grasp the essential trading rules and to be able to read options listings found online or in the financial press.

This chapter presents a broad overview of the options market as a starting point for folding an options strategy into an equity portfolio; identifying specific risks; and understanding how to mitigate or remove an equity-based *market risk*.

Attributes of the Option Contract

Options are intangible contracts, granting their buyers specific rights (and imposing obligations on sellers). The amazing attribute of options is that they can be used in many ways, covering the spectrum from highly speculative to highly conservative. Most investors cannot be classified as strictly speculative or conservative, but tend to operate within a range of risk levels. These levels change based on the circumstances, including market conditions, stock prices, and the amount of cash in a trading account.

With these variations in mind, options are perfect vehicles due to their flexibility. The degree of risk you can undertake based on how you use options is not fixed any more than your risk tolerance. The *leverage* of options is very attractive as well. However, depending on how that leverage is applied, it can increase or decrease your risk.

> **Key Point**
>
> Options are intangible contracts granting specific rights to their buyers and obligations to their sellers.

For example, options typically cost 3% to 5% of 100 shares of stock. So buying a single option is a highly leveraged way to benefit from favorable stock price

11

movement—or to suffer the risk of unfavorable movement. The percentage of option cost varies due to the specific terms of that option.

The flexibility of options is one of the primary attractions among investors. In addition to the pure speculator, many conservative investors with a buy-and-hold portfolio will trade options with a small portion of capital, as a form of "side bet" on the market. This not only brings up the chance for added profits, but also allows investors to take advantage of price movement in their stocks. Rather than sell to take profits, options can be used to capture those profits without giving up stock. And when a stock price is likely to decline, options can also be used to limit risks. In other words, options are flexible enough to allow you to manage portfolio risks while continuing to hold stocks in your portfolio.

The Leverage Benefit (and Risk)

Because option values are determined by price movement in the stock itself, the skillful use of options as a leverage tool presents many opportunities. For many, the option is an alternative to actually owning stock, so as a purely speculative tool, the leverage appeals to this group of traders. However, leverage also provides hedging value by setting up risk limitation as well as alternative forms of profit creation based on portfolio positions.

> **Key Point**
> Leverage is generally not conservative because it involves borrowing money to invest. Options are the exception, a form of leverage that does not involve borrowing.

Leverage is normally associated with borrowing and, in that regard, most forms of leverage are also high-risk investing strategies. Borrowing money to invest does not seem to most people like a prudent decision. However, even the most conservative investors trade on margin, meaning they can buy 100 shares of stock with 50% cash and 50% leverage. So even when you consider yourself very conservative, you might be using risky leverage in your own margin account.

This means that every investor trading in a margin account is exposed to the risk of leverage through borrowing. This approach might seem wise. You can buy 100 shares of a $50 stock for only $25 per share; as the stock price rises, the return on your $2,500 cash investment is twice as much as it would be when paying all cash. However, if the stock price declines, the loss also is accelerated. So if the $50 stock falls to $42, you lose $800, or 32% of the $2,500 you put at risk. However, you still owe your broker $2,500. Your leveraged debt is $2,500, but the cash portion of your investment has dropped to $1,700.

This demonstrates that leverage based on borrowing money means that both profits and losses are accelerated. So leverage (meaning borrowing money) can represent considerable risks. These risks are removed when you trade options as hedges against your portfolio. You can pay cash to buy options at a small percentage of the cost of 100 shares, and the most you can lose is the amount you pay, never any more.

Terms of Options

To completely understand how options provide hedging benefits, you need to master the jargon of this industry. Every option is uniquely defined by its four *standardized terms*. These terms define the option and always work in the same way, meaning all of the terms apply to all listed options (thus, they are standardized). So when you buy or sell an option, you know exactly what your contractual terms are for that asset.

The four terms are:

1. **Type of option.** There are two, and only two, "types" of options: *calls* and *puts*. A call grants its owner the right, but not the obligation, to buy 100 shares of stock, at a fixed strike price and by or before its expiration. A put grants its owner the right, but not the obligation, to sell 100 shares of stock, at a fixed strike price and by or before its expiration.

2. **Strike price.** This is the fixed price at which a call or a put can be traded. This price remains fixed for the entire life of the option regardless of the stock's price.

3. **Underlying security.** Every option is tied to a specific stock or other security (such as a stock index or exchange-traded fund, for example). This cannot be changed during the limited lifetime of the option.

4. **Expiration date.** This is the month and date when each option ceases to exist. Every option is identified by expiration month. In addition, listed options expire on the third Saturday of that month, and the last trading day is the third Friday.

Expression of an option is quite specific and is based on these four standardized terms. Here are two examples:

JNJ Oct 95 c (Johnson & Johnson, call with a 95 strike price, expiring in October)

MCD Mar 100 p (McDonald's, put with a 100 strike price, expiring in March)

The stock symbol for each stock (JNJ or MCD, for example) is used in an options listing or description. The expiration month is normally reduced to a three-digit summary without a period. The strike is always expressed at the price per share but without dollar signs.

> **Key Point**
> Options are expressed in a specific form of shorthand. Mastering these expressions is essential in options trading.

If the option is not a round dollar per share value, it is expressed as dollars and cents to two digits, also without dollar signs. So if the strike is 99.50, that means the strike is equal to $99.50 per share. In describing options and stocks, the use of dollar signs is always used to explain the price per share of stock, but never options. So a 99.50 option on a stock currently priced at $99.75 is how the situation is expressed.

The Price of Options

The price of each option is called its *premium* and it is always written as the price per share. So if the premium of a 99 call is $215, it is expressed as 2.15. Expanding the listing of an option to include the premium value, the following examples include premium:

> JNJ Oct 95 c @ 1.40 (Johnson & Johnson, call with a 95 strike price, expiring in October, with current premium value of 1.40, or $140)

> MCD Mar 100 p @ 7 (McDonald's, put with a 100 strike price, expiring in March, with current premium value of 7, or $700)

Figure 1.1 illustrates the terms of the option.

Figure 1.1: Terms of the Option

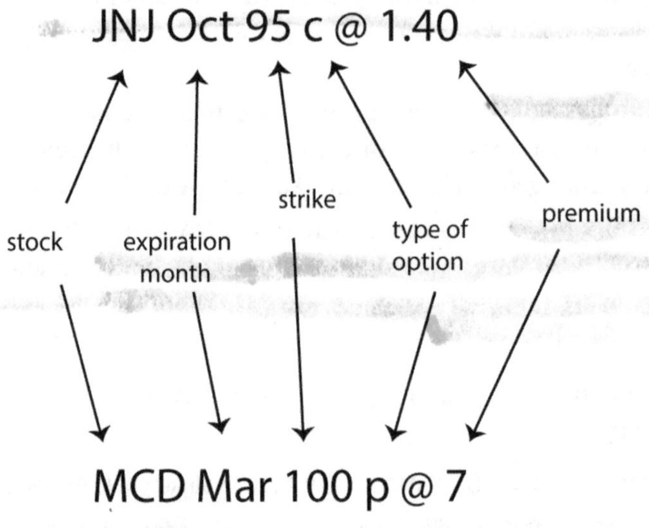

Like most securities, options also are expressed at both bid and ask prices. The ask is the price you pay to buy the option, and the *bid* is the price you receive for selling the option. For example, the JNJ Oct 95 c @ 1.40 is the bid price for that option, or what a seller receives. And the MCD Mar 100 p @ 7 describes a put worth $700.

Long and Short Positions

Expanding beyond the listing, every option can be either bought or sold. The bid price (what sellers receive) and the ask price (what buyers pay) are included in every options listing. When you buy an option, you are *long*; when you sell, you are *short*. The distinction is one of sequence. A long position is the well-known "buy-hold-sell" sequence. The short position is the opposite, or "sell-hold-buy."

This reversal of the sequence is confusing for many investors accustomed to first buying a security and then later selling. However, you can open a position that is either long or short with options, and the risks are different for each. Just as a buyer has the right to buy or sell 100 shares, the seller is exposed to the possibility of *exercise*, meaning a call owner will "call" 100 shares and the seller is required to deliver those shares at the strike, even when the market value is much higher. It also means a put owner will "put" 100 shares to the seller, meaning the seller is required to accept 100 shares at the strike, even when the market value is much lower.

The buyer of an option enters an opening trade, called "buy to open," and a later a closing trade, called "sell to close." Everyone who has bought and sold stock is familiar with these definitions. However, for those who enter a short position by opening with a sale, the opening trade is called "sell to open" and the closing trade is called "buy to close." These distinctions are important because the distinctions—buy versus sell and open versus close—define the action you take each time you trade an option. Many traders describe the closing of a short option as "buying back" the option. This is misleading and confusing, because the buy to close occurs based on the initial opening of a short position. There is no "buying back" action because the trader never owned the position to begin with.

To compare buying and selling consider the important differences between calls and puts and between long and short, illustrated in Table 1.1.

Table 1.1: Terms of the Options

Call	Put
Grants the right but not the obligation to buy 100 shares of the underlying stock before expiration and at the fixed strike	Grants the right but not the obligation to sell 100 shares of the underlying stock before expiration and at the fixed strike
Increases in value if the underlying security's price rises	Increases in value if the underlying security's price falls
Long traders want the underlying price to rise	Long traders want the underlying price to fall
Short traders want the underlying price to fall	Short traders want the underlying price to rise
Long positions are opened with a "buy to open" order and closed with a sell to close" order	
Short positions are opened with a sell to open" order and closed with a buy to close" order	

Where This Gets Confusing

Anyone new to jargon is going to struggle to grasp the concepts. With options, the opposites—call versus put, long versus short, buy versus sell—can be very difficult to put into context. To aid in clarifying these differences, keep in mind that:

- A call is the right to buy, and the put is the right to sell.
- Buyers of calls and puts gain the right to buy or sell, and sellers have an obligation to accept exercise if and when it happens.
- A long position starts with a "buy" order and ends with a "sell" order.
- A short position starts with a "sell" order and ends with a "buy" order.

Key Point
Options involve a series of opposites, so understand this is the
key to mastering options trading.

These definitions are of crucial importance in developing an understanding of the many potential hedging strategies you can apply to your portfolio. Among the difficulties faced by those new to options is the concept of profiting from a price decline. Most investors grasp the idea that investment is profitable when prices rise. However, thinking of the put as the opposite of a call, it becomes clearer why the put becomes profitable when the stock price falls.

The difficulty of jargon becomes clearer when specific strategies are introduced and aided by examples of outcomes. Price direction defines risk. So options working as hedges for portfolio positions (usually meaning long stock held in the portfolio) can involve either calls or puts, opened as either long or short trades.

The Option Premium's Three Types of Value

Every stockholder understands that stock has a single value: the price per share. This changes daily based on many influencing factors, but the value of a share of stock is universally agreed upon. With options, however, it is not as simple.

There are *three* distinct and separate types of value that make up the total premium of the option. Once you understand how these values interact, you will have a clearer understanding of why option-based hedging works so well. The influences on changing option value are not based only on movement of the underlying stock, but also on *volatility* and time.

Volatility of stock is often represented by *beta*, a measurement of how a stock's price follows or responds to the larger market. This comparison is made between the stock and a benchmark index like the S&P 500. A beta of 1.0 indicates that the stock will rise and fall at 100% of the rise or fall in the benchmark. A higher beta equals higher volatility, and a lower beta equals less responsiveness or lower volatility.

This is all relevant to option premium because the underlying stock's volatility (called historical volatility) is going to show up in the option as well. Whereas volatility is a clear factor in levels of option value, proximity between the option's strike and the underlying stock's price is another factor. So there are three key factors adding to value of the option: volatility, time, and proximity (between strike of the option and price of the stock). This proximity is called the *moneyness* of an option.

Every option may be in the money (when the stock price is higher than a call's strike or lower than a put's strike); at the money (when the stock price is exactly the same as the option's strike); or out of the money (when the stock price is lower than a call's strike or higher than a put's strike). Figure 1.2 illustrates the moneyness of options.

Figure 1.2: Moneyness of Options

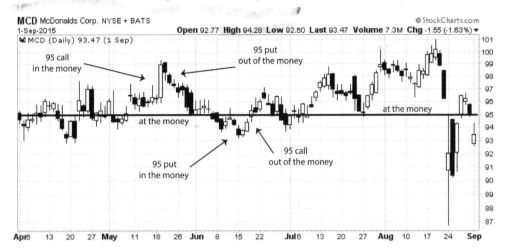

The chart demonstrates the moneyness of calls and puts. With strikes of 95, calls and puts are at the money (ATM) when the underlying stock is worth $95 per share. The in-the-money (ITM) and out-of-the-money (OTM) status are opposite for calls and puts.

> **Key Point**
>
> The "moneyness" of options determines option pricing and, more to the point, also identifies levels of risk.

With moneyness of options, it is easy to determine whether an option is in or out of the money. This leads to the definition of the first type of option premium: *intrinsic value*.

This value is easy to identify. For example, with a strike of 45, a call is 3 points in the money when the stock price is $48 per share. So the call has 3 points ($300) of intrinsic value. If the stock price is $45, the call is at the money; and any price below $45 per share means the 45 call is out of the money and has no intrinsic value.

For puts, the same rules apply but in the opposite direction. A 45 put is in the money by 2 points if the stock price is $43 per share. At a stock price of $45 per share, the put is at the money. And any time the stock price is higher than $45, the 45 put is out of the money and has no intrinsic value.

In trading options, the moneyness demonstrates that when proximity is close, there tends to be a more immediate reaction between overall option pricing and stock movement. When an option is in the money, intrinsic value changes point for point with movement in the stock. However, this does not mean the overall premium value tracks the stock precisely. The two other forms of option premium, time value and volatility, work together to also adjust the premium levels of options. With time value, increases in intrinsic value may be offset with a decrease, so the overall premium is not entirely responsive to stock movement. And volatility value also affects premium in either direction, depending on proximity and time.

Key Point
Time value is a depreciating form of price, and the closer the option is to expiration, the more rapidly it decays.

Time value is the portion of an option's premium directly related to the time remaining until expiration. It declines over the lifetime of the option, reaching zero by expiration day. As expiration approaches, the decline in time value (called *time decay*) accelerates as well.

Time value (like intrinsic value) is completely predictable. The curve of time decay increases toward the end of the option's life cycle, taking time value down to zero on the last trading day. This is shown in Figure 1.3.

Figure 1.3: Time Decay of an Option

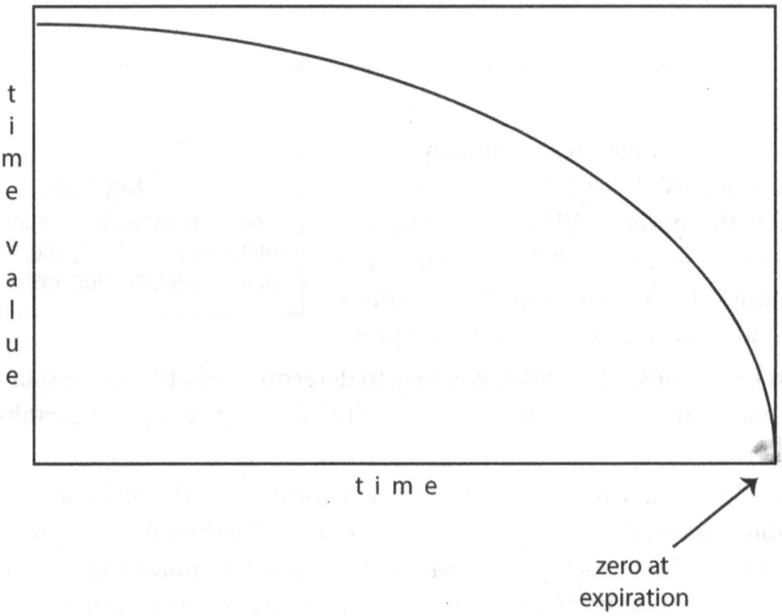

zero at
expiration

Time value affects overall premium in predictable ways, and you can see this effect in a study of an option's listing. For example, On October 1, 2015, IBM was trading at $142.64 per share. At that time calls and puts with three different expirations were trading at the following prices, as Table 1.2 indicates.

Table 1.2: IBM $142.64 – option premium levels

October (15 days)

Strike	Calls		Puts	
	Bid	Ask	Bid	Ask
140	4.40	4.55	1.82	1.85
145	1.59	1.62	3.90	4.05

November (51 days)

Strike	Calls		Puts	
	Bid	Ask	Bid	Ask
140	6.60	6.75	4.80	4.95
145	3.90	4.00	7.30	7.40

December (79 days)

Strike	Calls		Puts	
	Bid	Ask	Bid	Ask
140	7.25	7.50	5.75	5.85
145	4.70	4.80	8.00	8.25

Several interesting observations can be made about this summary. First, the differences in premium between the 140 and 145 strikes occurred because of the moneyness of the options. With a stock price between the two strikes, the 140 calls were all in the money; and the 145 puts were all in the money. The large differences in premium between these two strikes is explained by intrinsic value. For the 140 calls,

> **Key Point**
> A comparison of option values in and out of the money demonstrates how and why prices vary even for the same expiration month.

intrinsic value is 2.64 (142.64 – 140.00); and for the 145 puts, the intrinsic value is 2.36 (145.00 – 142.64).

Beyond intrinsic value, there remains a combination of time value and implied volatility. The effect of time value is easily observed. In the case of both calls and puts, overall premium increases with time. So 15-day, 51-day, and 79-day time remaining to expiration demonstrates the role of time in setting overall premium.

The final type of value is where all of the uncertainty comes into play. *Implied volatility (IV)* is the portion of option premium that varies based on volatility in the underlying stock and time remaining until expiration. This type of premium may also be termed *extrinsic value.*

Some options insiders lump time and intrinsic value together and call it "time value" collectively. This is a misleading characterization because time value is very specific, and intrinsic value may rise or fall during the lifetime of the option. When the two are classified together, it is possible for time value to increase based on higher volatility, and this confuses the distinctions between the roles of volatility and time. By keeping them separate, a focus on analysis can be limited to implied volatility, where all of the uncertainty will be found.

The distance to expiration determines how implied volatility works. When many months remain, movement of intrinsic value often is offset by changes in implied volatility, so very little overall change in premium will be seen. But the closer to expiration, the more "cause and effect" you see in the IV premium. Volatility declines toward the end of the option's life to a point where it—like time value—has little, if any, impact on the price of the option. By the last trading day, an in-the-money option will contain almost all intrinsic value without time or volatility. Any out-of-the-money options will have very little value remaining, and the further out of the money, the lower the premium value.

> **Key Point**
> Implied volatility (IV) is a reaction to the volatility in the underlying stock, but also to the time remaining until expiration of the option.

For options with several months remaining, volatility can be expected to change often, and rapidly. When the stock's volatility increases, so will option premium (due to its implied volatility). So as a timing strategy, many investors and traders try to time entry and exit based on changes in the implied volatility levels, buying at low volatility and selling at high volatility. This makes sense, but the rapid changes and unpredictability of volatility make this a difficult task to accomplish consistently. Combining volatility analysis with a study of the underlying stock's price chart may add more clarity and predictability to the timing of trades.

Volatility is studied by a series of calculations collectively called the **Greeks**. This name is used due to the definition of each with letters from the Greek alphabet. These calculations help determine the volatility levels of options and the level of reaction by options to the price movement in the underlying stock.

The first among the Greeks is **Delta**. This measures the change in option premium in comparison to a change in the underlying stock. A reaction level is affected by time remaining until expiration as well as by the moneyness of options. So an option whose strike is closer to the stock price is likely to be more responsive than one that is deep in or out of the money.

Delta is the most-used of the Greeks. It is a measure of the change in option premium relative to the change in the underlying stock. It ranges from –1.00 to 0 for puts, and from 0 to 1.00 for calls. With volatility at mid-level, an at-the-money option should have a Delta of 0.50 (for calls) or –0.50 (for puts). This is a fair measurement of whether a current option premium is reasonable. When at the money, if the call's Delta is higher or a put's delta is lower, it indicates an increase in volatility.

When the option moves in the money (meaning the stock price moves above the call's strike or below the put's strike), Delta should change by one-half of the degree of movement. So a 1-point move in the underlying stock would be accompanied by a 0.50-point change in Delta. As long as volatility levels remain unchanged, this rule will apply. Any variation points to higher or lower volatility. So Delta is a good measurement of this relationship.

> **Key Point**
> Delta is a reliable measure of the relationship between option price and stock market value.

As expiration approaches, Delta tends to change its rate of reaction to the stock price. However, a related concept, *volatility collapse*, makes volatility unreliable to measure during the final month of an option's life.

Closely related to Delta is *Gamma*, a measurement of the degree of change in Delta. When options are deep out of the money (usually defined as 5 points or more distance between strike and underlying price), Delta is usually quite low; but as those options move toward the money, Delta increases. The degree of increase is measured by Gamma.

Theta is a separate type of Greek. It measures the decline in time value. Although the tendency to accelerate time decay is entirely predictable, the speed of change is not the same for all options. So some experience rapid time decay while others move more slowly.

Theta normally is higher for out-of-the-money options when implied volatility is also higher than average. This would imply that volatility affects time value. However, because time and volatility value are often placed together as a single attribute of price, this indication is false. The change in what appears to be time value often is change in IV, which is a separate price element.

The next Greek is *Vega*. Although not a Greek letter, it is included as a "Greek" for the purpose of option analysis. Vega measures the rise or fall in an option's premium caused by IV. Two factors can be seen with Vega. First, it will change even when the underlying stock price does not move, due to changes in volatility. Second, as expiration approaches, Vega tends to decline. This can be best used to identify the speed of volatility collapse.

Calculation of the Greeks can be complex. The best way to find these indicators is to use the free calculator provided by the Chicago Board Options Exchange. This calculator enables you to identify all of the Greeks and to track their change over time; and also to identify levels of implied volatility.

Calculation of Option Return

> **Resource**
> To calculate the Greeks and implied volatility, use the free calculator at *http://bit.ly/28dQfkN*

It might seem that figuring out the return on an option trade would be quite simple. In fact, it is a challenge. In order to compare two or more trades, three inhibiting factors arise. First, what is the *basis* for the calculation? Second, how long was a position open? Third, do you base the calculation on options only, or do you include dividend income and capital gains as well?

Determining the Basis

The basis price for calculating returns should be used for each and every trade, so that the outcome will be expressed on the same terms. If you use the original cost of stock as the basis, you will get many different outcomes based on how much change has occurred between purchase date and option trade date; so this is not a reliable basis. The same problem is found in the current value of stock. This value will change by the time the option is closed or expires, so the outcome for different positions will also be inconsistent. The only reasonable basis for options trade is the strike. This price does not change, and it will be the price used if and when the option is exercised.

Making the Outcome Accurate

The basis is a good starting point, but how long will the position remain open? In order to reflect outcomes for two or more different options trades, you need to *annualize* the return. This means each return is calculated as if the position was open for one full year. This is necessary because a return achieved over a short period of time is worth more than the same net return over a longer period of time.

To demonstrate how this works, refer again to Table 1.2 on page 19.

To determine which option is a more profitable choice, do you pick the 15-, 51-, or 79-day contract? At first glance it looks like the 79-day call with a 140 strike is the best choice because it is worth significantly more money. However, when you annualize, you discover that shorter-term options yield much better annualized returns.

The steps in annualizing are:

1.   Calculate the net return, dividing option premium by the strike.
2.   Divide the return by the holding period.
3.   Multiply the result by a full year.

To accurate annualize returns, use the proper value (in the case of a long option, use the ask price; for short options use the bid). Next, estimate the transaction costs for options. Most online discount brokers charge approximately $9 for a single option, so throughout this book that is the trading cost level that will be used.

It is important to also understand that the cost is reduced for multiple contracts. For example, after the first option, the cost for additional contracts is quite small, so the more options traded, the lower the transaction cost. For example, Charles Schwab applies $8.75 for a single option and $0.75 for each additional contract traded (per *www.schwab.com*).

Table 1.3: IBM $142.64 – option premium levels

October (15 days)

Strike	Calls		Puts	
	Bid	Ask	Bid	Ask
140	4.40	4.55	1.82	1.85
145	1.59	1.62	3.90	4.05

November (51 days)

Strike	Calls		Puts	
	Bid	Ask	Bid	Ask
140	6.60	6.75	4.80	4.95
145	3.90	4.00	7.30	7.40

December (79 days)

Strike	Calls		Puts	
	Bid	Ask	Bid	Ask
140	7.25	7.50	5.75	5.85
145	4.70	4.80	8.00	8.25

For illustration of how this works, the following example is based on single option trades and rounding of transaction costs up to $9.00. Referring to the chart and assuming the sale of the 140 calls, the bid price for each were reported:

October (15 days) 4.40

November (51 days) 6.60

December (79 days) 7.25

When an option is sold, the transaction cost is deducted from the bid price (and when an option is bought, the transaction cost is added to the ask price). Converting these bid price premium values to dollars and then subtracting the transaction cost:

October (15 days) $440 – $9 = $431

November (51 days) $660 – $9 = $651

December (79 days) $725 – $9 = $716

Next, calculate the return based on the 140 strike for 100 shares:

October (15 days) $431 ÷ $14,000 = 3.08%

November (51 days) $651 ÷ $14,000 = 4.65%

December (79 days) $716 ÷ $14,000 = 5.11%

The initial outcome still makes it seem that the December options are the most profitable. However, once annualized, the outcome changes:

October (15 days) 3.08% ÷ 15 days x 365 days = 74.95%

November (51 days) 4.65% ÷ 51 days x 365 days = 33.28%

December (79 days) 5.11% ÷ 79 days x 365 days = 23.61%

Once the returns are annualized, it becomes clear that the shorter-term positions yield significantly higher returns. However, the purpose of annualizing is to make accurate comparisons, and should not be used to assume the outcome you should expect in your portfolio. The calculation does not promise you the amazing return of 74.95% every year on your options trades, but it does provide a good measurement of which trades are most profitable.

What Else Should Be Included?

> **Key Point**
>
> Capital gains should definitely be considered in the overall outcome, but option returns have to be kept separate to avoid distortions.

Annualizing returns adds accuracy to comparisons between option trades. But beyond the option, what about dividends and capital gains? These are certainly going to be significant in the overall return from options trades, especially if the trade is based on a combination of stock ownership and options trades. In each hedge discussed in this book, the assumption is that stock is held in the portfolio, and options trades accompany these positions. So dividends and capital gains cannot be ignored.

Capital gains on stock are often a big factor in overall return. However, in comparing options, the capital gain should be kept separate. If you buy 100 shares of stock at $25 and the value grows to $40 by the time you begin trading options, the 15 points represents a 60% increase in value. However, if you buy those shares at $38 per share and trade 40 strike options, you have only 2 points, or 5.3% gain based on the $38 purchase price. So capital gains can distort an otherwise-accurate comparison between different options.

Dividends often are included in the calculation of option profits. This is called the *total return* method, meaning the total of options and dividends together. In most calculations, you first calculate the annualized return and then add in the dividend yield.

To make the point about the impact of dividend, Table 1.4 compares three different stocks and their prices and option premium in early October 2015:

Table 1.4

Number of options	Cost	Cost per option
1	$ 8.95	$8.95
2	9.70	4.85
3	10.45	3.48
4	11.20	2.80
5	11.95	2.39
10	15.70	1.57

With 15 days remaining until expiration, the option returns (adjusted for trading costs) are:

ConocoPhillips (COP) 0.82 ÷ 48.50 = 1.69%

Occidental Petroleum (OXY) 1.42 ÷ 66.00 = 2.15

Exxon Mobil (XOM) 0.66 ÷ 73.00 = 0.90

To annualize and add dividend yield:

ConocoPhillips (COP) 1.69% ÷ 15 x 365 = 41.12% + 6.17% = 47.29%

Occidental Petroleum (OXY) 2.15% ÷ 15 x 365 = 52.32% + 4.55% = 56.87%

Exxon Mobil (XOM) 0.90% ÷ 15 x 365 = 21.90% + 3.93% = 25.83%

Based on this analysis, the October short calls are most productive for Occidental Petroleum, using the total return method. However, the dividend calculation has to also be made with awareness of when quarterly dividends will be paid. It is possible to enter into a trade with no dividend yield. This occurs when the time between entering the position and the expiration of options includes no ex-dividend date (the date on which the current dividend is no longer earned). In spite of the above calculations using 15-day options, none of the stocks receives a dividend during the period in question.

It is also possible to earn two full quarterly dividends when holding a stock from just before one ex-dividend date until the following ex-dividend date. Rather than a full two quarters of 180 days, this could occur in approximately 91 days, or about one-half of the six months associated with two quarters of dividends. So in calculating total return, it is crucial that the actual number of quarterly dividends be considered with the timing of dividend earnings dates in mind.

Key Point

Quarterly dividends are earned as long as you are the stockholder of record when dividends are earned. This means you can pick expiration dates to maximize dividend yield.

The Option's Life Span

Many types of options are issued on company stock. The traditional listed option lasts as long as eight months. However, many companies also have weekly options, which expire in between the monthly cycles. On the opposite end of the spectrum, some options last as long as 30 months. These are called LEAPS options (long-term equity appreciation securities).

Every company with listed options is classified into one of three annual cycles. This identifies the months in which options expire. The cycles are for the months of January, April, July, and October (JAJO); February, May, August, and November (FMAN); and March, June, September, and December (MJSD). For each cycle, options exist for all of the quarter months and, in addition, options will be found for every month during the year with expiration within 30 days. So there is great flexibility and variety within the range of listings.

Another consideration for options trading is the distance between strikes. Lower-priced stocks tend to have options at every round dollar amount. Options trading up to $100 per share have 5-point increments; and above $100, most trade every $10. However, for shorter-term expirations, the 5- and 10-point increment stocks may also have increments every 2.5 points or even every point. The closer increments of strikes adds to the flexibility of trading, especially for strategies relying on minimal price movement.

Collateral Requirements

Most stock investors are familiar with the concept of trading on margin. You can buy shares of stock paying one-half and getting the rest on margin. This is a form of leverage that can be a great advantage, but also comes with risks. However, "margin" is different for options trading. The margin for options is calculated depending on the type of option and on whether or not an offsetting position (in stock or other options) is open at the same time.

> **Key Point**
> Margin for options is not a form of borrowing as it is for stock purchases; option margin identifies the collateral you must maintain.

A covered call (a short call opened when you also own 100 shares of stock) contains no margin requirement because, if exercised, the shares are called away. However, for all short options, a margin requirement applies. As a general rule, a single short option requires 20% to be placed on margin, adjusted by the premium received and also adjusted based on the moneyness of the option.

For example, you sell an uncovered put with a strike of 30 when the stock is at $32 per share. You receive a premium of 2 ($200). The margin requirement is calculated as:

20% of current stock value of $32 per share	$640
Minus proceeds of the option	200
Margin collateral	$440

In this example, the put is out of the money. If a put is in the money, the margin requirement is calculated by adding the proceeds. For example, you sell an uncovered put for 4 ($400) with a 30 strike when the stock at $29 per share, or 1 point in the money:

20% of current stock value of $29 per share	$580
Plus proceeds of the option	400
Margin collateral	$980

The next chapter expands on the basics by exploring how hedging works and how options protect stock positions in your portfolio.

Resource

To calculate margin requirement for any position, use the free calculator provided by the CBOE at *www.cboe.com/tradtool/mcalc/*. To learn more about how margin is applied, download the free Margin Manual at *www.cboe.com/learncenter/pdf/margin2-00.pdf*.

2 | The Hedging Concept and Its Application

Options traders struggle endlessly with *risk*. Long-term options are expensive and short-term options expire too soon. How do you profit in this environment?

Hedging is an expansion of options combination strategies, designed to solve this problem. *This is a conservative program for options used to manage a stock portfolio.* By creating offsetting hedge positions, traders are able to generate profits in three conditions: underlying price rises, they fall, or they do not move at all. Safety within the hedge is created by the offsetting long/short and call/put option structures.

The Most Basic Hedge

With emphasis on profits in the markets, it is easy to overlook the equally important aspect of investing: protecting capital. This refers not only to the capital you have investing in building a portfolio, but also to protecting profits accumulated in well-chosen stocks. The dilemma is unceasing: Do you take profits when they occur, or do you wait for more?

> **Key Point**
>
> The desire for profits is accompanied by the equally important need to preserve capital. This is where hedging enters the picture.

If you chose stock well and want to continue holding shares, why take profits? If you take profits now, where do you invest next? The problem every stockholder faces is this question of when (or whether) to take profits. Those who do often end up with a portfolio full of shares that have not become profitable. This means that, by taking profits, you have removed the best positions from your portfolio and are left with your capital tied up in paper losses.

The hedge is the solution to this problem, and the most basic of hedges involves using options to generate income while protecting paper profits. With option hedging, it is also possible to take profits without needing to sell shares you would prefer to keep.

The first hedge to review is the covered call. In Chapter 6, a detailed analysis of the covered call's opportunities and risks is presented. For the purpose of the overview of hedging in general, the covered call is the most popular hedge and the most obvious way to augment your equity portfolio. This position, involving 100 shares offset by the sale of one call, sets up a very advantageous situation with three sources of profit: capital gains on stock, premium income from the short call, and dividends.

For many, the most basic option strategy is to buy either a call or a put. A call is bought when the stock price declines, on the theory that the price will rebound. If that occurs, the cycle of price changes in the stock results in added profits from buying a call and then selling it at a profit. A put is bought when the stock price rises, based on the same theory: The cycle of stock pricing is likely to come back around and leads to a decline. At that time, the long put can be sold at a profit.

For example, consider a choice of buying a call at 3 ($300) or buying a put at 4 ($400) on McDonald's Corp (MCD). With a strike of 95, the breakeven point for the call is at $98 per share; and the breakeven for the put is $91 per share. These are illustrated in Figure 2.1.

Figure 2.1

Considering the general range of this stock over six months, there were times in which the breakeven was reached on either side. In the case of the put, the only example occurred in late August, when a marketwide decline occurred briefly. So buying calls and puts is largely a matter of timing. It also relies on skillful selection of options based on both price and expiration. For example, if the call was purchased in late May with a June expiration, it would never reach its breakeven. Even though the call would be in the money most of this time (above 95), the cost of the call inhibits the price from ever exceeding the breakeven. Between purchase date and expiration, time decay erodes premium value and so the breakeven would never be reached.

For the put, the breakeven at $91 per share was never reached with the brief exception of August and September. In this case, buying a put in late May with an August expiration would be a losing trade. The last trading day in August was August 21, and the big drop in price did not occur until August 24. So even with three months between the date of purchase and expiration, the 95 put would end up expiring worthless.

> **Key Point**
>
> Long option trading is a challenge due to time decay and volatility in the underlying stock, which affects cost. Long options, consequently, by themselves are poor hedges.

These examples reveal the problem with long options. They are intended to hedge the short-term volatility in the underlying security, but that works only if the stock is volatile enough to yield a profit. Even if it is, you still have to decide whether to speculate on the upside (with a long call) or the downside (with a long put). In the example of McDonald's, the stock moved 5 points higher only in one session over six months; and it only moved more than 2 points below $95 per share in the large market decline, after which the stock price returned into its established range.

The point is that in deciding to hedge a stock's price with long options, there has to be a balance between price and volatility. A low-volatility stock will be hedged with low-priced options, and a high-volatility stock's options will be more expensive. This tendency, a form of point spread, makes it difficult to time options profitably.

The theory behind speculating in long options is logical at first glance. A trader may rationalize that there is plenty of time before expiration and breakeven is only a few points away. However, long options are poor hedges due to one inhibiting factor: Time value declines, so that the value of the long call or put will fall as expiration approaches. So even if the stock price moves in the direction you need in order to make the option profitable, growth in intrinsic value is going to be offset by decline in time value. If you buy a very short-term option it will be cheap; however, time decay is accelerated and you will need a significant change in the stock's market value just to overcome the time value problem. If you buy a longer-term option, it will be more expensive, meaning you have to put more capital at risk. In that case, you still need significant point movement in the stock to offset the cost of the option.

The problems associated with long options—both short-term and long-term—make them poor hedges. It is difficult to produce a profitable outcome in the basic long option, so for consistent hedging you need to look beyond. This is why the covered call is the most popular option strategy. It solves two problems. First, because the call is short, a decline in time value is advantageous. A large number of covered calls are closed at a profit due primarily to the decline in time value. So it is sold to open and later bought to close for less, producing a net profit.

The second problem solved by the covered call is profit-taking. When a stock's price rises, the temptation is to take profits. However, selling a covered call at a strike near the current price yields an attractive premium. If the stock price retreats, the call can be closed at as profit. If the stock price remains at or below the strike, the short call will expire worthless. If the stock price rises, the call will be exercised and three forms of profit result: The call premium is yours to keep after exercise, so it represents a total profit. As long as the strike is higher than your basis in the stock, you also earn a capital gain when the stock is called away. Finally, you profit from all dividends earned while you held the stock.

This seems to present a winning situation no matter what happens. However, the covered call is not without risk. If the stock price falls below your **net basis**, you end up with a paper loss. Net basis in a covered call is the price per share, discounted by the sale of a covered call. When that occurs, the call will expire worthless but you end up with depreciated stock. This can be rationalized by arguing that without the covered call, the stock would have lost value and that the premium from the call reduces the paper loss.

Key Point

Covered calls are a popular and basic form of hedge, but as a first step, the company should be picked based on its fundamentals.

This does not mean that covered calls are poor hedges. In fact, they are excellent hedges when the alternative of simply holding stock is considered. If you are a long-time holder of shares, the paper loss will be of less concern than if you just want to get a profit and get out of the position as soon as possible.

The market risk of the covered call is mitigated by careful selection of a company whose stock you purchase. Every stockholder is wise to qualify a company based on its fundamental attributes and historical volatility, as a first step. This applies whether you just hold shares for the long term or you write covered calls. By picking exceptionally strong companies (in terms of fundamental strength over many years), the likely gyrations in stock price are going to be less of a factor than if the stock you buy is a fundamentally weaker company, whose price volatility is much higher. This is a common mistake made by investors who want to write covered calls. Intent on getting the highest possible premium, they are drawn to higher-risk companies. Consequently, they get a rich premium for the covered call, but they are exposed to higher market risks as well. A prudent covered call strategy works best when the company is selected as a first step based on its fundamental strength. The options will not yield as high a return for these more stable companies, but overall, the lower market risk makes this a sensible strategy.

A closely related hedge, and another alternative to buying calls or puts, is the uncovered put. This is counter-intuitive at first glance. Most investors consider any uncovered option to be high risk, but the uncovered put is not. Any option that is "uncovered" is not offset by a different position. The covered call is considered a safe strategy because the short call is covered by 100 shares of stock. If the call is exercised, 100 shares are called away at the strike. A short put cannot be covered in this way, so it has to be uncovered.

The uncovered put's market risk is identical to the market risk of the covered call. When you consider the risks of both, it is a downside movement that presents problems, both for the covered call and the uncovered put. In the case of the covered call, a decline below net basis creates a paper loss. For an uncovered put, a decline below the strike represents an exercise risk. Most investors think of covered calls in terms of upside risk, but this is inaccurate. The thinking is over-simplified. It goes like this: If the stock price declines, the call loses value and will eventually expire worthless, and that yields a profit. However, if the stock price rises above the call's strike, shares are called away and the added profit (points above the strike) is lost. So this *lost opportunity risk* is where the covered call emphasis is placed.

If the call's strike is higher than your basis in stock, exercise is one of several possible outcomes and produces a net profit. So it is a positive outcome. However, you should enter into a covered call strategy only if you are willing to have shares called away.

For the uncovered put, the perception in the market is also misplaced. The thinking is that if the underlying price declines below the put's strike, the put could be exercise, resulting in being forced to buy shares above current market value. This perception of the uncovered put as high risk is inaccurate. The put can be closed or rolled forward to avoid exercise. Considering that a price decline produces the same loss in either a covered call or an uncovered put, the characterization of the put as high risk is not accurate. As an alternative to the covered call but with the same market risk, the uncovered put is more flexible because it can be rolled without concern for the strike. Because there is no stock at exercise risk, the put can be replaced with a lower-strike put. The risk of the short put occurs when the stock price falls many points and results in exercise. This is the same risk as owning 100 shares of stock; the result of a decline is a loss of value in both cases.

Table 2.1 summarizes a comparison between covered calls and uncovered puts.

Table 2.1

Covered Calls	Uncovered Puts
The call is matched with 100 shares of stock.	No stock is held.
Stock can be purchased with 50% margin.	Uncovered puts require collateral.
Dividends are earned at long as stock is owned.	No dividends are earned.
Stock is called away when its price is higher than the call's strike.	Stock is put to the seller when its price is lower than the put's strike.
In-the-money calls can be rolled forward, but the strike should be higher than the net basis in stock.	In-the-money puts can be rolled forward to any strike.

Key Point

The covered call and uncovered put are stronger basic hedges than long calls or puts.

So as a basic hedge, the covered call and uncovered put are the starting points for a conservative hedging program. The more widely held belief that long calls and puts represent the basic conservative hedge overlooks the actual risk: With time decay, the long option is a long shot. If you buy an option expiring in the near future, time decay is accelerated. If you buy an option with more time remaining, the time value makes it a more expensive position to enter.

Combining Calls and Puts in a Hedging Position

Some traders recognize that stock prices are likely to move, but they are not sure of the direction. In this case, the combination of two or more options has a certain appeal. However, many of these strategies are speculative. There is a big difference between speculation and hedging.

Speculation is risk-taking, making a move with high risk in the hopes of making a big profit. In comparison, hedging is a more conservative set of strategies designed to place a cap on risk and also generating additional income.

So in considering a combination of calls and puts, this distinction has to be kept in mind. Some market insiders claim that risk cannot be avoided and is a fact of life. These insiders believe that investors have to diversify their holdings or enter into a program of **asset allocation**. **Diversification** is a worthy concept, but it does not always work. It often leads to bland returns or even losses. For example, the mutual fund industry, based entirely on a diversified portfolio placed under professional management, has a dismal record. Funds traditionally have performed below the benchmark market indexes. "Because of their excessive annual fees and poor execution, approximately 80% of mutual funds underperform the stock market's returns in a typical year," according to an article on Motley Fool (Bill Barker, "The Performance of Mutual Funds").

So what is all of the fuss about diversification? The professional management of mutual funds has notoriously been unable to deliver a net benefit better than market averages, so investing in an index fund that tracks the market is probably a better way to go.

Asset allocation is a similar tactic to diversification, but attempts to divide a portfolio into holdings by type (stocks, bonds, real estate, commodities). However, asset allocation is a responsive tactic, often determining how to divide up holdings after the problems have emerged. In many applications, asset allocation is not truly effective, but is used in some financial planning programs to convince clients that expertise can and does beat the market.

Key Point

Portfolio management based on diversification or asset allocation acknowledges the need to spread risks. Hedging challenges this and presents methods for reducing or eliminating risk.

Simply accepting risk as unavoidable is what leads to the decision to buy mutual fund shares, or to trust an institution to mandate how your holdings should be allocated. The idea is to accept the inevitability of risk and to spread it out. In comparison, hedging does not accept this idea, but presents a different argument: *Risk can be limited or eliminated with the right strategies.*

So rather than accepting risk as inevitable, or trusting a mutual fund management team to manage risks for you, the alternative is to seek ways to actually limit risk. This is by no means a revolutionary idea; it is simply the recognition that risk can be managed, anticipated, and controlled with hedging.

When options traders consider this idea, do they pick a speculative set of strategies or do they design a true hedging strategy? A speculative move involves taking a gamble that a stock price will move enough points before expiration, to exceed a breakeven price. Some speculative strategies include:

1. **Long spreads and straddles.** In its most rudimentary form, the spread involves a long call and a long put with different strike prices and the same expiration date. The risk level of the straddle is the combined cost of both options, plus transaction fees. To be profitable, the stock price has to move more points in either direction than the cost of the position. The point move must occur above the call's strike or below the put's strike.

   The straddle is a similar configuration, but the long call and put have the same strike. So the degree of price movement is not as much as the spread, but accomplishing a profit remains challenging. The soon-to-expire straddle is cheap but price has to move quickly; the later-expiring straddle has more time but is more expensive.

2. **Short spreads and straddles.** For those investors wary of long options and the disadvantage of time decay, the short spread or straddle appears to offer a solution. The fact that you receive money for opening a short position means that as long as price does *not* move too far, it will become profitable. The problem here is that risks are considerable and the maximum profit is limited.

   A short spread involves selling a call and a put with different strikes, which expands the profit zone. In comparison, a short straddle is opened with both sides at the same strike. Because both sides are short, the position is highly speculative.

3. **Uncovered calls.** The covered call is considered a conservative strategy, but the uncovered call is one of the most speculative strategies available. In this position, you sell a call but you do not have stock. The risk is unlimited, at least in theory. The potential loss occurs when a stock's price rises above the call's strike. The loss is calculated as the difference between market value and strike, minus the call premium. For example, if you sell a 35 call for 4 ($400) and the stock rises to $48 per share, the call will be exercised. The loss is: $4,800 − $3,500 − $400 = $900

All of these speculative applications of options contain a common element: None of them have any influence on an equity portfolio position. All exist outside of the stock portfolio and are based on an attempt to make a profit based on price movement, in exchange of accepting a high (often a very high) risk that the price will move in the wrong direction or will not move far enough.

In comparison, a combination that hedges portfolio equity positions is more conservative because risks are *managed* as part of the options positions that have been opened. Chapters 8 through 12 examine the combination hedges in great detail, and demonstrate the differences between high-risk speculation and conservative portfolio management.

> **Key Point**
> Speculation and hedging are entirely different strategies. A speculator *takes* risks, whereas a hedger *manages* risks.

The short straddle is high risk because no matter how the underlying price changes, one side or the other is always at risk. This problem is solved with the covered straddle. Even though the call and put are both opened with the same strike, the risk is not the same as the short straddle's risk.

The covered call and uncovered put have the same level of market risk. The actual risk is a downside risk. If the stock price falls, the uncovered put goes in the money and is at risk of exercise; this makes the uncovered put risk identical to the risk of owning stock. With the covered call, a decline beneath net basis represents a net loss as well.

On the upside, the risk is quite different. The uncovered put will expire worthless as long as the underlying stock's price is above the put's strike. The covered call will be exercised if the stock price is higher than the call's strike. This is not going to generate a loss as long as the call's strike is higher than the original basis in stock. Even so, the in-the-money covered call can be closed or rolled forward to avoid exercise.

So the covered straddle introduces two different positions with identical market risk. Why not just open two uncovered puts or buy another 100 shares and sell two covered calls? The answer is found in the evolving changes in both time and intrinsic value. For the covered call and the uncovered put, time value erodes over time, accelerating as expiration approaches; so both positions are advantageous due to time decay.

> **Key Point**
> The covered straddle creates two forms of option income while enabling the investor to manage risks in a conservative manner.

On the intrinsic side, the two options act differently. If the stock price rises above the strike, the call gains intrinsic value. If the stock price falls below the strike, the put gains intrinsic value. In both instances, the opposite option has no intrinsic value and can be closed at a profit or allowed to expire worthless. The risk management attribute addresses the option that is in the money.

The call can be left alone and allowed to exercise, in which case the 100 shares of stock are called away at the strike. Or the call can be closed or rolled to avoid or defer exercise. The put that has gone in the money can be closed to avoid exercise, or rolled forward. It can also be left alone and allowed to get exercised. This makes sense when the in-the-money points are lower than the premium received for selling the put. For example, you opened a covered straddle with a 35 strike and received 3 ($300) for selling the uncovered put. At expiration, the stock price is $34 per share or one point in the money. The put is exercised and 100 shares are put to you at $35 per share. This is one point higher than current market value; however, because you received $300 for selling the put, your net gain is still $200 points below the net:

35 strike – $34 per share = $100 loss

Put premium $300 – $100 loss = $200 net gain

After this, what else can be done? Having acquired an additional 100 shares, you now have a total of 200 shares. This leads to additional hedging potential in the form of covered calls or covered straddles based on two options and 200 shares of stock.

Another type of hedge involves long and short positions opened with the same strike or with different strikes. The synthetic long or short stock strategy sets up positions on the same strike and value mirrors movement of the underlying stock. A collar involves 100 shares along with a short call and a long put, both out of the money. This combines insurance with a covered call. Both the collar and the synthetic stock strategy are explained in detail in Chapter 10.

Why Hedge?

Options traders are aware of the effect volatility has on option pricing. The lower the stock's historical volatility, the lower the option premium tends to be—the relationship called implied volatility. So a low-volatility stock is going to experience much different options pricing activity than a high-volatility stock.

You might have examples of both types of stock in your portfolio. So as a means of managing risk for both types of stock, various options-based hedging techniques not only help manage risk, but may also generate additional income without adding substantially to levels of risk. An investor holding a portfolio of fundamentally strong stocks will not be concerned with short-term volatility, at least in theory. The idea is to identify quality based on fundamental strength (revenue and earnings growth, high dividends, low or level long-term debt), and wait for the long term. However, even the most conservative investor with the ability to pick and buy high-quality stocks is going to be aware of short-term price changes and may want to exploit those price movements to generate short-term income.

This is at times a speculative move made by investors willing to take risks with a small dollar amount of capital. However, at times, it also contains elements of hedging as part of a conservative outlook. For example, you own 100 shares of stock in a company you consider a strong prospect for long-term growth. The company pays a strong dividend of 3.5% and you reinvest your quarterly in additional partial shares. The history of the stock price has been strong as well. However, the latest earnings report included a negative earnings surprise. The company missed its estimates of revenue and earnings by a small amount. On the day of the announcement, the stock price fell 3 points.

The tendency for stock prices to overreact to earnings surprises (positive or negative) can be observed reliably. As a stock price moves against the surprise, it also tends to self-correct within two to five sessions. A fundamentally strong company with low volatility and consistent returns may fall 3 points when it misses analysts' targets, but it is likely that the price will rebound very quickly. In this situation, a buy-and-hold strategy dictates that no action should be taken. However, even the most conservative trader can take many actions in this situation to exploit what is probably an exaggerated price movement of short duration. These actions can include:

1. Close any open covered call positions and take the profit. When the stock rebounds, sell a new covered call. This takes advantage of the price decline on both sides. Taking profits after the decline yields a small profit; opening a new covered call after the rebound brings in a higher premium.

2. Buy a long call to benefit from a rebound in the stock's price. This is a speculative move based on the belief that the rebound is likely to happen. As with all forms of speculation, it does not hedge your stock position, but the timing of the move is prudent given the likelihood of a price rebound.

3. Sell an uncovered put to benefit from a rebound. Remember: The uncovered put has the same market risk as a covered call. This is one of those situations where the two sides, even with the same market risk, will behave differently. When the stock price declines, it is not the time to open a covered call, but it is a good time to open an uncovered put—both observations based on the likely rebound in stock price.

> **Key Point**
>
> A popular form of hedging is timed to coincide with stock patterns following earnings surprises. The tendency is for price to move in an exaggerated manner and to correct itself very quickly.

The same strategic application of options strategies applies after a positive earnings surprise. If the revenue and earnings exceed expectations, the tendency is for the stock price to rise and to then retreat within a few sessions. At these times, you can take advantage of the price change by closing any long calls currently open. Or you can buy a long put to add insurance to your position, a popular hedge that cements the gain in the stock price; this is also known as a *married put*.

If the stock price does decline, you can sell the long put and take profits, meaning the benefit from the exaggerated price movement is converted into a new form of income. Finally, immediately after an exaggerated price movement, the timing for opening a covered call is excellent. If the stock price declines, the call can be closed and profits taken; if the stock price does not decline, the higher strike translates to higher profits if the short call is exercised.

These examples demonstrate that, based on short-term price movement in your stock positions, the risk management attributes of hedging are preservation measures that either limit or erase paper losses. Hedging protects your stock portfolio, and is a more prudent and profitable system than diversifying or asset allocation. Under those systems, risk and loss are accepted as inevitable. With hedging, you do not eliminate loss completely, but you do reduce its impact on your stock positions. Whether you hedge to reduce loss or to generate additional income, the results are the same: higher value in your portfolio and better preservation against market risk.

Hedges are not guarantees. Most forms of hedging cost money or limit your potential profits. So a hedge usually will involve a trade-off between cost and risk reduction. This is a conservative policy as part of portfolio management, because it is a means for limiting losses and the willingness to pay for the protection or offset gained through the hedge. So the choice is not between hedging and diversification. The real choice is in the degree of hedging you want to put in place for the cost it involves. A buy-and-hold strategy may be entered with the long-term view that in spite of short-term price movement, the well-selected company's stock will grow. Hedging may not be necessary, but it is a method for managing the uncertainty of short-term price movement and also for limiting longer-term risks.

Many theories have been developed to articulate and quantify the value of hedging. In a "perfect" hedge, for example, the hedge offsets risk by exactly 100%. For example, a long put costs 3 ($300) and the stock declines by a net of 3 points. The loss in stock is offset 100% by the net cost of the put. This "inverse correlation" is intended only to distinguish between profits and losses. A hedge that costs more to open than the risk it eliminates is not worth opening, and a hedge that generates a profit clearly provides added benefits. For the purpose of comparing outcomes between hedges, the theory of the *perfect hedge* is useful. It helps you to decide whether a particular hedging strategy is worth the risk.

The perfect hedge is not possible most of the time, but it sets a standard for minimum outcomes. However, certain inhibiting factors may create a net loss for hedges in spite of the intended risk-reducing benefits that hedging provides. In these cases, the net loss can be thought of as the insurance you pay for to prevent loss in the event the loss occurs. It is similar to homeowner's insurance, in which you protect against cata-

> **Key Point**
>
> Some traders resist long hedge positions because it requires spending capital. However, it is similar to other forms of insurance: Its value is in the benefit if and when price moves against the stock position.

strophic losses, even though the chance of these occurring is quite low.

In the market, the factors leading to likelihood of negative outcome include:

1. **Time decay of long options.** Any hedge involving long options has to consider the impact of time decay. Even when both sides remain at the same risk levels, time decay erodes the market value of the long option. This is why offsetting long and short options is desirable as a form of

hedge. Time value works against the long position, but it works in favor of the short position. The net result is likely to be mitigated well enough so that you do not suffer from time decay overall.

2. **Changes in implied volatility levels.** When IV is high, option premium tends to increase. So if you open a hedge with long options at such times, some of the value will decline as volatility retreats. If a hedge involves the use of short options, the opposite problem occurs when the hedge is opened when IV is low. If IV increases, so does the premium value of the short option; this is a disadvantage because it means the option is less likely to become profitable.

3. **Price drift.** In spite of earnings trends and supply and demand for stocks, many theorists have observed that stock and stock index prices tend to rise over time. This so-called price drift affects options as well, especially near the money. For example, as a stock's price drifts upward, the premium value of long puts will decline.

Another View of Hedging

An argument can be made that you do not need to take specific actions in order to hedge. For example, staying out of the market with a portion of your capital kept in cash can be called a hedge. In practice, staying out of the market hedges only the market risk, but not the equity positions you hold. So in that regard, keeping cash may be conservative in an uncertain market, but it is not a hedge under the usual definition.

Another way to hedge is through rotating stocks from one sector to another. Every sector experiences cycles and many are easily identifiable. So the idea of rotation is to move equity into company stocks most likely to benefit from the high end of the cycle. As rational as this idea might seem, even if you can call the cycles correctly, there is no automatic guarantee that stock prices will act or react to cyclical timing. Beyond sector-specific trends, every individual stock acts based on its own influences. These may be fundamental or technical, and economic influences also play a role. For example, a company with a large share of its revenue and earnings overseas may react more to currency exchange rates than to its sector cycles. The economic influence is very difficult to anticipate and is just as uncertain as the rise and fall in currency prices.

So even with the defensive character of rotation in mind, calling a move from one sector to another is going to succeed or fail based on much more than cyclical timing. Rotation often becomes more speculative than you would like, so as a form of hedging, it is as reliable as diversification in other forms. Rotation is not a true hedge, but merely an attempt to time positions based on annual cycles.

One strategy is based on shorting equity positions. If you believe the market in general is heading down, or that an individual stock's price is weak, you can either short the stock or invest in an "inverse equity" *exchange-traded fund (ETF)*. This type of ETF gains value when its basket of holdings loses value. It is shorting the basket, unlike most ETFs and mutual funds, which hope for increased value. Some inverse ETFs are also leveraged, meaning that for every dollar of decline, the ETF holdings gain two or even three times the move. These are speculative and often high-risk, and though some describe them as hedge strategies, they do not provide the safer and less expensive benefits found in options. For example, a long put is likely to provide the desired insurance against price decline, perhaps more so than an inverse ETF. Even if you own the basket of securities through ETF shares, most ETFs also allow hedging with options. So rather than taking higher risks with inverse or leveraged ETF shares, the simple solution of buying puts is both cheaper and safer.

With hedging in mind as a core strategy for the use of options, how do you manage your portfolio? More to the point, how do you manage portfolio risks? Options are valuable in this quest and may be used in a rich variety of strategies. The elements of time to expiration, proximity between stock price and option strike ("moneyness"), and even consideration of another type of proximity (stock price and patterns in proximity to resistance or support) all affect the methods selected to hedge this risk. In Chapter 5, this second form of proximity is examined and demonstrated. The next chapter continues the discussion of hedging with an analysis of option valuation and its relationship to portfolio risk.

3 | Option Valuation and Portfolio Risk

Investors are constantly looking for the signals pointing to higher or lower risks. This is especially true after taking positions in stock. The expression "Wall Street climbs a wall of worry" is accurate.

The reason for this concern about risk—specifically the risk that a newly opened position will decline in value—can be traced back to an assumption some investors have, whether verbalized or not. This assumption is that the entry price is the zero value or starting point. In other words, if you buy share at $45, you expect the price per share to rise, but not to fall. The optimistic assumption is destructive, however. Every price is part of an unending struggle between buyers and sellers, and this means the price may rise or it may fall.

> **Key Point**
> The entry price of any trade is part of constantly changing prices, not your individual "zero" price.

Everyone knows this, of course. But something more important than knowledge is how you act on that knowledge, or, when it comes to stocks and risk, how you may easily overlook some of the obvious forms of risk. For this reason, options are tools for managing portfolio risk and for identifying the actions to take using options to mitigate, offset, or eliminate risk.

The Nature of Market Risk

Every investor has experienced the negative side of market risk. A position is opened and the price immediately declines. Now what? Do you take your losses quickly; wait out the price, hoping for a rebound; or try to hedge the position?

These are core issues for every investor. Risk often appears when least expected, even though it should *always* be expected. It's the nature of investing. Even so, one form of risk, which may be called *conformity risk*, is the tendency to go along with

43

the majority. In the market, this often is a big mistake. The "herd mentality" of the market often is wrong, and at the very least, its belief often is based on the wrong assumptions.

The tendency to conform is strong. Human instinct tells you that the majority must be right just based on the numbers; but the majority is not always right. In some cases, the majority is dead wrong, and that's the point. Why does a majority make decisions as it does? The answer: The majority acts on emotions and not on logic. The prevailing market emotions are fear and greed. The majority (the "herd") becomes fearful when prices fall, so the emotional impulse is to cut losses and sell even at a loss. When prices rise, the majority acts emotionally once again, in greed. With prices on the price, the majority develops the opinion that they will miss out on more profits if they don't act immediately.

The outcome of this herd mentality is to buy high and sell low, instead of the opposite sage advice to buy low and sell high. As obvious and logical as this sounds, the market acts on emotions and not on logic.

Conformity risk, as much as market risk, explains why so many investors end up timing their trades poorly. The alternative is to practice *contrarian investing*, which is developing a logical basis for when and why you trade. Many think a contrarian goes against the majority just to be different, but this is not the case. Contrarians are coldly logical and analytical, and as a result they make fewer mistakes and time their trades based on facts rather than on feelings. This discipline also helps the contrarian to ignore and avoid crowd thinking.

Key Point

Contrarians are able to resist the common problems based on opinion, because they restrict their decision-making to logical analysis.

Contrarian investing brings up a related spectrum of risk. By proceeding logically instead of emotionally, you can avoid some of the common mistakes investors make. For example, some investors fall into the trap of feeling superior to the crowd. Anyone who starts out with a series of winning trades is susceptible to this misguided sense of superiority. There are numerous problems with this, including a tendency to ignore warning signs of poor judgment. For example, a trade is made with poor timing and it becomes apparent right away. Do you cut your losses and get out? Or do you wait for price to turn around? An investor with a sense of superiority will not be willing to accept input, whether from others investors or from the market itself.

Closely related to a sense of superiority is stubbornness. If an investor develops an opinion and acts on it successfully, how can that stubbornness be changed? For example, many investors in the past were stubborn about their loyalty to a specific company, such as General Motors, Eastman Kodak, or Enron. All of these examples, once considered stellar blue chip investments, failed. However, long before they failed, warning signs were there. A contrarian is able to recognize logically what those warning signs reveal; a contrarian is not blindly loyal to a company or to an idea. The same logic applies to strategies. A favorite strategy is not going to work in every case, and stubborn loyalty to that strategy is blinding.

Contrarians are also aware of the problems of **confirmation bias**. This is the tendency to seek confirmation of a previously established idea without remaining objective. For example, you invest in a company's stock based on many positive signals. The stock begins a slide downward, and you are concerned. But in studying the chart, you find many signals that confirm your bullish opinion about the company and the stock. This is a lack of objectivity, when the smart choice would be to either cut losses or turn to options to hedge any further declines. A true contrarian will understand confirmation bias and be able to avoid it with cold logic.

Contrarians also understand the final type of risk, that of **magical thinking**. An investor who follows this thinking believes that when making a trade, wearing a lucky shirt or undergoing a specific ritual will lead to success. It is not a rational mindset, but it is common among investors just as it is among faithful fans of sports teams.

> **Key Point**
>
> Anyone relying on magical thinking to invest makes the mistake of assuming that being a good person means they deserve profits and being a bad person means they deserve losses.

Magical thinking also contains an element of religion. The ritual is part of a belief that being a good person leads to a reward in the form of profits. This is not faith in the religious sense, but superstition. But it feels like faith, and the "true believer" may not consciously examine the illogical assumptions being made.

All of these forms of risk are less tangible than the well-understood market risk. All contain a similar element, however. They are forms of risk common among the majority of "the market," where the herd mentality rules the decision-making process. In comparison, the contrarian approach involves making decisions logically and based on analysis of both fundamental and technical trends; and then making trade decisions based on observed trend movement and reversal.

Leverage Risk

Another well-known form of risk involves a combination of capital and borrowed money. Any time you borrow to invest, you are taking on risk. If a leveraged account rises in value, profits also rise; but if that account loses value, the losses are accelerated as well.

For example, you can buy stock with 50% cash and 50% margin. This is one widely used form of leverage. However, ask any investor if they would borrow to invest and most will say they would not. So what happens to that 50% of leverage? If you buy 100 shares at $60 and you place $3,000 in your margin account, the remaining $3,000 is loaned to you by your broker. If the price rises, this leveraged investment also becomes profitable, as Table 3.1 shows.

Table 3.1

SharePrice	Value of investment	Amount of leverage	Percent of leverage
$62	$6,200	$3,000	48.4%
64	6,400	3,000	46.9
66	6,600	3,000	45.4
68	6,800	3,000	44.1
70	7,000	3,000	42.9

As the value of shares rises, the percentage of the total remaining leveraged falls. So the net profit is accelerated as well. With the original share price at $60 per share, paying 100% in cash yields a $1,000 profit when the stock price reaches $70. But with 50% leverage, the same move in price produces $4,000 in profit ($7,000 total value minus $3,000 borrowed).

This looks attractive, but what happens if the share price declines? Then the overall picture is far different, as Table 3.2 indicates.

Table 3.2

Share Price	Value of investment	Amount of leverage	Percent of leverage
$58	$5,800	$3,000	51.7%
56	5,600	3,000	53.6
54	5,400	3,000	55.6
52	5,200	3,000	57.7
50	5,000	3,000	60.0

Now, with the borrowed amount remaining unchanged, the original 50% leveraged has risen to 60%. If you had paid 100% for the stock, the loss would be $1,000 ($6,000 – $5,000). However, with leverage of one-half, the net loss rises to $2,000 ($5,000 – $3,000).

Investors often buy shares on margin without stopping to think about how much that increases their risk. Leverage in the form of margin provides greater profit potential while also placing greater loss potential on the position.

Lost Opportunity Risk

The "lost opportunity" of what could have occurred is often on the minds of investors. This comes in several forms.

For stock positions, a lost opportunity arises when prices rise and profits are taken too early. The dilemma for anyone taking profits too quickly is not only that an otherwise-sound investment is lost, but so are profits. If you purchase stock because you believe the company is fundamentally strong and offers growth potential in the future, then taking profits too early does bring up a lost opportunity. If you were to close out all positions as soon as they became profitable, your portfolio would end up with nothing but shares of stock that had declined in value.

Key Point
Taking profits as they appear means you end up with a portfolio of depreciated stocks.

That action—taking profits on worthwhile stocks while holding onto losing stock—is poor portfolio management. It is self-defeating and so the lost opportunity is the actual health of the portfolio.

In the alternative, it makes more sense to sell shares of stocks that have declined or not moved at all, and reinvest in more shares of stock with a robust growth curve underway. This emphasizes movement and profits, but those profits accumulate. Once you take profits, you next have to decide where to reinvest the capital.

Another type of lost opportunity is found on the other side of the portfolio equation. If you fail to close out positions because the market value has fallen, what do you do if it continues to fall even further? A stubborn investor might hold on in the hope of a reversal, so that those paper losses turn into profits. Unfortunately, this often results only in larger losses. The lost opportunity is the limitation on losses that could have been put into place.

A third version of lost opportunity relates to options trading in several ways. The most readily apparent way is the covered call. Those who oppose covered calls argue that if the stock price rises, the call limits profit and the lost opportunity represents the higher price per share that you would have had if you had not written a covered call. However, anyone writing a covered call needs to understand the pro and con of the position. On the pro side, you keep the option premium and, upon exercise, you also profit from capital gains. Finally, you earn dividends as long as you earn the stock. Properly selected covered calls yield double-digit annualized returns. On the con side, the occasional loss of further profits makes the covered call less profitable than just owning stock.

The problem with this version of lost opportunity it that is does not occur in every case. Many covered call writers use the same 100 shares to sell and profit from calls over and over, generating income from the call premium while being willing to risk the stock being called away. It is a judgment call, but the emphasis is on the wrong risk.

The true risk involved in covered call writing is not the lost opportunity risk on the upside, but the market risk on the downside. This risk is the same as the basic risk of just owning stock, but it is reduced by the call premium. So it is a more desirable downside risk than just owning stock. When this is factored in to the upside lost opportunity risk discussion, the value of covered call writing becomes clearer, even with that lost opportunity risk.

Other Types of Portfolio Risks

The usual emphasis among investors is on market risk. This is understandable. Of course, everyone wants their investments to become profitable and also would like to beat the averages. Three specific additional forms of risks come into the picture, however, and these cannot be ignored as all influence whether or not it will be possible to generate profits.

Knowledge and Experience Risk

> **Key Point**
>
> You do not have to become an expert at reading financial statements to master a few fundamentals. Using long-term trend summaries is adequate.

Knowledge and experience risk refers to every investor's understanding of markets. This includes everything from the economic limits on profit based on supply and demand, to the larger analytical methods by which companies and their stocks are studied. Fundamental analysis involves a large body of knowledge about how financial statements are put together and what they reveal. Fortunately for the average non-accountant investor, online brokerage services offer nicely summarized fundamental trends in services like the *S&P Stock Report*, provided free of charge by many brokerages.

Experience is closely associated with knowledge. For most investors, "experience" is what happens when they were expecting something else. In other words, losing money is a great form of experience, but it's by no means desirable. However, loss is instructive because it brings up the false assumptions an inexperienced investor starts out with; the worst aspect of those assumptions is that they are not obvious until a loss occurs. So some of the best experience is also expensive, but a small loss early on in an investing career can prevent larger losses later.

With options trading, knowledge and experience risk is even more severe than for stock investors. Options are characterized by highly specialized jargon, trading rules, and restrictions. Because options leverage stock price movement, both profits and losses can occur rapidly. This is where selection of conservative strategies is sensible, especially when the purpose is to manage portfolio risk through hedging, and not just to make fast money through speculation.

Tax and Inflation Risk

Tax and inflation risk surprises many investors, because it is easy to overlook the significance of these risks. Added together, inflation and taxes mandate the net return you need from your investments just to break even. This breakeven yield is higher than most people assume. It is a severe risk, for two reasons. First, if your net return is lower than your breakeven rate, you are losing spending power every year. Second, if you end up taking higher market risks to reach or exceed breakeven, you face the prospect of greater losses as well.

This type of risk is well managed by hedging with options. Even the most basic hedge, such as a covered call, is likely to offset the double impact of inflation and taxes. The covered call is an excellent hedge for this reason. It consistently yields double-digit annualized returns just from option premium, as demonstrated by the following example.

On October 9, Exxon Mobil (XOM) was trading during the session at $79.68. The owner of 100 shares may consider a covered call with a strike of 80. Without considering capital gains or dividends, the premium income from the covered call would be:

November (49 days) 80 call bid 1.92 (less $9 costs) = 1.83

Yield: 1.83 ÷ 80 = 2.29%

Annualized yield: 2.29% ÷ 49 days x 365 days = 17.06%

December (71 days) 80 call bid 2.35 (less $9 costs) = 226

Yield: 2.26 ÷ 80 = 2.83%

Annualized yield: 2.83% ÷ 71 days x 365 days = 14.55%

January (99 days) 80 call bid 2.78 (less $9 costs) = 269

Yield: 2.69 ÷ 80 = 3.36%

Annualized yield: 3.36% ÷ 99 days x 365 days = 12.39%

These outcomes demonstrate that annualized return for shorter-term options annualizes to a higher annual return than for longer-term options. But do these outcomes beat the double impact of inflation and taxes? Yes.

To calculate your breakeven yield, identify the inflation rate you believe is in effect. Divide that by your net income after deducting federal and state income taxes. If your combined federal and state income tax rate is 36% (33% federal and 3% state, for example), your after-tax income is 72% (100 − 36). If you assume inflation is 3%, the calculation of breakeven requirement is:

> **Key Point**
> Few investors have analyzed what they need to truly break even. The breakeven yield for most people is higher than their average yield. This is where conservative hedging with options helps.

$$I \div (100 - E) = B$$

I is inflation and E is effective tax rate; breakeven is the rate you need to earn to offset taxes and inflation. So in the previous example, the calculation is:

$$3\% \div (100 - 36) = 4.17\%$$

You need to earn 4.17% in your portfolio just to break even. Most investors realize that to accomplish this rate or better, higher risks need to be taken on. However, with options used not only to hedge risk but also to generate income (with covered calls, for example), this breakeven rate can be surpassed easily. In the example of

Exxon Mobil, the annualized yield on a covered call was 17.06%, well above a typical breakeven yield.

Table 3.3 shows breakeven requirements at various tax rates and inflation rates.

Table 3.3

Tax Rate	Breakeven Rate				
	1%	2%	3%	4%	5%
14%	1.2%	2.3%	3.5%	4.7%	5.8%
16	1.2	2.4	3.6	54.8	6.0
18	1.2	2.4	3.7	4.9	6.1
20	1.3	2.5	3.8	5.0	6.3
22	1.3	2.6	3.8	5.1	6.4

The hedge value of options used in even the most basic conservative strategy is perhaps one of the only ways to beat the inflation and tax breakeven rate consistently. Alternatives will usually result in higher potential yields accompanied by much greater risks.

Impatience Risk

Impatience risk is a form of risk that most investors experience. In the desire to earn profits quickly, and to move from one position to another, the market does not always move at the speed desired. As a consequence, the impatient investor closes one position and replaces it with another that has seen more price action in recent weeks. By chasing profits like this, the likelihood of poorly timed trade decisions increases. Any investor acknowledging their own impatience will also recognize the risk that comes with it. An old investing adage promises that "the market rewards patience."

Hedging as an Alternative to Diversification

The widely accepted assumptions about investing are that risks are inevitable, that they have to be spread among many different products, and that a diversified investment program will beat the market averages.

To the first assumption, inevitability: Yes, risk is inevitable unless action is taken to ensure positions, place a floor on potential loss, and otherwise hedge portfolio positions so that risk can be *managed* or *eliminated*. If this is accomplished, then risk and its inevitability are defeated through good management.

The second assumption, that you have to diversify: There clearly is value in investing capital in several different places, but diversification itself has to be done effectively. For example, buying shares of three different stocks with identical risk factors is not diversification. Secondly, over-diversification leads to poor overall net returns, meaning that the investor (or mutual fund) ends up with reports *below* the market average.

The third assumption is the most dangerous of all, that a diversified program will beat market averages. As the previous exercise demonstrated, the double problem of inflation and taxes showed you need an exceptionally large rate of return just to break even. This

> **Key Point**
> The popular assumptions (risk is inevitable, diversification is the solution, and diversification beats the market) are all incorrect.

means that under the usual program of diversification, you need to take higher than average risks; unfortunately, this means making or beating breakeven is much more difficult to accomplish consistently.

Investors relying on professional management through mutual funds might beat the market in some years, but not in others. Buying shares of ETFs might accomplish the same thing, but the risk there is that the basket of securities will net out to an average return, which might not consistently beat the market. Diversification is not the answer to the problem of wanting to maintain capital value and reducing risk. The solution to the issues is to figure out how to apply hedging consistently and effectively to portfolio positions.

When this is designed properly, the outcome is that conservative hedging does beat inflation and taxes, while yielding returns above the average of the market. Diversification is a sound practice just to avoid big losses due to problems in a single security; in spite of how this idea has been sold to the public, diversification is only one aspect of investing, but it does not solve the risk challenge.

Coming chapters describe a limited number of conservative strategies to hedge equity positions, or strategies that can be used as hedges in some situations, but not in all. Some positions are high risk in some applications and moderate or low risk in others. This is an essential aspect to recognize in developing hedges. No single strategy can be labeled in terms of risk in every case. For example, a covered call is a smart strategy for low-volatility stocks or for stocks whose price has recently peaked (especially when the signals indicate coming reversal). However, when a stock's price has spiked in the opposite direction and you expect price to turn upward, the covered call is not a wise strategy. At that time, the uncovered put (with the same market risk as the covered call) makes much more sense.

Another example is the uncovered spread, which is widely assumed to be a speculative high-risk strategy. In this strategy, you sell a call and a put, so there are two uncovered options open at the same time. As long as the price remains between the OTM (out-of-the-money) strikes of the higher call and the lower put, a profit will be earned, and both positions can be closed at a profit or allowed to expire. But if the price moves beyond either strike, the exercise risk becomes more severe. However, this can be a very low-risk strategy in one specific situation. When a stock has been trending sideways in a *consolidation trend*, it is described as "range-bound," meaning neither buyers nor sellers are able to move the price higher than resistance or lower than support.

Many investors view consolidation as a pause between trends, in which trading cannot be done because there is no dynamic trend to reverse. However, specific signals do foretell breakouts from consolidation. These include triangles, wedges, and others. As a basic hedge, the existing consolidation that lacks breakout signals may last many months or even years. For example, the one-year chart for Johnson & Johnson (JNJ) shown in Figure 3.01 includes a four-month consolidation trend from January to May. The end of this trend was signaled by a double top forming above resistance; and following that, resistance began declining against level support, forming a bearish descending triangle. In September and October, price settled into a new consolidation range, including strong new resistance formed by a flip of the support price. When a flip like this occurs, the new range tends to be stronger than average.

Figure 3.1: Consolidation Trend

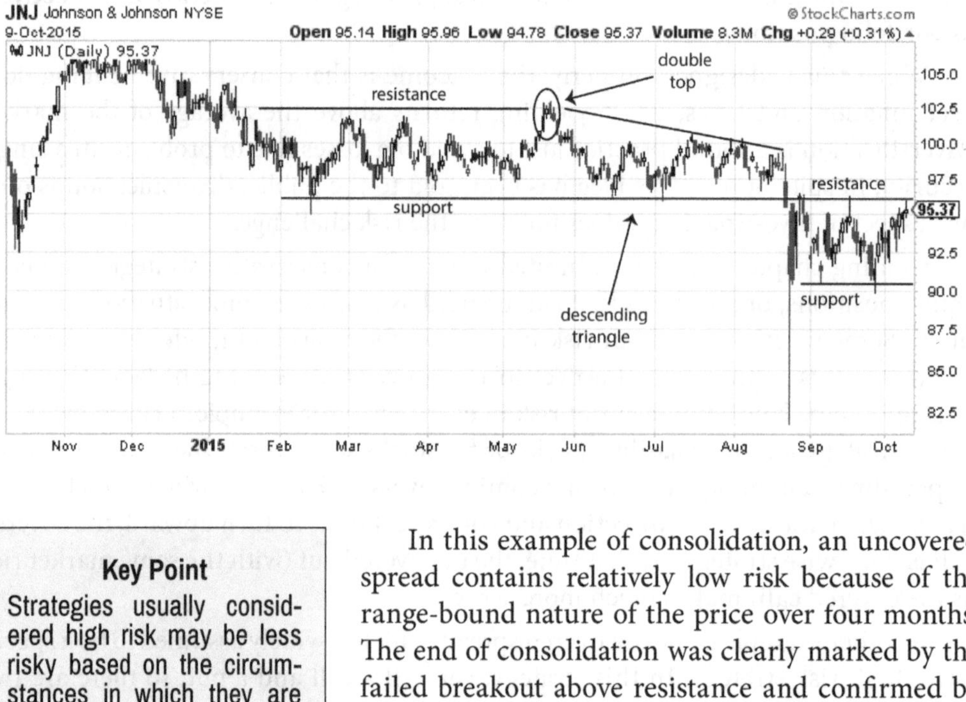

In this example of consolidation, an uncovered spread contains relatively low risk because of the range-bound nature of the price over four months. The end of consolidation was clearly marked by the failed breakout above resistance and confirmed by the descending triangle. So during the period in which JNJ was range-bound, an uncovered spread could have been opened once the consolidation was established. For example, by mid-March, a position could have been opened using short options with April expiration. Keeping expiration within one month for short positions is wise, because time value falls an accelerated speed in the final month; with consolidation possibly ending at any time, the shorter-term options are manageable until the price range evolves and changes (as it did beginning in June).

> **Key Point**
>
> Strategies usually considered high risk may be less risky based on the circumstances in which they are used.

An example of an uncovered spread opened in March could include an April 105 call and an April 95 put. This strike range of 10 points is at or beyond the range-bound area between resistance and support. Because consolidation tends to be difficult to break from, this is not a high-risk strategy.

In comparison, an uncovered spread on a much more volatile stock would be high risk. Figure 3.2 is a one-year chart for Alphabet (GOOG). The stock was in a consolidation trend from February through June. During this period, three breakout attempts all failed, but there was no specific price decline below the established support price of $520. In mid-July, a 70-point upward gap moved price from $580 to $650.

Figure 3.2

The volatility of Alphabet would have made an uncovered spread unwise. For example, a short call with a 560 strike and a short put with a 520 strike would set up a 40-point buffer zone, which sounds very safe, especially when that zone is expanded for the premium received. However, the 70-point move in a single day demonstrates that volatility stocks are poor candidates for uncovered short positions.

The comparison between JNJ and Alphabet (GOOG) demonstrates that a specific strategy may be conservative or high-risk depending on where and when it is deployed. Alphabet is a high-volatility and high-priced stock, and big price moves are not uncommon. Johnson & Johnson is a more stable, low-volatility stock. Its one-year price range was less than 20 points from $90 to less than $110, compared to Alphabet's 200-point spread from $480 to $680.

Hedging and Market Inefficiency

In using options to hedge, whether in an uncovered straddle, a covered call, or any other strategy, the degree of risk relies on volatility in the underlying, but also on a tendency for markets to behave inefficiently.

As option expiration approaches, notably in the last week, underlying prices tend to move toward the closest option strike. This phenomenon, call ***pinning the strike***, does not always occur, but it occurs often enough that it will affect the value of soon-to-expire hedge positions.

> **Key Point**
>
> Finding trading opportunities does not always take a lot of time. Online sources provide information you can use to time smart trades.

The short-term inefficiency of the market is even more glaring after even small earnings surprises. One worthwhile options strategy involves tracking earnings reports and looking for surprises, and then exploiting the overreaction in price. With a small amount of research, you can reasonably identify candidates for earnings surprises.

An example is shown on the chart of Pepsi (PEP) in Figure 03.3.

Figure 3.3

The procedure was not complicated. The day before earnings were reported (October 5), an analysis of Pepsi's earnings history revealed consistent positive earnings surprises:

Quarter	Surprise %
9/14	5.4%
12/14	3.7
3/15	5.1
6/15	7.3

Based on this, it was assumed that yet another earnings surprise would occur. So the recommendation was to buy an October 94.50 call @ 1.33 (net cost $142). One week later, the call could be sold @ 4.65 (after trading costs, a net of $456), a profit of 221%. Why sell at this point? The chart revealed a number of

signs that the expected rise in price had peaked. The flip from support to resistance was followed by a price move above resistance on the day earnings were reported, including strong upward gaps. However, the Relative Strength Index (RSI) moved into overbought (above the index value of 70), the first time that had occurred over the six months shown on the chart. This combined set of signals was enough to warn that a price correction might be on the way.

The fact that a stock's price will react strongly to an earnings surprise is one example of market inefficiency. In most instances, a strong upward move after a positive surprise (or downward move after a negative surprise) will be followed within a few sessions by a turn back to price levels near those before the earnings announcement. By realizing this, you can take advantage of the inefficiency in price activity by making relatively inexpensive options trades.

A long option expiring in the near future is not generally considered a conservative strategy. However, in this situation, knowing how prices act after earnings surprises make the long call an "educated guess" and a good one. The same would apply after a negative earnings surprise. Anticipating a downward move, you would buy puts and then sell after a decline took place. This could be based on a track record of four past quarters in which outcome always fell short of analysts' predictions.

Specific to options pricing, volatility collapse, which works as another form of inefficiency. Implied volatility also tends to spike before earnings announcements, especially if a surprise (positive or negative) is anticipated. However, among the many forms of inefficiency, options traders may observe that near the end of the cycle (especially in the last week before expi-

Key Point
Options traders relying on volatility analysis are at risk as expiration approaches. At this time, it makes sense to reply more on price charts of the underlying security.

ration) any type of reliance on volatility can be misleading. At this point in the cycle, it makes more sense to time options trades based on technical analysis of the underlying stock's price chart.

An example of how knowing this can produce profitable outcomes on very short-term swing trades: Knowing that both volatility and time value will end up at zero on the last trading day of the option cycle, analysis of option premium on the previous day (the third Thursday of the month) will point out potential bargains. For example, if an at-the-money or out-of-the-money option reports strong growth in premium on

Thursday, you know that it will disappear on Friday. This points the way to trading opportunities, but these are going to be limited.

Most instances of such premium spikes are going to be minimal, so that the trading costs to enter and then exit a trade could consume part or all of the profit. A single option should cost about $9 to trade, so a **round trip cost** will be about $18. So if an option is only valued at 0.18 on the third Thursday, it will not be worth trading. Making matters worse, the **price spread**, the difference between bid and ask, will also reduce potential profits. So a spread of 0.03 with pricing of 0.21 nets out to breakeven at best based on the cost to move in and out of a position.

Yet another form of inefficiency relates to the option's time value. You know that time value ends up at zero by the end of the last trading day. However, because you cannot trade options when the market is closed, you also know that time value will depreciate most rapidly on the last Friday. Whereas options cannot be traded in off hours, time decay should be expected to apply even when the market is closed. So the change between Thursday and Friday will be significant. In examining the price of options on Thursday, any premium for at-the-money or on-the-money options will consist of a mix between volatility and time value. It is not possible to identify how much of each applies, but it doesn't matter either. You know that by the end of trading on the next day, both of these values will be zero. The entire ATM or OTM premium will disappear the following day.

The next chapter expands on the question of portfolio risk with a comparison between speculative and conservative strategies. This comparison is difficult for some investors, notably those who consider options as high risk in most situations. The emphasis on identifying safe hedges points the way to success in portfolio risk management.

4 | Speculation With Options vs. Conservative Strategies

In order to create a system in which options are used *conservatively* to hedge portfolio equity positions, it is first necessary to settle on definitions. Many traders describe themselves as conservative but at times execute highly speculative trades.

This problem is especially applicable to the options world. With a vast array of possible strategies, even experienced stock traders may easily fall into the trap of violating their own investment standards. Options traders need to resist temptation to veer from their self-imposed risk profile; this is not as a simple as it sounds.

> **Key Point**
> Every investor faces the possibility of violating well thought-out standards developed as part of a risk profile.

As a starting point in developing an effective program involving options as hedges against portfolio risk, the definition of conservative has to be articulated.

What Is "Conservative"?

The definition of a **conservative** profile contains a degree of variation, based on several factors. Many readers will be surprised to discover that risk profile itself contains variables, and that an individual risk profile is going to change over time based on these factors as well as on changing attitudes toward investing. The key factors in this equation include:

1. **Experience.** If you have been trading for many years and have developed a reliable system for picking stocks and determining when to continue holding or when to sell, it is more likely that a similar level of discipline will be applied in the addition of options to hedge. If you are an experienced investor, you know that research and complete understanding are essential in the creation of a safe program and in being able to hedge based on well-articulated risks.

2. **Capital.** The level of cash available to invest also affects risk profile, even though it might seem that this should not be a variable. However, if you have a very small amount of capital, you will have to allocate those scarce resources cautiously and cannot afford loss. The addition of options as hedges is desirable but might also be further restricted by capital limitations. If you have a larger dollar value to the portfolio, you also have more flexibility to diversify, and can also afford losses more readily. Adding option hedging is affordable in the larger portfolio. This does not mean that losses are "acceptable" in a larger portfolio, but they are more affordable. This changes the risk tolerance level as well.

3. **Goals.** The purpose for investing has a significant influence on risk profile. This changes with age, as it should. If you are a younger investor, you are concerned with job security and being able to start a family and buy a home. If you are an older investor, you are more likely to think about investing to build a retirement fund and, once children are grown and on their own, you may consider some forms of insurance to be less important than the younger investor. Goals affect your risk profile because as these change over time, your attitude about levels of risk also changes. The tendency is that as you grow older, you will tend to become more conservative and have lower risk tolerance than you did when younger.

4. **Portfolio contents and diversification.** If you own 100 shares of one company's stock, you will benefit 100% from rises in price and suffer 100% from declines. This is not a portfolio but a position, a starting point. There is not much you can do to diversify a one-stock position, but it can be hedged. However, if you own shares of many stocks in different sectors, your diversified portfolio will behave with a mix of price changes. In this case, the positions in the portfolio can be hedged in different ways, depending on *historical volatility*, percentage of holdings in the overall portfolio, and the effectiveness of diversification. Most investors think a broadly diversified portfolio makes it a safer and better-managed portfolio. However, this is not always the case. Being able to hedge a more concentrated mix of holdings is often more profitable than diversifying widely and hoping that the mix of holdings will outperform the broader market. So the diversification policy itself may *increase* risks, whereas hedging a smaller, less-diversified portfolio may *decrease* risks.

5. **Market conditions.** Finally, all investors are at risk based on market conditions. If you consider current market conditions relatively stable, you might think hedging is not as necessary to protect your portfolio. If you think the market is very volatile, hedging makes more sense. Ultimately, it is not the volatility in the overall market that matters, but the volatility in your portfolio positions. If you own stocks that all tend to be volatile, your market risk is greater than average. However, even in a volatile

portfolio, conservative hedging can improve management over risk and allow you to limit losses due to fast and unexpected price swings. Your selection of high-volatility or low-volatility stocks defines your risk profile and whether or not you are truly investing in a conservative manner.

The Role of Trends and Fundamentals in a Hedging Program

If option hedging can be effective to manage portfolio risk, it has to be based on analysis of price trends in the underlying stock; and the levels of risk requiring hedging depend on the fundamentals of each company. This includes appreciation of overall trends in the market; however, the trend in the single stock is a separate issue and—apart from market trends and volatility—serves as the central feature

> **Key Point**
> A hedging program based on fundamentals of the underlying stock as a starting point brings order to the selection process and reduces technical risks.

of the hedging program. A starting point for this analysis is comparison among many companies of the fundamental strength of the organization and its long-term fundamental trends.

Your portfolio, consisting of shares of stock in companies, was selected on some basis. Most conservative investors look at the fundamentals—the dividend, P/E ratio, revenue, earnings, and debt—in selecting stocks. These are worth some limited analysis here, if only to demonstrate the differences between companies in terms of how fundamentals define risk in your portfolio. To many options traders, this seems contradictory. A preference for technical analysis does not exclude the fundamental side as a requisite. Both analyses are enhanced when the fundamentals are also studied.

Analysis of fundamentals is best performed as part of a trend over time. Looking at any financial result for a single year does not reveal whether the company's fundamentals are improving or declining. A longer-term analysis of a few key fundamentals reveals levels of *fundamental volatility*, a form of risk going to the very beginning of how a portfolio is constructed and managed. Many fundamental indicators are available and can be studied online without needing to reconstruct financial statements. Many online brokerage services provide free fundamentals summaries. Many allow their investment customers free access to data-rich reports like the *S&P Stock Reports*, which includes 10 years of fundamental data for thousands of publicly listed companies.

These tests are essential to developing a hedging program. The level of volatility in the company's fundamentals is reflected in the volatility of the stock price, which also represents market risk. Finally, the historical volatility in the stock price affects option premium and, as a result, the cost or profit from a hedging position. Of course, the higher the volatility, the more valuable the hedge as long as it truly reduces or eliminates market risk.

Following is a summary of fundamental tests based on dividend indicators, P/E ratio, revenue and earnings, and debt capitalization.

Dividend Analysis

Three specific and separate dividend indicators are worth studying as part of a long-term trend. These are dividend yield, dividends per share, and payout ratio.

The **dividend yield** is the annual percentage represented by the dollar amount of dividends, divided by price per share. For example, if share price is $75, and dividend is $3.50 per share, dividend yield is: 3.50 ÷ 70 = 5%. However, in calculating dividend yield, you should base it on the actual price you paid originally. As the stock price moves, dividend yield changes. However, your effective yield is always based on your original price per share no matter how much price moves. As price declines and dividend per share remains unchanged, dividend yield rises:

3.50 ÷ $68 = 5.15%

3.50 ÷ $66 = 5.30%

3.50 ÷ $64 = 5.47%

> **Key Point**
>
> A high dividend is not always a reflection of exceptional value. It may be the result of a large decline in the stock's price, so the reasons for this decline should be studied before deciding to purchase share.

This means that a high current dividend yield is not always good news. You need to check stock price over many years to decide whether the fixed dividend per share is occurring while the company's stock is losing value, or whether the company has increased dividends over the years.

Dividends per share is normally expressed as the total per year. However, most dividends are paid quarterly. So if a company has declared a dividend of $3.50 per share, the quarterly dividend payment will be 87.5 cents per share (one-fourth of the annual dollar amount).

The **payout ratio** represents the percentage that dividends represent of total earnings per share. For example, if a company is paying $3.50 per share each year and total earnings per share was $5.00, the payout ratio is 70% (3.50 ÷ 5.00 = 70%). The ratio is important when studied as part of a trend, because this lets you see whether the payout is growing or shrinking.

Dividend trends for three companies reveals a comparative summary over 10 years. These companies are AT&T (T), paying 5.66% dividend in October 2015; ConocoPhillips (COP), paying 5.73% dividend yield; and GlaxoSmithKline (GSK), with dividend yield of 5.92%. All of these were selected as examples of companies yielding more than 5.5% dividend, and are summarized in Table 4.1

Table 4.1

Year	ATT		COP		GSK	
	Dividend per Share	Payout Ratio	Dividend per Share	Payout Ratio	Dividend per Share	Payout Ratio
2014	$1.84	155%	$2.84	62%	$2.65	142%
2013	1.80	53	2.70	42	2.96	86
2012	1.76	141	2.64	45	2.48	85
2011	1.72	--	2.64	29	2.21	67
2010	1.68	52	2.15	28	--	--
2009	1.64	77	1.91	59	1.85	55
2008	1.60	74	1.88	--	2.18	73
2007	1.42	73	1.64	23	2.06	55
2006	1.33	70	1.44	15	1.74	47
2005	1.29	91	1.18	12	1.53	54

The analysis of trends in these dividend indicators over a 10-year period provides a context to the latest entry in that trend. Comparisons made among three companies, each paying approximately the same attractive dividend, adds additional insights into the levels of volatility and hedging potential for each.

> **Key Point**
> Most indicators are more accurately understood when studied over a period of years, rather than only for the latest year.

For example, AT&T (T) increased its dividend every year over the entire decade. When this occurs, the company is classified as a "dividend achiever," because long-term and consistent growth in the dividend is considered highly desirable as a fundamental test. However, the company clearly has set a policy of increasing the dividend by four cents per share each year over the past seven years, and this explains the volatility in the payout ratio. A desirable outcome is a consistent ratio, meaning the same portion of earnings is paid out each year. However, when emphasis is on increasing the annual dividend per share but earnings rise and fall from year to year, the payout ratio is more volatile. In fact, AT&T's earnings were also volatile during this period, which explains why payout ratio is so inconsistent.

ConocoPhillips (COP) increased dividends per share in nine of the 10 years, and the single year reported no increase or decrease. This places COP in a category close to "dividend achiever." However, with earnings reported at a lower level of volatility, the payout ratio grew over the 10-year period.

GlaxoSmithKline (GSK) was far less consistent in year-to-year dividends per share. However, the payout ratio rose throughout the period. A degree of volatility made the GSK results less consistent and more volatile than the other two companies.

This analysis summarizes how dividend data can be compared and studied over a decade. The consistent rise in dividends per share is very desirable, and while all three of these companies paid exceptionally high dividends, the increases in T and COP were stronger than those in GSK.

P/E Ratio Trends

> **Key Point**
>
> The P/E ratio is a hybrid, combining a technical value (price) with a fundamental one (earnings). Thus, the time periods for each will be different.

The price/earnings (P/E) ratio is one of the more popular indicators. However, it is an oddity in the sense that it compares a technical value (price) to a fundamental outcome (earnings). With this in mind, the time frame for each side is also dissimilar. Price represents the latest known price, which changes daily and is available instantly. Earnings, however, might be many weeks or months out of date, because the latest reported earnings are for the latest reported fiscal quarter.

Some attempts to fix this disparity include use of the forward P/E, which compares current price to estimated current earnings. This is a problematic method, as the estimate of earnings might be quite inaccurate.

The solution to the odd comparisons and time are found in the long-term analysis of the annual high and low P/E. This provides you with a more accurate idea of how a company's stock has been priced over time. By dividing price by earnings, the resulting number, called the multiple, represents the number of years of earnings (based on latest known earnings) reflected in price. For example, if the P/E is 15, it means the current price per share is equal to 15 years of earnings for the company.

The generally accepted middle rate for well-priced stocks is a multiple somewhere between 10 and 25. A multiple under 10 indicates a lack of interest in the market. And when the multiple moves above, it indicates that the stock is overpriced. By analyzing 10 years of the annual range from high to low P/E, you get a good idea of how the stock has been priced over a decade, and how the price trend has behaved—high or low volatility.

The three companies previously studied for dividend trends can also be studied for their P/E ranges. Table 4.2 summarizes the range of multiples for each.

Table 4.2

	ATT		COP		GSK	
Year	High P/E	Low P/E	High P/E	Low P/E	High P/E	Low P/E
2014	32	27	19	13	30	22
2013	12	10	12	9	16	13
2012	31	23	13	9	16	14
2011	48	41	9	7	14	11
2010	9	7	9	6	44	32
2009	14	10	18	11	13	8
2008	19	10	--	--	18	10
2007	22	16	13	9	16	13
2006	19	13	8	6	16	14
2005	18	15	7	4	19	16

In the case of AT&T, the multiple was consistently within the moderate range for most years, with the exception in 2011 with exceptionally high levels of P/E multiple. The 2014 and 2012 high multiples were also out of the middle range. However, in addition to checking the high and low levels, the span between the two is also revealing. AT&T's high and low span was under 10 points for every year during the decade, which indicates that the yearly range of changes in both price and earnings are not volatile. However, the high levels in specific years does reveal a lot of volatility in earnings levels.

COP reported a range of multiples in the middle range for the entire period, and the span between high and low never exceeded 6 points. This indicates that based on volatility in revenue and earnings, COP's stock price was reasonable within the decade.

GSK reported spans of 8 points or less every year. The jump in the multiple, revealing some years in which the stock price was too high, is a reflection of a natural tendency in the market to see stock prices move too high, only to correct in following periods. This is good information for any investor with a long-term portfolio in two respects. First, a big change in a fundamental indicator like the P/E ratio is likely to self-correct in time. Second, those periods of changes in the stock price and resulting value through P/E and other indicators, points to the need for specific types of hedges when the trends begin to change.

Revenue and Earnings

The best-known fundamental indicator is the combination of revenue and earnings. However, these combined trend values also are easily misinterpreted or misread.

In an ideal growth pattern, revenue will grow every year, consistently and with a predictable curve of growth, also reflected as a percentage of year-over-year dollar value. However, that ideal situation rarely occurs. There is a tendency in every trend to eventually slow down and level out. This is not a problem as long as earnings keep track with revenue.

Just as the dollar value of revenue should grow every year, the **net return** should remain steady or improve as well. Net return is the percentage that earnings represent of revenue. It is not realistic to expect to see net return increase indefinitely because there is a ceiling on the percentage that can be expected. However, as revenue grows, so should the dollar amount of earnings.

These assumptions are affected by changes in the mix of business and market share. When one company acquires or merges with another, the trends will change as well. So in analyzing long-term trends, make sure that the reported values are adjusted to reflect new realities once a company has merged with or acquired another, or after a company disposes of part of its operating revenues by selling off segments.

No one wants to invest in a company that is losing market share. However, just as declining revenue and earnings are negative trends, some trends are not as visible. For example, even when revenues and earnings are both increasing, is the net return keeping pace? When you see increasing revenue with declining net return (even as the dollar value grows), it signals a decline in internal controls, a negative trend for the organization.

For example, in Table 4.3, the annual dollar values (in millions of dollars) for revenue and earnings are summarized over a 10-year period for the three companies in this study.

Table 4.3

	AT&T (T) in $millions		ConocoPhillips in $millions		GlaxoSmithKline (GSK) in $millions	
Year	Revenue	Earnings	Revenue	Earnings	Revenue	Earnings
2014	132,446	6,224	55,419	5,738	37,875	4,661
2013	128,752	18,249	58,248	7,978	41,439	8,799
2012	127,434	7,264	62,004	7,411	41,883	7,517
2011	126,723	3,944	235,265	12,502	43,905	8,750
2010	124,280	19,085	175,752	11,358	43,855	2,862
2009	123,018	12,535	149,341	4,858	44,238	8,625
2008	124,028	12,867	240,842	(16,998)	44,649	8,438
2007	118,928	11,951	187,437	11,891	45,446	10,431
2006	63,055	7,356	183,650	15,550	42,734	9,916
2005	43,862	4,786	179,442	13,640	39,367	8,522

The AT&T (T) trend is strong in terms of revenue, with the dollar amount growing in most of the years shown. Earnings were more volatile. However, a great problem is in the net return. In the period between 2005 and 2009, net return was consistently reported between 10% and 11%. After that, net return was quite volatile, with three of the most recent years all below 6%. In 2014, net return was only 4.7%, less than half the average of the net return in the first five years.

ConocoPhillips (COP) has experienced declining revenues in the most recent three years, and during this period earnings have also been on a general decline. Considering the condition of the oil and gas industry, this trend is not surprising. However, it remains a troubling aspect of the long-term trend that the dollar value of revenue has declined to levels less than one-third of revenue levels 10 years ago, and earnings have also declined considerably.

GlaxoSmithKline (GSK) has reported no substantial growth in revenue throughout the decade, although earnings have been inconsistent. In 2014, earnings were about one-half on the decade's average. This reveals weakness in the fundamentals of the company.

Debt Capitalization

The final fundamental indicator is the **debt capitalization ratio**. This is a percentage of **total capitalization** represented by long-term debt (with the remainder represented by stockholders' equity).

When you see a trend of long-term debt increasing over several years, it is a troubling change. The more long-term debt a company is carrying, the more future earnings will have to be spent on debt service, and the less remaining for dividends and growth. An examination of the three organizations in Table 4.4 reveals some very different kinds of long-term debt trends.

Table 4.4

Year	T	COP	GSK
2014	46.8	29.2	73.9
2013	43.2	27.6	64.2
2012	41.8	32.0	65.6
2011	36.7	—	49.9
2010	34.6	27.4	58.3
2009	38.8	—	57.9
2008	38.7	30.6	62.5
2007	33.2	19.3	41.6
2006	30.3	21.6	31.8
2005	32.3	14.1	39.3

> **Key Point**
>
> The debt capitalization ratio studied over many years reveals whether reliance on long-term debt is rising or falling. A rising level of debt is a negative signal.

The debt capitalization ratio for AT&T (T) rose during the decade, from levels around 30% up to more recent levels in excess of 40%. This occurred during the time of net return declining significantly. So in combination, the net return and debt capitalization ratio paint a picture of a negative trend.

ConocoPhillips (COP) also saw debt capitalization ratio double from 14.1 in 2005 to 29.2 by 2005. At the same time, levels of both revenue and earnings were also on the decline. When the debt capitalization ratio is taken into account with the revenue and earnings trend, the signs were not positive.

GlaxoSmithKline (GSK) reported the most alarming debt trend of these three companies. Revenue levels did not change much during the decade, and earnings were stagnant. However, long-term debt grew from less than 40% in 2005 to more than 70% by 2014.

In summary, all of these companies appear to be strong on a fundamental level. However, the weaknesses in many fundamentals (especially seeing trends in combined negative movement) eventually should be expected to affect the stock price and volatility, and that in turns also affects option pricing and the need for hedging.

> **Key Point**
>
> The analysis of fundamentals should be performed before buying an equity position; these should be monitored periodically to ensure that initial assumptions still apply.

Assumptions Used in Trend Analysis

Once a company is selected as appropriate for your risk tolerance, it may be added to your portfolio. However, this is not the end of the process, but the beginning. While trends apply to fundamental strength or weakness, they play at least as much of a role in tracking stock prices. Your portfolio is rarely permanent. Yesterday's strong and seemingly safe stock might be a less attractive choice tomorrow or next month.

Anyone who doubts this may want to review the history of General Motors, Eastman Kodak, or any other company that was once considered a bulletproof blue chip stock, only to end up bankrupt and worth only a fraction of its previous value.

Assumptions rule trend analysis, and the skillful analysis of the current stock trend relies on how accurately those assumptions are applied and interpreted. The first broad assumption worth considering is that some type of trend is always in effect. Is this even true?

A *trend*—consistent directional movement in price over time, within a well-defined range, and continuing until signals forecast an end—may not always exist for a particular stock. Periods of high volatility often throw trends into chaos and it is difficult to determine the direction price is likely to move next.

As chaotic as this situation is for stock investors, volatility presents opportunities for options traders to hedge positions with high probability of profits. Some specific option strategies are perfectly suited for these times of price volatility and unclear direction. See chapters 8 through 12 for some of the many varieties of options strategies well suited to hedging within volatile price patterns.

In tracking prices of stocks, one assumption that may easily mislead you is the assumption that your entry price is the "zero price." In other words, once you buy shares of stock, you expect the price to rise as if you were starting out at zero. In fact, whatever price you pay for shares of stock, it is part of an endless series of increases and decreases in price. These change daily and can move in either direction. As obvious an observation as this seems, many investors act on the unspoken assumption that they buy shares at "zero."

A third popular assumption is that price trends are a reflection of supply and demand for shares of stock. This is partly true, but there is much more at play in the overall influence of prices for stock. If supply and demand were simple and easily identifiable matters, anticipating and forecasting prices would be simple. A stock's market value could be appraised just like real estate and a fair price set based on changes in supply and demand. This does not happen because many variables come into the pricing of stock. These include forecasting of earnings, changes in product or service mix, mergers and acquisitions, rumors about the company, changes in management, and specific management decisions affecting stock prices. Supply and demand is part of the picture, but the total picture is much more complicated.

Yet another assumption is that trends are reliable for some predetermined period of time. In fact, though, trends cannot be predicted. Their duration varies considerably, some very short and others lasting for years. The only type of prediction that can be made is a likely end to the trend. This is based on locating reversal signals and secondary signals confirming a likely change in direction. Even that is far from completely reliable. There are too many variables that cause a stock's price to continue moving or to suddenly reverse and move in the opposite direction, to be able to call the end of a trend predictably.

Another trend involves perceptions of the market, and tracks how a majority of traders act based on news. The most important form of news is earnings. A popular activity among analysts is to estimate the price per share of revenue and earnings that will be reported. If the outcome is anything other than the prediction, the *earnings surprise* is likely to cause a big move in price. Even missing estimates by one penny per share can cause a 4- or 5-point move in the stock price. However, whether the news is good (earnings surpass estimates) or bad (earnings fall short), the resulting jump in price usually self-corrects within one or two sessions. So a 4-point jump is likely to be followed by a three-point move in their direction. Stock prices tend to overreact and then to correct very rapidly. This points to the timing for options-based hedges with exceptionally good chances to exploit short-term price movement.

A majority of market traders act and react emotionally rather than logically to surprises. This "crowd mentality" is what causes the short-term price chaos. However, a *contrarian* is an investor who understands this overreaction and tends to make decisions logically rather than emotionally. So the bullish tendency is to act out of greed and buy shares expecting further price increases; the bearish tendency is to act out of panic or fear and dump shares before prices decline further. A contrarian does not make decisions just to do the opposite of the majority, but based on a rational and unemotional analysis of what is taking place.

The contrarian tends to follow the advice to "buy low and sell high," but the majority does the opposite. Acting out of greed or panic, the more common tendency is to "sell low and buy high."

Speculation as an Alternative to Conservative Investing

Contrarians recognize the value of price patterns on charts and are able to act on what they see. This can be a conservative approach because it is based on analysis rather than on emotion.

For the purpose of hedging portfolio positions with options, following price trends of stocks makes more sense than the alternative: calculating the volatility levels of options. For the options *speculator*, volatility is the key to timing of trades. Because volatility changes over time, the theory is that long or short trades—speculative trades—can be accurately timed. This system may work to a degree, but it is focused solely on the option.

The alternative of timing conservative hedging trades based on stock charts and price signals makes more sense—because when tracking the signals in the stock price, your focus is on the market risk of the stock rather than on the ever-changing premium value of the option. As a result, option trades are timed based on exposure to market risk or exploitation of opportunities based on price movement in the stock.

Speculators share common attributes that do not address the risk reduction benefits of hedging. These attributes include:

1. **Short-term thinking.** The speculator often is also impatient. Speculation is focused on very quick in-and-out trades. A speculator is not likely to hold onto equity positions unless that is part of a speculative move itself. Because of this, the speculator—unlike the conservative investor—creates trades offsetting profits and losses, but does not hold onto equity positions any longer than they need to in order to play out the speculative purpose.

2. **Focus on the immediate pattern, not the long term.** For a conservative investor, the focus is on holding value investments over a period of time and hedging market risk. So this affects how a conservative investor looks at trends and price patterns. It is all part of how price behavior affects value. If the price behavior indicates a change in the long-term trend, a conservative might decide to sell equity and move cash to a different

position. The speculator is concerned only with the immediate pattern and how that can be timed to create an immediate profit.

3. **Chasing fast profits at the risk of fast losses.** The great flaw of the speculator is focus on fast profits. If you talk to speculators, you will hear all about how they doubled their money in a single session by getting in at 10 a.m. and getting out by 2 p.m. But you are less likely to hear about all of the other times when similar trades ended up in big losses.

4. **A tendency to keep score of outcomes between trades.** A speculator who loses on today's trade is likely to double up on tomorrow's trade to recapture the loss. This means their risk level is doubled up. A wiser method is to accept losses as they occur, keep risk levels at the same profile already established, and move on to the next trade. The "double or nothing" approach to investing more often than not leads to bigger losses, not recapture of lost profits.

Conservative investors are quite different in the sense of how price patterns are interpreted. When option hedging is based on management of equity risk, patterns in price are more reliable. A longer-term perspective reveals likely price movement based on historical trends (the past six to 12 months, for example) and how those price patterns are likely to behave in coming weeks and months. The speculator is looking at price patterns and anticipating movement over a matter of days or even hours, so their perspective is very short-term. And short-term price behavior is invariably chaotic and difficult to understand.

A conservative charting technique is based on recognition of signals and confirmation through other signals. Speculators certainly use similar techniques, but such combinations of signals do not always occur within a short span of time, which is the speculative focus. A conservative analyst understands that each current price pattern is unique and, even with reliable signals, behavior depends on circumstances, not only related to the stock being studied but also in the broader market in the moment.

The speculative assumption often is based on a belief that a correlation will be found between one set of price patterns and another—in other words, that price behavior is predictable even in the short term, and price movement reacts in the same way at all times. This is a blind spot for speculators. Some patterns are likely to repeat

> **Key Point**
> A common flaw among speculators is to assume a correlation between price patterns, even when no such correlation can be established.

most of the time, but relying on it occurring all of the time is a high-risk assumption. It makes more sense to look at all of the current signals and indicators.

A final note about speculation: Although it is a method enjoyed by many traders, the risk of loss makes speculation a difficult system to profit from consistently. Even speculators who track signals tend to suffer from confirmation bias. So a speculator who spots a bullish reversal is likely to look for confirmation of a bullish move. They may easily ignore divergence between signals or clearly bearish indicators.

Contradiction in signals is not unusual, but it should be taken as a warning signal of confusion in the market. If not confusion, contrary signals also reveal a fact about price patterns. Some patterns are simply coincidental and others just fail some of the time. So confirmation bias is a blind spot to be aware of whether adopting a conservative or speculative view of a current trade. No one will profit 100% of the time, but prudent chart analysis and conservative timing of trades—especially applying a contrarian logic to decisions—will tend to improve trade outcomes more than the alternative of speculating on short-term price patterns.

To understand investor behavior within a charting method for timing trades, it is useful to understand the basics of trend theories, including the Dow Theory, the efficient market hypothesis (EMH), and the random walk hypothesis (RWH).

The Dow Theory

The best-known theory of trends is the **Dow Theory**, named for the founder of the *Wall Street Journal* and one of the two originators of the Dow Jones Company, Charles Dow. He developed a system aimed at anticipating fundamental trends within companies. He was a fundamental analyst and did not anticipate applying his beliefs to stock prices directly. He developed not only the concept of trend analysis, but also formed one of the first stock averages. This was an index containing nine railroads, a shipping line, Western Union, and a small number of other companies traded publicly.

It was not until after Dow's death in 1902 that the idea of the Dow Theory was formalized and applied to marketwide trends. The well-known Dow Jones Industrial Average (DJIA) as well as the transportation, utility, and composite averages, were devised by Dow's successor, William P. Hamilton. Today's DJIA consists of 30 industrial stocks and, for many market watchers, represents "the market." However, it holds only 30 stocks out of thousands, and as of late October 2015, according to Dow Jones & Company, four companies represented nearly one-fourth of the total weight of the DJIA:

Goldman Sachs	7.19%
MMM	5.94
Boeing	5.56
IBM	5.29
Total	23.98%

This price weighting is the result of how components are calculated. When a stock splits, for example, the weighting increases. This means that a few companies tend to have greater influence over the 30 included in the index. So in this example, four companies represent nearly one-fourth of "the market," as interpreted widely. This points out the importance for equity investors of focusing on the indicators for individual companies in their portfolio. The overall market certainly influences price movement in the short term, but for a more conservative opinion about the value of your portfolio, the fundamental and technical indicators of those individual stocks you own are more important in the long term than activity in the overall market, however that is measured.

> **Key Point**
>
> The weighting of the DJIA gives considerable influence to a handful of companies. Even so, many consider this index representative of "the market."

The DJIA and related averages form the basis for how the Dow Theory works. As currently applied, the Dow Theory has six major points, or tenets:

1. **The market consists of three movements.** The movements (of duration of trends) consist of primary, or major trend, lasting up to several years; medium, or secondary trend, lasting up to three months; and minor, or swing trend, lasting between a matter of hours and a few days. The normal explanation of a "trend" is that it can be bullish or bearish. However, a period of consolidation, in which prices are range-bound and move sideways, may extend from a matter of weeks to several years. This is a third type of trend beyond bullish or bearish, but it is clearly a form of price movement. The consolidation also brings up many options trades and offers the potential to hedge range-bound prices to create short-term profits.

2. **Trends have three distinct phases.** In bull markets, these are accumulation (the purchase of shares by investors who understand the markets), public participation (the time when the majority follows the lead of those investing earlier), and the distribution phase, in which the bull market comes to an end and investors sell shares. During the public participation phase, speculation tends to increase in the belief that the current trend is likely to continue. However, more price movement tends to occur in phases one and three, which also offers guidance for the timing of hedge trades. In a bearish market, the first phase is distribution, followed by public participation, and finally by accumulation, a sign that the bear market is coming to an end. During a consolidation trend, the three phases cannot be spotted, making timing of trades more difficult but also providing good opportunities for hedging with options.

3. **News is discounted by the markets and this is reflected in prices.** This portion of the theory assumes an *efficient* market, in which prices always reflect current news and even rumor. This might be true, but "efficiency" should not be confused with "accuracy." The discounting of news does not make the current prices fair or accurate, especially given the inclusion of rumor and gossip as forms of news, and the tendency for markets to react in an exaggerated fashion to the unexpected, such as earnings surprises.

4. **Trends reflected in averages have to be confirmed by the same trend in other averages.** This basic concept of reversal and confirmation is clearly an effective means for timing hedges based on price behavior in

individual stocks. Under the Dow Theory, the DJIA trend changes direction, but that is not established as a clear reversal until confirmed by one of the other averages. This is most commonly viewed in the Dow Jones Transportation Average; when it reverses in the same manner as the industrials, it serves as confirmation.

For example, Figure 4.1 summarizes the one-year record of the Dow Jones Industrial Average.

Figure 4.1: Dow Jones Industrial Average Index, 2014

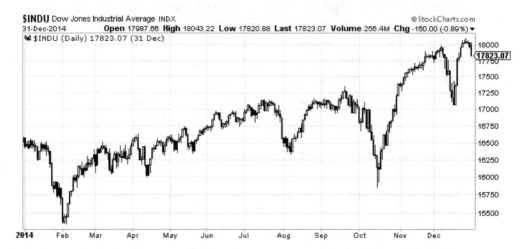

Compare the pattern in this to the pattern of the Dow Jones Transportation Average shown in Figure 4.2. The similarity reveals the accuracy of the theory that the averages confirm one another.

Figure 4.2: Dow Jones Transportation Average Index, 2014

5. **Trends are further confirmed by volume.** The mood of the overall market is seen in changes in trend direction and then confirmed by changes in levels of volume. By the same argument reversal signals in individual stocks often are confirmed by single-session volume spikes or by one of several volume indicators. This form of confirmation strengthens the timing of option trades intended to hedge market risk associated with trend reversal.

6. **Trends continue until signals appear indicating reversal.** This might seem obvious, but it is a key to understanding how trends behave and how timing of hedge trades can be improved. As long as a clear trend has been established, it will not just stop without signals. On the basis of an individual stock, this is valuable information. Timing of hedges should be based on recognition of a reversal signal and confirmation of a likely change in direction.

> **Key Point**
> The Dow Theory forms the basis for modern technical analysis, notably about signals within market trends.

The Efficient Market Hypothesis (EMH)

The Dow Theory formed the basis for modern technical analysis. However, it is focused on the broad averages and the trends established within the 30 industrial stocks. To some degree, these 30 do represent the larger market. Not only do the 30 stocks represent a large percentage of overall market capitalization, the trends also tend to lead the market, so trends in the DJIA are often closely followed by other companies.

The Dow Theory led to some additional theories about the market, including the *efficient market hypothesis (EMH)*. This theory is based partly on the tenet of the Dow Theory concerning the efficient discounting of all news. However, an accurate definition of EMH should clarify that the market is *informationally efficient*. In other words, all information known to the public, in theory, is reflected in current prices. However, this does not mean the market accurately values stocks, or that it does not contain overreaction to news. In fact, the tendency for price movement in individual stocks is very inefficient and chaotic in the short term. However, this is a symptom of a market that is informally efficient—because not all information is reliable or accurate.

Some observers point to EMH as evidence that stocks are always accurately priced. They are not. They are efficiently priced based on a combination of supply and demand coupled with efficient discounting of all news, both accurate and inaccurate. EMH has always been controversial, partly because it is not properly understood and partly because a natural conflict has arisen between those who believe you cannot accurately predict price movement and those who are devoted to price signals. Once you understand what efficiency means (specifically how accurate *and* inaccurate information affects prices), the theory makes sense. However, EMH is best understood in the context of how markets react to and discount news, and not as a basis for claiming the markets price stocks efficiently.

Even if you accept the theory that markets incorporate news efficiently, this does not mean that participants in the market (whether speculators or conservative investors) always apply sound judgment. How do investors respond to information? The overreaction to earnings surprises begs this point. A predictable tendency of prices to move too far and to then retreat after earnings surprises reveals that efficiency is not the same as accuracy. In other words, an efficient reaction to news does not always lead automatically to an efficient or accurate response by the market.

The Random Walk Hypothesis (RWH)

The Dow Theory also led to the development of another idea closely related to EMH: the *random walk hypothesis (RWH)*. Under this belief, all price movement is random and cannot be accurately or consistently forecast by any methods of study. Under RWH, the initial assumption is that markets are informationally efficient (as expressed by EMH), so it follows that all price movement occurs within that informationally efficient environment. In other words, if the market is efficient, it follows that price activity will be random.

If RWH were accurate, all stocks would move upward 50% of the time or downward 50% of the time. Overall value would never change. A review of any stock chart shows that this random tendency is simply not the case. In a truly random environment, like roulette, nearly half of all spins will land on black and nearly half on red (outside of this, some spins land on zero or double zero). A counter-argument can be offered that over the entire market, price movement is a 50/50 proposition. However, history has shown that, over time, stock values have tended to grow, but to remain in a range of random outcomes.

RWH believers claim that a balance between supply and demand explains the random nature of the markets. These economic forces tend to balance out against one another. However, in order for RWH to work in the real world, you would need agreement between all buyers and sellers about the fairness of current stock prices. As a result, any movement above or below those levels would be truly random. This is not how markets can ever operate, however. Too many variables are in play, including changes in competitive position and earnings, mergers and acquisitions that change a sector's membership, and, more than anything else, the irrational behavior of investors and traders. Yet another reality is that the forces of demand and supply are rarely equal, and are in constant movement and change based on trend duration and strength.

An Option Hedging Theory of the Market

In comparison to EMH and RWH, the markets work in very predictable ways. A new theory of hedging includes the use of options to offset risk and contains a few observable points:

1. **Reversal signals, if confirmed, reliably forecast price behavior.** The general observation about use of reversal and confirmation can be demonstrated as effective. In spite of EMH and RWH theories about the impossibility of price predictions, the science is reliable. No one can claim to generate 100% success, but finding strong reversal and confirmation signals and timing trades as a result will improve overall trading success. For an investor with a portfolio of equity securities, this does not mean you want to move in and out of positions; it does mean you can use option strategies to hedge risks and generate income at a better than average rate based on locating strong reversal and confirmation signals. This has to be qualified by the following key points.

2. **The strength of a trend has an effect in the strength of reversal signals.** As you observe how reversal actually occurs, you will discover a statistical reality. Price movement contains many random variables, but there is a direct correlation between the strength of a trend and the strength in reversal signals. "Strength" refers to the speed of price movement as well as to the rate of price movement. Stronger trends under this definition tend to end with stronger-than-usual reversal and confirmation signals. It also follows that weak trends (characterized as slow-moving and with a marginal degree of price change) tend to lead to weaker and less-reliable reversal and confirmation signals. It also follows that the levels of strength or weakness in trends and in reversal and confirmation signals are also correlated in the strength or weakness of the trend that develops after the reversal occurs. This observation is crucial to the selection of option hedges and to the timing of their entry and exit. An understanding of the stock trend leads to a better understanding of how to hedge with options.

3. **The proximity of signals to resistance and support identifies the likelihood of successful forecasting.** Another observable fact about trends is that the trading range matters. The tendency is for stock prices to adhere to the defined borders of resistance and support, whether trending upward, downward, or sideways. Reversal signals occurring at these borders or moving through them are more likely to succeed than the same signals occurring at midrange. This proximity effect should not be ignored. Resistance and support define the trend as well as place limits on how prices behave. When price moves through resistance at the top of support at the bottom, it may also set up a new and stronger continuation trend. This is easily observed by the lack of a reversal signal and the emergence of strong continuation signals and confirmation indicators.

4. **No matter how strong a set of signals, some are going to fail.** All signals may succeed or fail. Even the strongest, best-placed reversals, with equally strong confirmation with multiple added signals, will not act as

expected 100% of the time. This fact points to another essential practice in the use of options to hedge risk: The level of a trade should be limited to what you need, hopefully at about the same dollar level for a series of trades. In this way, a failed reversal is not catastrophic, but merely the expected outcome in which some portion of trades do not end up profitably. However, even a strong believer in RWH will admit that creating profits in more than 50% of trades is "better than random." Applying the principles of reversal location and confirmation should produce even better results than a minimal 51%. It is entirely reasonable to assume that even with some failures, properly discovered, timed, and executed option trades will hedge stock position risks, and yield better results than the average of the market.

The next chapter explores the specifics of chart analysis and demonstrates how to identify strong reversal and confirmation signals. This is based on a belief that the stock trend is what matters, and that an options trend should be based on timing to mitigate the market risk in the stock position, not out of a desire to speculate but in the interest of putting conservative principles into action.

5 | Charting and Trade Timing

Price charts include a wealth of information, which leads to good timing for both stock trades and option hedges.

Options trading can and should be based on analysis of the stock's price chart, on which current trends and reversals can be spotted and acted upon. The proximity to trades in relation to the current trading range is a critical aspect of skillful timing. This chapter examines many crucial charting attributes and explains how they work. This information is at the core of proper timing for option hedging strategies.

Included in the following pages are basics of chart signals, both Western (well-known technical price patterns) and Eastern (Japanese candlesticks). The candlestick chart is today the default charting medium for stock price analysis, although the specific types of candlestick signals are not always well understood. Also included is a discussion of options

> **Key Point**
> Charts are the starting point for technical analysis, combining price and non-price indicators to spot signals and anticipate price behavior.

trading based on identified reversal and confirmation signals involving price as well as volume, moving averages and momentum oscillators.

Most investors are familiar with candlestick charts, as these have gained popularity in recent years. Before widespread use of the Internet, candlestick charts were difficult and time-consuming to construct, so most traders relied on the simpler OHLC (open, high, low, close) chart. On this chart, a vertical line extends from the high to low range of trading during a session. A small horizontal line extending to the left identifies the opening price, and a small horizontal line to the right marks the closing price.

The chart of US Steel in Figure 5.1 shows the appearance of an OHLC chart.

Figure 5.1: US Steel—OHLC Chart, 3 Months

A second form of chart used in the past was a simple line chart. This could be based on either opening or closing prices. Figure 5.2 is a revised chart showing closing prices for STOCK.

Figure 5.2: US Steel—Line Chart, 3 Months

Both of these old-style charts are difficult to read in comparison to a candlestick chart. With this form of chart, you can quickly identify the price direction (white for upward days and black for downward days); the daily open and close (marked by the borders of a rectangular box called the "real body"); and the extent of trading above and below the open and close, better known as the trading range (identified by the full extent of vertical lines called shadows, extending above and below the real body).

Figure 5.3 is a chart for US Steel using candlesticks in place of OHLC or line systems.

Figure 5.3: US Steel—Candlestick Chart, 3 Months

The Meaning of Reversal

Later sections introduce many popular reversal signals that appear on price charts. This is a sample among dozens of possible reversal signals. By definition, *reversal* means a current trend is likely to end and be replaced by a new dynamic trend. So a current bullish trend will end with a bearish reversal; and a current bearish trend will signal a change with a bullish reversal signal.

This general rule is easily understood for dynamic trends (bullish or bearish). For a consolidation trend, the rule is slightly different. The sideways-moving, range-bound price behavior eventually will break out either above or below. The breakout identifies a possible new trend and at this point a reversal signal, accompanied by confirmation, indicates that the new trend will succeed. So for a continuation pattern, "reversal" means a change from sideways to either bullish or bearish movement. This observation is controversial, because many technical analyses describe consolidation as a period in between trends but not as a trend itself. If this were true, it would be impossible to identify a change (meaning the beginning of a new bullish or bearish trend) until the new trend was already underway.

If you accept the premise that "reversal" is not strictly directional, the use of reversal signals makes sense. The signal identifies the reversal of a trend, but not always its direction. For example, a current bullish or bearish trend may end with a reversal signal, with

> **Key Point**
> The definition of a reversal can be expanded to mean any change in a trend's movement, including movement into or out of consolidation.

the resulting trend moving sideways into a consolidation pattern. So in this case, "reversal" is defined as a change from dynamic to sideways price movement. These distinctions become important when identifying the most advantageous option strategy to use for hedging the price action of the stock held in your portfolio.

The Meaning of Continuation

Not as widely acknowledged as reversal signals is the **continuation** signal. This is a specific price pattern, found in either Western technical signals or Eastern ones (candlesticks). In a continuation signal, the apparent direction of a trend is confirmed as likely to continue.

The continuation signal is most useful when it appears after a breakout above resistance or below support. The big question at this moment is whether or not the price will reverse or continue moving in the same direction. At this moment, an option hedge makes good sense as long as you know the likelihood of reversal or continuation. So a continuation signal is a strong forecast that the breakout is going to succeed. A second location for continuation signals follows a reversal. For example, a downtrend concludes with a bullish reversal signal, price begins moving upward, and then a continuation signal appears. This confirms the initial signal and adds confidence that the new direction is likely to succeed. The same applies to a bearish reversal after a bull trend. The price pattern moves downward and is confirmed if a continuation signal appears.

> **Key Point**
> A continuation signal works in all types of trends, but often is strongest following breakout from a continuation trend.

When the trend is not dynamic (bullish or bearish) but is a range-bound consolidation trend, breakout followed by a continuation signal has even greater value. A breakout from the consolidation range does not necessarily provide any reversal indication, so it is not easy to know whether the breakout will reverse or succeed. However, if a continuation pattern appears, this adds confidence to the likelihood that the breakout will succeed. In consolidation, many attempted breakouts are likely to occur, only to fail; so finding a continuation signal with breakout is perhaps the only sign that should increase confidence. This timing—breakout from consolidation—is one of the difficult patterns to read, so the continuation signal has special value as this breakout occurs. The inclusion of a continuation pattern points to the best timing for an option hedge in what appears to be a new dynamic trend.

Both reversal and continuation signals may be short term in nature. However, even though the outcome is uncertain, as a conservative investor you can make judgment calls about protecting positions and hedging risk as these crucial patterns emerge. Without the hedge, stock investors are on a roller coaster, but without knowing how high or low the ride will move. Options hedging timed for reversal and continuation signals levels out the ride and controls market risk in the equity position.

Western Technical Signals

The first set of signals is widely understood by chartists accustomed to spotting signals on charts. As with all chart interpretation, the danger of confirmation bias affects judgment and may easily lead to incorrect beliefs. So you need and depend on strong signals *and* strong confirmation in order to support a belief about how price is behaving. The purpose in looking for signals is to anticipate price movement before it happens. With the short list of popular **Western technical signals**, a remarkable consistency can be experienced in price behavior based on testing of resistance or support. As a general rule, when price tests those price levels without successfully breaking out, the most likely next step is a price movement in the opposite direction.

The first of these signals is called the **head and shoulders**. This price pattern has three parts. The first and third are price spikes and are named the shoulders. The middle is a higher price spike and is the head. The theory of head and shoulders is that this three-part attempt at moving price higher fails, so it is likely to be followed by a price decline.

This can also occur as a bullish pattern, or as an **inverse head and shoulders**. In this case, the three parts are at the bottom, and are expected to be followed by a rise in price. Figure 5.4 shows examples of both head and shoulders and the inverse pattern.

Figure 5.4: Head and Shoulders/Inverse Head and Shoulders

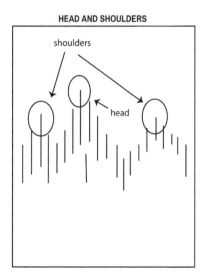
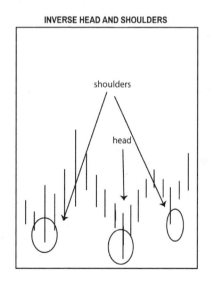

Another frequently viewed pattern is the **double top**. This is a double spike in price at the top of a current price range, and a test of resistance. As this attempt to break out fails, price behaves as expected and is likely to decline. Likewise, a *double bottom* consists of double spikes at the bottom of a downtrend, and is expected to lead to a bullish result. Figure 5.5 includes a double top and a double bottom.

Figure 5.5: Double Top/Double Bottom

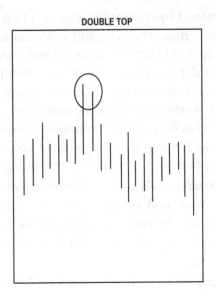
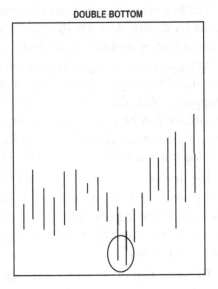

A *gapping pattern* is characterized by single or multiple price gaps between sessions. There are many types of gaps, but the most significant ones for the purpose of timing option hedges are those that move price through resistance or support. These two events—the gap itself and the move outside of the established trading range—set up a likely signal of coming reversal, when price is expected to retreat back into range.

Figure 5.6 shows an example of the gapping pattern on the chart of Weyerhaeuser.

Figure 5.6: Gaping Pattern

The gaps followed a short and gradual time of rising support. Gaps appeared in four consecutive sessions. The final gap is the strongest, from the close of the black session at about \$27.60 to the opening of the larger black session at about \$28.10. A problem with gapping price behavior is that a correction in the opposite is likely to occur, or the rapid price movement may lead to consolidation, as it did on this chart. The one-month consolidation ranged only one point and, after price spiked higher, it appeared to return to this range-bound trend.

The next form of signal is the wedge. A *rising wedge* is a bearish pattern. Both resistance and support trend upward but the trading range narrows. As the range reaches its narrowest point, price is expected to decline below the rising level of support. A *falling* wedge does the opposite, with both sides narrowing downward until price breaks out and rises. Figure 5.7 shows both wedge types.

Figure 5.7: Rising Wedge/Falling Wedge

RISING WEDGE

FALLING WEDGE

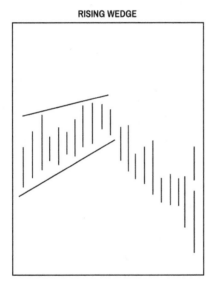
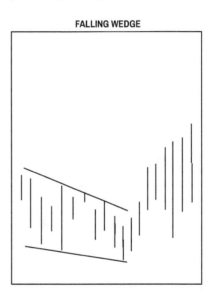

The triangle is similar to the wedge and often is only slightly different. However, whereas the wedge is a reversal pattern, the triangle is a continuation pattern, meaning it indicates a continuation of the current trend. An ***ascending triangle*** consists of a level resistance price with a rising support price, and a ***descending triangle*** has level support with a declining resistance. As the triangle narrows, price is expected to break out in the direction indicated, continuing the trend. An example of both of these patterns is found in Figure 5.8.

Figure 5.8: Descending Triangle; Ascending Triangle

DESCENDING TRIANGLE   ASCENDING TRIANGLE

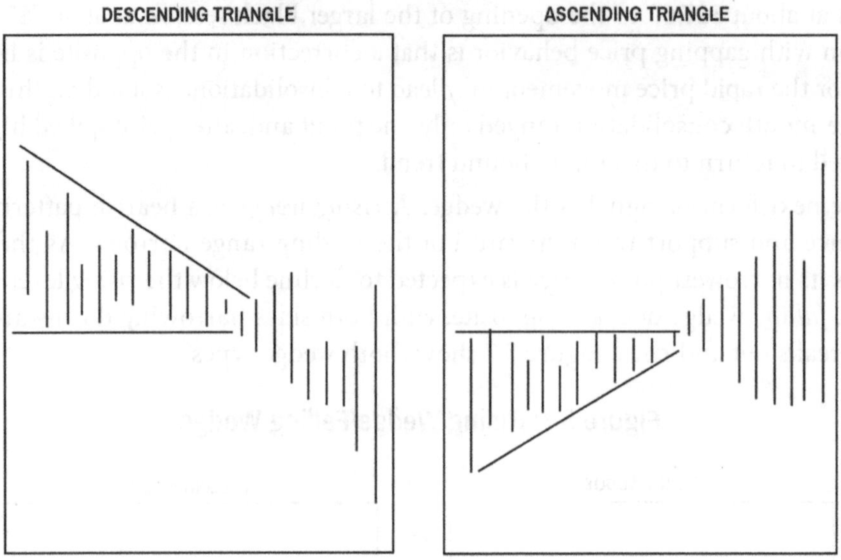

An important distinction between wedges and triangles is their opposite meaning. Wedges lead to reversal away from the previous trend and triangles are expected to indicate continuation. Given the fact that the two types of signals are very similar (but contain different meaning) it is easy to misread what they forecast. So you need to find strong confirming signals before acting on either a wedge or a triangle as it appears on a chart.

Candlestick Basics

Beyond the familiar Western reversal and continuation signals are a broad range of dozens of candlesticks, also classified as *Eastern technical signals*. In this and following sections, several popular and frequently seen candlestick patterns are introduced. These include 26 reversal signals and six continuation signals. They represent a small portion of the candlestick universe.

As a starting point, you will need to become familiar with all of the information a candlestick reveals. Figure 5.9 summarizes the attributes of the candlestick, including the names for each of the parts of the session.

Figure 5.9: Candlestick Attributes

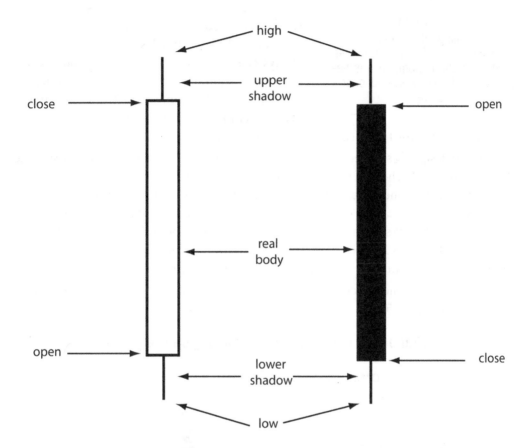

The candlestick is a powerful charting tool because of its visual aspects. Not only single candlestick sessions, but an entire chart range becomes immediately clear as to range and strength as well as general direction of movement. A white candlestick means the price moved up during the session, from the bottom of the rectangular real body up to the close at the top. The black candlestick is a downward-moving day, opening at the top and closing at the bottom. The upper and lower shadows reveal the full trading range during the session, from high price to low.

Both reversal and continuation signals should be confirmed independently, by additional candlestick indicators, or by Western signals (head and shoulders, double top or bottom, gaps, wedges, triangles, for example). An important principle about candlesticks is their placement. Many of the writings about candlesticks report that a reversal signal in the wrong location is a continuation signal. This is not the case. If a reversal signal appears in the wrong location, it is not a signal at all. For example, a bullish reversal signal should appear at or near the bottom of a bearish trend; and a bearish reversal should appear at or near the top of a bullish trend. These "rules" are basic and can be observed on actual charts. It also follows that improper location of signals provides no value at all and might even mislead you into an erroneous interpretation.

Single-Session Reversal Signals

The first set of signals involves only single sessions. Although relying on a single session to find reversal may imply less strength, this is not always the case. However, single-session reversal signals should be confirmed independently. Remembering that some formations are going to occur as coincidence, it is not wise to act on one indicator alone, until confirmation has been found.

The first signal is called a *long candlestick*. The definition of "long" is specific to the chart itself. There is no specific number of points defining a long candlestick versus a "normal" one. A session is long when it exceeds the typical size of preceding sessions. This point can be observed in the fact that the scaling of a chart affects the length of candlesticks. Some charts employ one-quarter-point increments; others are as high as 10 or even 20 points. So "long" is a visual outcome based on a comparison between sessions found on the chart and based on how price is scaled.

A long white candlestick is bullish and a long black candlestick is bearish. Both are shown in Figure 5.10.

Figure 5.10: Long Candle (White)/Long Candle (Black)

LONG CANDLE (WHITE)   LONG CANDLE (BLACK)

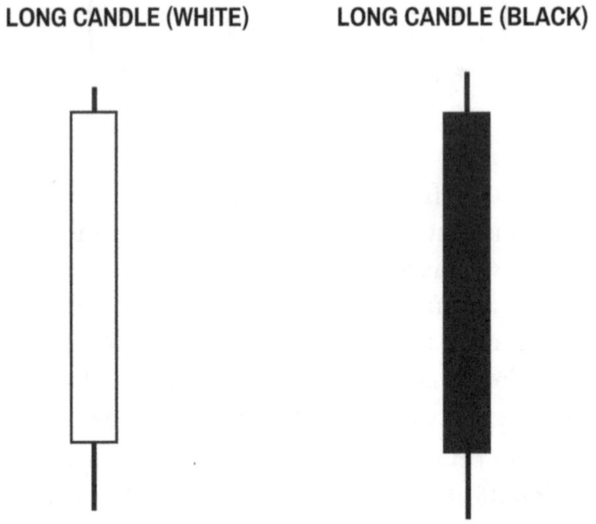

Another single-session reversal is found in the form of a *doji*. The doji is a session with the same or very close opening and closing price, meaning that instead of a rectangle, you find only a horizontal line. The doji includes a horizontal line and a shadow, but the significance relies on the placement of both. A *dragonfly doji* is bullish and has the horizontal line at the top with a long lower shadow; the *gravestone doji* is bearish and has the horizontal line at the bottom with a long upper shadow.

Two additional types are significant depending on where they appear in a trend; at the bottom of a trend, they tend to be bullish and at the top they are bearish. *The* **long-legged doji** has both an upper and lower shadow; and the **spinning top** is also known as a near-doji because instead of a horizontal line, it has a small real body. The

> **Key Point**
> Many signals, including the long-legged doji and spinning top, may be bullish or bearish depending on where they appear and how they are confirmed.

upper and lower shadow should both be longer than the spinning top's real body. All four of these are shown in Figure 5.11.

Figure 5.11: Dragonfly Doji/Gravestone Doji/ Long-Legged Doji/Spinning Top

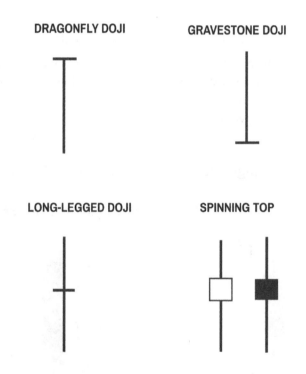

DRAGONFLY DOJI

GRAVESTONE DOJI

LONG-LEGGED DOJI

SPINNING TOP

The **hammer** and **hanging man** are examples of single-session patterns with a small real body of either color and a long lower shadow. Although both are identical in appearance, they take on different meaning depending on where they appear in a trend. A hammer appears at the bottom of a

> **Key Point**
> The hammer and hanging man are identical in appearance, but the proximity to bullish or bearish trends creates an opposite meaning.

trend and is a bullish signal. The hanging man is bearish and appears at the top of a trend. Both are shown in Figure 5.12.

Figure 5.12: Hammer/Hanging Man

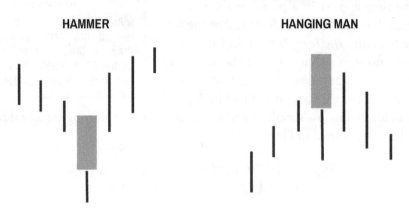

Double-Session Reversal Signals

Among two-session reversal signals, one of the strongest is the engulfing pattern. A **bullish engulfing** consists of a black session followed by a white session that extends both higher and lower than the previous session's real body. A **bearish** engulfing is the opposite: a white session followed by a larger black session. These are shown in Figure 5.13.

Figure 5.13: Engulfing Pattern (Bull)/Engulfing Pattern (Bear)

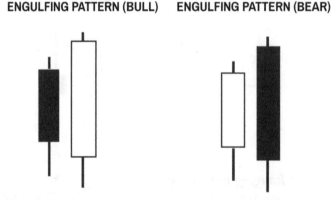

The engulfing appears often and is one of the most reliable of candlestick signals. So when you see one of these and can also find confirmation, it is a strong indicator that a current trend is likely to reverse and begin moving in the opposite direction.

A harami is the opposite of the engulfing. It consists of a first session followed by a shorter session of the opposite color. The **bullish harami** begins with a long black session followed by a smaller white session, with opening and closing prices both within the range of the previous day's real body. The **bearish harami** is the opposite: a long white session followed by a shorter black session. Closely related is the **harami** *cross.* This is like a harami, but the second session is a doji. All four of these are summarized in Figure 5.14.

Figure 5.14: Harami (Bull)/Harami (Bear)/Harami Cross (Bull)/Harami Cross (Bear)

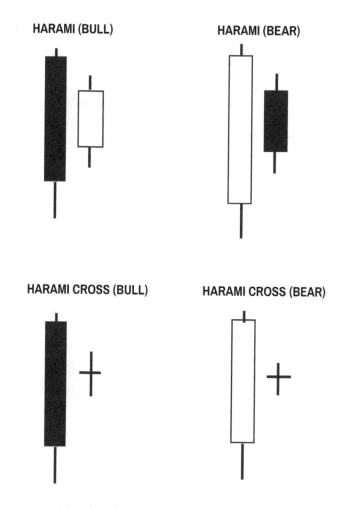

The harami by itself is not an especially strong signal. However, when confirmed by other signals, it helps strengthen reversal signals. In addition, greater strength is seen when the first session is longer than average.

The next two-day signals are the meeting lines and piercing lines. The **bullish meeting lines** declines in the first gap, and gaps to open lower on the second day with a closing price the same as the day before. The **bearish meeting lines** sees movement in the opposite direction and reversal of colors.

A very similar formation is seen in the piercing lines signal. The exception is that the second session closes within the range of the first. The **bullish piercing lines** begins with a black day, followed by a white day opening lower but closing higher than the close of the previous day. The *bearish piercing lines* starts out with a white session, with the second day opening with a higher gap but closing within the range of the previous day. All of these patterns are shown in Figure 5.15.

Figure 5.15: Meeting Lines (Bull)/Meeting Lines (Bear)/Piercing Lines (Bull)/Piercing Lines (Bear)

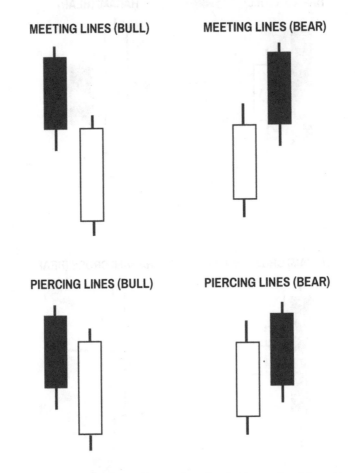

Another two-session candlestick signal is the doji star. In this pattern, the second session follows a gap and forms as a doji. The *bullish doji star* begins with a black session, then a downside gap and a doji. The *bearish doji star* begins with a white session and is followed by an upside gap and a doji. This should be found at or near the top of an uptrend. An example of each is shown in Figure 5.16.

Figure 5.16: Doji Star (Bull)/Doji Star (Bear)

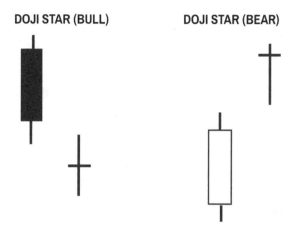

Triple-Session Reversal Signals

The final group of reversal signals consists of three consecutive sessions. In many respects, the three sessions tend to be stronger than the one- or two-session signals, simply because they involve more trading sessions to form the indicators.

> **Key Point**
> Three-session reversals may be stronger than others; however, many of these appear often and can reliably forecast reversal in the current trend.

The first among these is called *three white soldiers* and *three black crows.* The three white soldiers is a bullish signal made. Each session opens higher than the opening price of the previous session and also closes higher. The *three black* crows is the opposite: It is a bearish session. Each one opens and closes lower than the preceding one. Both are shown in Figure 5.17.

Figure 5.17: Three White Soldiers/Three Black Crows

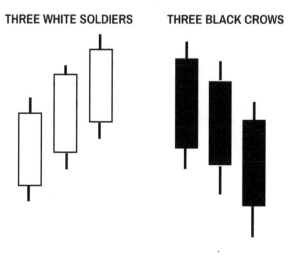

Another set of three-session reversals appears as a ***morning star*** (a bullish signal) or an ***evening star*** (a bearish signal). Both of these appear with gaps between each of the sessions. Very similar is the ***abandoned baby.*** The difference is that the middle session is a doji in both bullish and bearish versions. These four reversal signals are shown in Figure 5.18.

Figure 5.18: Morning Star/Evening Star/Abandoned Baby (Bull)/ Abandoned Baby (Bear)

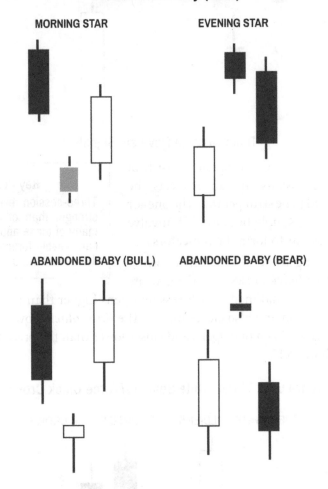

These patterns often are set up as part of a set of trading sessions above or below the current trading range, set off by gaps both before and after. This period is known as an ***island cluster,*** a series of sessions outside the established range and marked by gaps.

Continuation Signals

Numerous candlestick continuation signals are found on charts. Following are the most common categories of continuation, the two-session thrusting lines, and three-session tasuki gap and gap filled.

The **bullish thrusting lines** reveals a likely continuation of the current trend. It consists of a white session that "thrusts" into the price range of the second session's black real body. The **bearish thrusting lines** has the opposite configuration and the colors of the two sessions are switched. This is found during a downtrend and forecasts that the trend will continue in the same direction. An example of each is shown in Figure 5.19.

Figure 5.19: Thrusting Lines (Bull)/Thrusting Lines (Bear)

THRUSTING LINES (BULL)   THRUSTING LINES (BEAR)

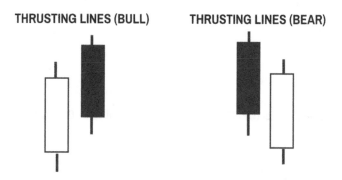

Continuation may also appear in the form of three-session signals. The tasuki gap consists of two sessions separated by a gap and then an opposite-color session moving in the opposite direction. It forecasts continuation of the current trend. A **bullish tasuki gap** starts with two white sessions separated by an upward gap and then a black session moving into the range of the gap but not closing it. The *bearish tasuki gap* begins with two black sessions separated by a downward gap and then a white session moving back up into the gap's range.

The gap filled is similar to the tasuki gap with the exception that the third session closes within the range of the second day, absorbing the entire gap that precedes it. The **bullish gap filled** starts with two white sessions separated by an upside gap, and a third, black session moving down to absorb the gap. The **bearish gap filled** consists of two black sessions separated by a downside gap and a third day as a white session moving to absorb the gap. All four of these continuation patterns are shown in Figure 5.20.

Figure 5.20: Tasuki Gap (Upside)/Tasuki Gap (Downside)/ Gap Filled (Upside)/Gap Filled (Downside)

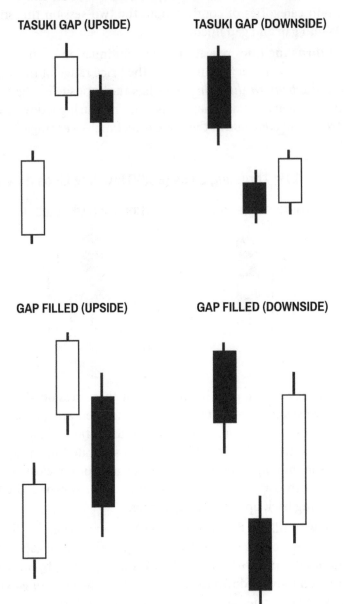

TASUKI GAP (UPSIDE)

TASUKI GAP (DOWNSIDE)

GAP FILLED (UPSIDE)

GAP FILLED (DOWNSIDE)

The reversal and continuation patterns described here are most commonly found, but they are not complete. Dozens of other signals will also appear, and the science of candlestick analysis as part of a charting technical theory involves more than 100 different signals.

> **Key Point**
> Continuation is as valuable as reversal, especially when located close to resistance or support. It indicates a likely successful breakout.

Candlestick Limitations

The candlestick signal is a powerful tool that serves as a guideline for picking and timing option hedges. However, these are not foolproof. Some specific limitations of candlesticks should be kept in mind. These include:

1. **Interpretation is not a simple matter.** The strength or weakness of many signals might not be well understood or, even more troubling, might vary from one case to another. A lot depends on the speed and strength of preceding trends and the amount of time those trends have been in effect. Interpretation becomes quite complex, however, when a similar pattern is strongly confirmed but the precise attributes of the preceding trend are dissimilar. This means that to aid in interpretation, it is useful to seek out additional confirmation beyond a single indicator, and to also check non-price indicators as additional forms of signals that may help clarify what price patterns reveal.

2. **Perfect patterns are not always found.** The appearance of the perfect pattern is an ideal discovery, but it does not always occur. Some conforming patterns meet the criteria but only minimally. The stronger the shape and relative size of patterns to the ideal, the stronger the pattern tends to be. A minimally conforming pattern might also tend to be weaker than many similar signals. With this in mind, the importance of strong confirmation should be emphasized to ensure that the reading of a pattern is as reliable as possible.

3. **All patterns fail at times, even strong ones.** The strong pattern aided by equally strong confirmation will succeed most of the time and will point to good timing for option hedging trades. However, there are no absolutely guaranteed patterns, and at times they will fail. This is true for all indicators. The purpose of relying on strong patterns and confirmation is to increase the ratio of profits to losses, striving to beat the averages. The purpose should never be to try for a "perfect" system for timing trades. Indicators and confirmation should increase confidence in the timing of the hedge, but this is not a promise that the timing will yield profits in every case.

Non-Price Signals and Confirmation

Beyond the numerous price patterns and signals, a comprehensive option-based hedging strategy should also rely on volume, moving averages, and momentum oscillators. These indicators are good sources for confirmation, but they are more likely to not work as leading indicators. For the lead reversal or continuation signal, it makes sense to rely on price signals and then confirm them with other price signals or non-price indicators.

The science of charting is intended as a replacement for the better-known options trading method, based on a study of volatility. This is a fast-moving and at times unreliable method. For example, in the final month before option expiration, volatility collapse makes volatility analysis ineffective. Because many option hedging strategies focus on short-term expiration, the use of implied volatility of options as a means for timing trades is a speculative and risky approach to option trading.

Because your purpose is to manage risks in your equity portfolio, the stock chart and its signals is the most logical source for the timing of hedge trades; and options are an excellent vehicle to accomplish this purpose, as the timing is based on patterns in the stock price.

The next chapter introduces the most popular form of hedge, the covered call. In this conservative strategy, you create current income from options without adding market risk to your stock position. So with the covered call, you earn profits from option premium, stock-based capital gains, and dividends.

6 | The Basic Covered Call

The most popular option hedge is the ***covered call***. This in its most basic form has two parts: 100 shares of stock held in your portfolio, offset by a short call. If that call is exercised, you are required to give up 100 shares at the fixed strike, even if the current market value is higher. At the time you open the covered call, you receive the call premium and it is yours to keep, whether the call is exercised, expires worthless, or is later closed.

This is the starting point for developing a hedging strategy. The premium you receive for selling the call reduces your net basis in stock and creates a downside cushion. When you own 100 shares of stock, your market risk level is any price below your cost. With a covered call, the risk level is reduced by the premium. For example, if you buy 100 shares at $50 and sell a call for 3 ($300), your breakeven price is $47 per share.

The strategy is simple at first glance. However, several aspects of writing covered calls have to be considered in order to convert this strategy into a true hedge. These considerations include selection of the company whose stock will be bought and held; your own objectives and attitudes about the strategy; specific attributes of the covered call; moneyness of the strike you pick; and many variations on the strategy.

When you first study the covered call, some obvious features are seen at once. For one thing, it is attractive because it involves three sources of profits: option premium, capital gains, and dividends. In addition, the covered call is clearly less risky than just owning stock, assuming the strike selected is higher than your original basis,

> **Key Point**
> Although covered calls appear very basic at first glance, it contains several aspects that have to be considered to use it as a true hedge.

because the option premium lowers your breakeven price for stock. Third, picking stock with a higher dividend appears a sensible idea, even though this is not always the case.

As a straightforward strategic use of stock in your portfolio, the covered call may be used as a "cash cow" in the sense that repetitive positions can be opened and allowed to expire, closed at a profit, or rolled forward. For the investor interested in creating additional income, this is a conservative strategy that you can employ, assuming you also accept the limitations of the strategy. The covered call limits your capital gain if and when it is exercised. So a compromise may be to pick very short-term calls out of the money and monitor them carefully, to allow those calls to expire, or, if they move in the money, to quickly take action to avoid exercise.

Because the stock price can move either up or down, the outcome of the covered call can take several forms. However, maximum profit is limited, and maximum can range considerably farther. The maximum profit is:

Strike – stock basis + premium

Breakeven, however, can in theory be greater than maximum gain. It is equal to:

Basis in stock – premium

This means that loss could be a big number, assuming the stock price might fall indefinitely. The overall catastrophic maximum loss is equal to:

Basis in stock – zero + premium

This means that if the stock price falls to zero, you lose the entire investment. (By the way, just owning stock presents an identical risk of catastrophic loss.) The only difference here is that the call's premium discounts the loss.

The breakeven price is itself a hedge. When you buy stock, your breakeven price is the net amount paid. The call premium discounts this and lowers the breakeven. However, this points out the risk in covered call writing. If the underlying price falls below your breakeven (basis – premium), you have a paper loss. You need to accept this loss, wait out a hoped-for reversal, or devise a new hedging strategy to recover the loss.

In the straightforward use of the covered call—meaning closing the call once it loses value and becomes profitable—exercise is clearly a possibility. So as part of a specific hedging strategy (versus a more basic money-making strategy), you need to decide whether exercise is an acceptable outcome. Properly structured, exercise should be profitable in every case, without exception. So one point of view is that creating double-digit annualized returns justifies the occasional calling away of shares. With this goal in mind, the ideal covered call situation is when the underlying price remains in a narrow consolidation range, meaning it trades sideways with little movement up or down. You just wait out the decline in time value and then close the call at a profit and replace it with a later-expiring one. The problem, though, is that exercise remains a possibility if and when the underlying rises above the call's strike. If you are happy with the mix of holdings in your portfolio, having shares called away creates three problems:

1. **Tax consequences** including capital gains, often short term. This may be worth avoiding by also avoiding the sale of shares, at least until the one-year deadline has been passed.

2. **Need to replace called-away shares.** Do you repurchase shares of the same company? Or do you look for a bargain-priced replacement? If you want to hold on to shares, exercise is worth avoiding, either through rolling or closing short calls; or finding different hedging strategies.

3. **Loss of dividend income.** A conservative investing strategy is likely to include selection of companies whose dividend is higher than average. So a covered call exercised shortly before ex-dividend date also means you lose the quarterly dividend. The period

> **Key Point**
> You probably would prefer to not have shares called away. However, the event causes several problems involving taxes, replacement, and loss of dividends.

right before ex-dividend date is the most likely time for *early exercise*, so the timing of expiration for your covered call has to be carefully timed to avoid in-the-money positions in the month that dividends are earned.

As with all hedges involving long positions in stock, the starting point is selection of the right stock.

Picking the Right Stock

If you already own shares in your portfolio, especially appreciated shares, this clearly affects your selection of a covered call strategy. This also raises additional questions. For example, do you want to create a covered call designed to augment income or have shares called away at a profit? If so, the selection of a strike and expiration will be likely to change. This possibility is examined later in this chapter.

If you want to buy shares and, as part of a hedging strategy, sell a series of covered calls to increase income, the selection of a company is of the utmost importance. The greater the historical volatility of the stock, the richer the option premium. So some investors pick stock based on the level of option premium, without realizing that the market risk of the stock is also much higher. As a conservative investor, the analysis of fundamental trends and also of fundamental volatility leads to a more balanced selection of the company. Covered call premium will be lower, but the entire position will also be safer. The purpose of a hedge is to reduce and control risks, not to increase them. So picking a safe stock for covered call writing involves the same basic steps as those for picking stock to hold in your portfolio.

Chapter 4 included detailed analysis of a short list of fundamental trends and how evaluation can be conducted. This concept applies to every option hedge, without exception. All of the positions in your portfolio can be studied based on fundamental trends and their strength or weakness; and if a once-strong fundamental investment has changed and moved into negative territory, a smart move is to sell those shares and replace them with a safer, stronger company.

For covered call writing, a less-volatile stock will offer lower premiums. However, you will also notice that less-volatile stock prices reflect safer fundamental trends. Companies whose revenue and earnings are on the rise, with a healthy and growing dividend, and a stable or falling debt capitalization ratio, tend to also see long-term stability in the stock price. The two aspects—fundamental strength and stock risk—are directly connected. However, with marketwide trends often influencing stock value, especially short-term, it is easy to overlook this reality.

For example, those stocks classified as "dividend achievers" (companies increasing dividends every year for 10 years or more) tend to also see consistent growth in the value of stock over the long term. This reflects the fact that the company has managed its cash well enough to afford to make dividend payments, and that profits are more likely to occur than losses. These are basic ideas.

> **Key Point**
> The analysis of dividends involves not only yield, but annual dividend trends and the payout ratio.

Beyond the dividend per share measured by the dividend achiever standard, the dividend payout ratio is an equally important test. This is the percentage of earnings paid out each year in the form of dividends. It is possible to see dividend payments increase along with a drop in the payout ratio. This means that the company is growing its earnings every year but paying lower dividends in terms of the payout ratio. You cannot expect the ratio to increase indefinitely, but it should remain consistent from one year to the next.

Another fundamental test is more difficult to spot, especially if you focus solely on dividend payments. A consistently higher dividend paid each year appears to be a positive trend, but how is this possible if earnings are flat or falling? What if the company reports a net loss but the dividend is still increased? This is where comparisons between dividend payments and long-term debt are crucial to understand how to select a company as part of your long-term portfolio. If dividends are increasing every year but earnings are flat or falling (or net losses are reported), where is the money coming from? If you notice that the debt capitalization ratio has been increasing during the same period, this is a troubling trend. It means the company is financing higher dividends with higher long-term debt. So future earnings will have to be used to pay debt service, meaning less will be available for growth and dividend payments.

The point here is that picking a company for covered call writing involves the same careful analysis as picking stocks for your portfolio even if you do not intend to hedge the market risk. Isolating the selection to one set of criteria without looking at the full picture can easily lead to false assumptions. So picking a company because dividends are increased every year is one test; but also check revenue and earnings trends, and the debt capitalization ratio, to make sure that the dividend history reflects growing earnings and long-term cash management, and not replacement of equity with debt capitalization.

The Downside Protection Aspect

One hedging attribute of the covered call is quite apparent. Compared to just buying 100 shares of stock, the combination of 100 shares and a short call involves a discount. The option premium reduces the net basis in stock. However, it also places a cap on maximum profit. This is equal to the strike minus basis in stock plus option premium.

On the downside, this hedge is important but minor in the larger scheme of risk management. For example, if you buy shares and sell a call for 3 ($300), your basis is hedged by three points, and so is your breakeven point. However, if the stock price continues moving downward below your breakeven price, the result is a paper loss. You either have to wait out the price, hoping for a reversal, or take further hedging action.

In other words, downside protection matters, but it only reduces risk; it does not eliminate it altogether.

Waiting out price reversal often works, especially if the company has been selected wisely and you believe in long-term value. Riding out the price swings will validate the strategy, but there are cases when the price will simply not recover or, if it doesn't, the recovery will take many months. With this in mind, expansion of the covered call

> **Key Point**
> Hedges in the form of bearish defensive moves accompany the covered call as contingencies in the event of price slide after the call is opened.

into a balanced strategy makes sense as a more protective form of hedge. Strategies may include the insurance put for matching of stock price decline with option intrinsic value growth, a covered straddle to increase the downside protection, synthetic strategies, or collars.

These defensive moves can be entered if the stock price begins to slide, and at the same time the short call can probably be closed at a profit. However, as long as the market risk works against your equity position, the conversion from covered call to downside protective hedge has to be acted upon quickly. In coming chapters, the issue of hedging when prices are on the decline is a core element of the discussion. Chapter 7 provides an alternative to the covered call with the same market risk but greater flexibility. A comparison of this topic (uncovered puts) with covered calls provides a deeper view of the covered call idea than most investors have. This is true due to the bias against uncovered options, including uncovered puts.

An example of a fairly simple hedging technique when stock prices begin to slide is to close the covered call and replace it with an uncovered put. This replaces one option with another but does not change the market risk. It is a method for hedging the downside risk without having to sell shares. However, it is always true that maintaining shares in your portfolio rests on a broad assumption that you continue to believe in the long-term value of the company and its stock. If this belief has changed, shares should be sold and replaced with stronger equity candidates.

Objectives and Investor Attitude

The decision to pick a particular company and write calls, and the policies you set for yourself about when or if to close, roll, or accept exercise, all reflect your objectives in writing covered calls, and your attitude concerning the hedge itself.

Your first objective probably is a combination of two things: achieving downside protection (to the extent of the call's premium) while generating additional income. Writing a series of short-term calls over the period of a year accomplishes both of these objectives; and selection of a strike out of the money will yield lower premium but drastically reduces the odds of exercise. A popular example of this is writing a series of monthly calls; the strategy makes sense because time value evaporates rapidly during the final month, so chances of exercise are slim when out of the money calls are used in this manner.

As an alternative, some option series are available on a weekly basis, so you can write calls expiring in only a few days. In this case, time decay will be maximized. Whether you use monthly or weekly options, with rapid time decay, you can create consistent income as long as the underlying stock does not rise dramatically. Two suggestions to minimize this threat: Avoid the week of ex-dividend date and the week when earnings will be announced. Both of these usually come up quarterly, and are likely to occur in different months and weeks.

The period right before ex-dividend is the most likely period for early exercise, especially the day before ex-dividend. That is the last day to be stockholder of record and earn the current dividend, so the owner of a call that has moved in the money is likely to exercise and take shares to earn that dividend. It does not always happen, but it can happen, so it is worth avoiding. Once the ex-dividend date arrives, the early exercise threat is over. "Ex-dividend" means "without dividend," meaning you do not earn the current dividend until the following quarter.

Earnings announcement dates are also troubling if you have already opened a covered call. An earnings surprise can send stock prices higher (positive surprise) or lower (negative surprise). Although the price usually self-corrects within a few sessions, the change in the call's status presents an exercise threat.

> **Key Point**
>
> One requirement for writing covered calls is the willingness to have the call exercised. It is one of several possible outcomes.

The underlying stock can rise quickly and at any time, but as long as you pick out-of-the-money calls with strikes above your basis in stock, the risk is minimal; and if the call is exercised, you profit from option premium and capital gains. This leads to yet another important objective in covered call writing: A wise covered call strategy is one in which you accept exercise as one possible outcome. Because your true objective is to create a hedge against market risk, you probably prefer to maintain equity in your portfolio and to use covered calls as hedges. However, one risk to the covered call hedge is exercise, so this has to be acceptable, even though it is not desirable.

Setting objectives as part of your covered call strategy is good portfolio management. Without clearly defined objectives, it is too easy to focus on the three forms of income (capital gains, option premium, and dividends) and to ignore the reality of downside risk; it is also possible to overlook the clear advantages of hedging because upside profit is capped at the call's strike. This awareness of lost opportunity risk translates to a limitation in thinking. A call can be closed or rolled forward to avoid exercise, or the profit—even though limited—is a positive outcome even though not the desired end result.

The lost opportunity risk should not be ignored. In some market conditions, owning stock without writing calls will perform better than a covered call position. As a general rule, the covered call reduces the market risk of just owning stock. However, if the market is strongly bullish and stock prices are rising, avoiding covered call writing—at least until market volatility ends or slows down—makes more sense. For example, after a large price decline, stock prices are likely to rise back into the previous range. Writing covered calls at the bottom of this trend is poor timing.

For example, on August 24, 2015, the overall market declined in a one-day drop. Many stocks experienced rapid price decline as well, and the pattern can be seen on numerous charts. The Boeing chart shown in Figure 6.1 is an example.

Figure 6.1: Covered Call Timing

The stock had been trading in a consolidation trend with a range of 10 points, between $137 and $147 per share. The dramatic drop down to as low as $115 on October 24 was severe; however, as it often occurs in sudden price moves, the trading range returned to the previous consolidation range within two months.

For the purpose of covered call timing, this chart is instructive. The hedge works best during a period of consolidation. The range-bound price lends itself to short-term profits from covered calls that will not move in the money as long as consolidation holds. So writing a series of very short-term covered calls hedges the situation well. Consolidation is frustrating for investors; nothing is moving, so the stock is not profitable. However, generating consistent profits through short-term options solves this problem. In fact, consolidation adds safety to the covered call, because the price is range-bound.

At the top of this range, at-the-money calls are very profitable. As of early November (closing values of Friday, November 6), the stock price was still within the consolidation range established the month before. The stock closed at $147.94. Table 6.1 shows the covered calls were available at that time.

Table 6.1

Call description	Expiration	Bid Price
1 week ATM	Nov 13 (7 days)	1.30
2 week ATM	Nov 20 (14 days)	1.94
3 week ATM	Nov 27 (21 days)	2.28

These three calls make the point. (The first and third were weekly, and the middle was the November monthly contract.) As long as Boeing remained in consolidation, it was possible to generate premium income repeatedly.

Once the price moved below the support price of consolidation, which happened on August 20, it was time to stop writing calls. Any open calls could be left to expire worthless, but given the decline in price, no new covered calls should be opened, especially at lower strikes. The likelihood of a reversal back into range is quite high once support is violated.

The August 24 decline was unusual, but, as expected, price did return to range. This occurred in a set of three very strong bullish moves. It took two months to recover completely from the decline, but this pattern of short-term volatility points to a period when the covered call hedge did not make sense. During this time, different hedges would have been more profitable. At the very bottom on August 24, buying calls (or selling uncovered puts) would have yielded profits. As a contrarian strategy, making bullish moves at a market bottom demands nerves of steel, because at such times most investors are concerned (and some panic) that prices might continue falling. The contrarian understands that such fast and violent price declines are most like to rise. A bullish hedge contains minimum risk at this point, because the maximum loss of a long call is the premium, which will be quite low if a strike is selected slightly out of the money.

Once price reaches the range of consolidation that held until mid-August, a short-term covered call program can be resumed. The consolidation resistance level of $147 to $148 is likely to hold, making the short-term covered call a worthwhile hedge.

Rules for Writing Covered Calls

A few important rules should always be observed when writing covered calls. In order for the strategy to work as intended, these are essential:

1. **Pick companies as part of a <u>portfolio</u> strategy, not an <u>option</u> strategy.** The starting point for a covered call hedge should be based on your portfolio priorities and risk profile. So if you prefer low-volatility companies, avoid high-volatility alternatives just to gain more profits on covered calls.

2. **Always keep original basis in mind.** Your basis in stock is a "line in the sand," and writing covered calls with strikes at a lower level creates capital losses in the event of exercise.

3. **Be aware of ex-dividend date and earnings date.** To avoid early exercise, avoid having in-the-money calls exposed in the week leading up to ex-dividend. This is the most likely time in which early exercise can occur. To avoid short-term volatility, also avoid keeping covered calls open in earnings week. Any earnings surprises can cause short-term spikes above or below the strike of the call.

4. **Adjust the strategy for marketwide peaks and valleys.** Once markets turn volatile, the covered call hedge is not going to be as advantageous, or as easy to control, as it is during lower-volatility periods or during consolidation trends.

5. **Accept the lost opportunity risk.** As a basic requirement for writing covered calls, be ready to accept the loss of what could have been without the profit capping of the call. If stock prices rise above the strike and stock is called away, this additional profit is lost. A successful covered call strategy accepts this in exchange for the certainty of the three-source income (capital gains, option premium, and dividends). Although the purpose—based on the portfolio objectives—is to *not* have shares called away, it is one of several possible outcomes.

6. **Take profits when they occur, and write new contracts.** Once the covered call approaches expiration date, it will rapidly lose its time value. During this time, especially during the last week, the premium value is likely to decline enough to create a profitable difference between the opening sold price and current value. At this time, you can wait until the position expires and then write a new call; or you can take profits by closing the short call and replacing it with a later-expiring one. There is never a bad time to take profits; this enables you to generate more short-term income by continually taking profits and replacing one short call with another.

7. **Choose expiration dates with time decay in mind.** The longer-term expiration tempts the covered call writer with a higher premium; however,

> **Key Point**
> To succeed with a covered call hedging strategy, the basic rules have to be followed consistently.

on an annualized basis, more will be earned by focusing on the shorter-term contracts. This is true for one primary reason: Time decay accelerates as expiration approaches. With this in mind, picking the shortest term possible not only generates higher net return, it also makes exercise less likely due to shorter periods of exposure.

Another rule worth observing, apart from the strategy itself, is to use the proper terminology when describing covered calls and other option strategies. These "style guide" rules include:

1.   **Use dollar signs for stock prices.** The proper expression for stock price is on a per-share basis and with the use of dollar signs. For example, a stock is current at $55 per share (not 55 or 55.00); or the price might rise to $55.25 (not 55.25). Decimal places are always used to two places for expressing value of stock, and always expressed in price per share.

2.   **Express option premium in value per share.** For options, dollar signs are never used. So the strike is 55 or 55.25. The decimal places are used only when premium is at a level other than round dollars. Premium is also expressed without dollar signs and on a per-share basis. So a premium of 2.30 translates to $230 for one option on 100 shares. If the premium value is at a rounded number, it is expressed without decimal values. So a premium of 2 is $200.

3.   **Use proper buying and selling terms, especially for short options.** The best-known description of opening a long position (in either stock or option) is "buy to open," and for a sale it is "sell to close." When dealing with a short option, the terminology is reversed. An opening transaction is "sell to open" and a closing one is "buy to close." You will see the closing price described in other places as "buying back" the option. This is inaccurate and confusing. When you close a short option, you are not "buying it back" because you never owned it in the first place. Although this might seem like a minor point, it is important to use the right terminology to avoid confusion.

Moneyness of the Call

The selection of a particular strike based on its moneyness determines to a large degree the effectiveness of the hedge. As long as the strike is higher than your basis in stock, you can decide to write in-the-money, out-of-the-money, or at-the-money covered calls. Each will have a different hedging profile and likely outcome.

The chart of Exxon Mobil shown in Figure 6.2 illustrates the status of a 72.50.

Figure 6.2: Moneyness of the Call

The out-of-the-money call contains greater potential profits but lower downside protection; and vice versa for in the money, in which case profit potential is reduced but downside protection is greater due to higher call premium. The final outcome also relies on time remaining until expiration, so the moneyness is only one-half of the strike selection decision. Perhaps the optimum strike—assuming your purpose is to hedge downside risk minimally and to create an income stream with minimal exposure to exercise—is either an at-the-money call expiring in a few days, or an out-of-the-money call expiring in less than one month. Both of these contain an element of safety in terms of likely exercise, and both can be managed to avoid movement in the money where exercise is a distinct possibility.

Compare premium values for Macy's (M) as of the closing prices of November 6, 2015, consisting of two expirations and five strikes, as shown in Table 6.2.

Table 6.2 – Macy's call prices, two expirations

Nov 13 (weekly, 7 days)	Bid
48	2.40
48.50	2.26
49	2.06
49.50	1.84
50	1.60
Nov 20 (weekly, 14 days)	Bid
48	2.94
48.50	2.66
49	2.42
49.50	2.16
50	1.95

Source: Options listings, Charles Schwab & Co.

The differences between the moneyness levels and time to expiration are clear. All of the one-week options are cheaper, meaning opening one of these will accomplish faster expiration but less money. However, the difference is slight. The closest to the money contract of 49 yields 2.06 in the seven-day option, or 2.42 for the 14-day, a difference of only 0.36, or $36. Is it worth an extra week of exposure for an added $36 in premium income? Considering how any stock price can move in a short period of time, the added days of exposure do not yield enough added income to justify the exposure. The at-the-money contracts make more sense when opened for the shortest possible term. Earning 2.06 (approximately $197 after deducting estimated $9 for trading costs) in only one week is not only advantageous income but a 2.06-point hedge as well.

The in-the-money calls yield more premium, but also are exposed to greater exercise risk. For example, the one-week 48 contracts were big at 2.40 versus 2.94 for the two-week contracts. This raises a strategic question: How do you analyze the interaction between time decay and potential profits between two different options? With one point in the money for both of these, the shorter-term option will expire quite soon but will lose approximately 1.4 points if the stock price does not move. This means that the time decay will be rapid, so even though the call is in the money, the potential profit due to time decay is considerable. In comparison, the two-week option bid at 2.94 will lose nearly two full points in the next two weeks. The chances of exercise are identical to the one-week calls, but with more time to act and react, greater profit is also possible.

With short-term in-the-money covered calls, it is possible to earn a profit even if the stock does not move, and even if the call remains in the money. This is because time decay will be rapid, so the position can be bought to close at a profit even though it remains in the money.

An out-of-the-money strategy is the safest. Even though it yields less premium, chances of exercise are very remote, notably for the one-week contracts. For example, you can sell a 50 covered call expiring in one week for 1.60 (net about $151 after $9 trading fees are taken). This call is over a full point out of the money, and expiration is in one week. With all attributes considered (time to expiration and moneyness), this is the lowest-yielding dollar amount of the range of options analyzed; however, it is the one most likely to expire worthless (or to lose enough value to be profitable with a buy to close order within a few days).

In selecting one hedge over another, moneyness is a consideration that will determine the likely profitability of a short-term covered call. Combined with time to expiration and the certainty of rapid time decay, a covered call hedge can be structured to yield consistent profits, even if executed using one-week expiration terms.

Covered Calls With an Expiration Series

Moneyness and time to expiration have to be taken into account when writing a single covered call against 100 shares. However, this idea can be expanded into a more elaborate form of hedge when you own more than 100 shares, utilizing a series of expiration dates and strikes.

Returning to the example of Macy's, the two next expiration cycles (including one a weekly option), consider expanding into several. If you owned 300 shares of Macy's valued at $48.90 as of the close of November 6, 2015, some interesting hedge potential is opened up when expanding the basic covered call idea. Table 6.3 expands the expirations to be considered.

Table 6.3 – Macy's call prices, three expirations

Nov 20 (14 days)	Bid
50	1.95
52.50	1.05
55	0.50
Dec 18 (38 days)	Bid
50	2.61
52.50	1.69
55	1.04
Jan 158 (66 days)	Bid
50	3.30
52.50	2.42
55	1.67

Source: Options listings, Charles Schwab & Co.

In this expanded list, two dates have been avoided intentionally. Earnings were scheduled to be announced on November 11, so on the "action date" of November 6, the possibility of an earnings surprise made this immediate strike less attractive. The week on December 11 also contained weekly options, but that same week concluded with an ex-dividend date. This was also avoided as potentially a time for in-the-money early exercise.

Key Point

An option series allows you to vary the strike while maintaining attractive premium levels. This may be preferable to writing strictly short-term options with a single strike.

A series of options is based on current value of the underlying and its basis, and on the premium values. This is an excellent hedging device as long as you intend to hold shares for the long term and want to exploit time decay to create current income. Assuming your basis in this stock was the November 6 closing price of $48.90, and that you bought 300 shares, the following option contracts represent one way to set up a series:

November 50 @ 1.95 (minus $9 trading costs)	$186
December 52.50 @ 1.69 (minus $9)	$160
January 55 @ 1.67 (minus $9)	$158
Total premium	$504

This total is lower than the income you could have received for selling three November 50 calls. These were out of the money by 1.10 points and expired in 14 days, so that would be a reasonable covered call and hedge. The total net premium for that trade would be $558. However, by expanding into the subsequent months *and* changing the strike, you avoid the possibility of short-term exercise in the immediate term. At the same time, for slightly less income, you set up the series so that if the stock were to rise higher than the strikes, the capital gain on the December and January contracts would be higher (by an additional $250 for December and $500 for January). The lost opportunity risk of exercise is offset to a degree with this "upside protection" feature of the option series.

Even if the underlying price were to rise during this period, time decay will make it very likely that some or all of these positions could be closed for less premium than the initial sale, making this a profitable hedge based simply on time decay. This can work as a rolling series as well. For example, once November options expire or are closed, they are replaced by a new option expiring in February. However, that will also be a month in which earnings are again reported, so this is a factor to keep in mind when picking expiration dates. However, at the point the November contracts were set to expire, February is in the distant future; so selecting out-of-the-money contracts with attractive levels of time value offsets this problem.

The option series takes the basic covered call for 100 shares, and expands it for higher numbers of shares owned. It takes advantage of time decay and enables you to either roll forward or close at a profit when the underlying price rises. As a hedge, this reduces current income on an annualized basis but provides smart management over strikes and creates an income stream that works well. During times of consolidation, this form of hedge is particularly attractive as it continues to generate income even though you cannot know when the consolidation will end on which direction price will move. If price did break out of consolidation and move downward, currently open calls lose value and eventually expire; at the same time, if you continue to believe the shares are worth keeping in your portfolio, you also will assume the price decline is cyclical. If price breaks out of consolidation to the upside, open calls are likely to move in the money. If possible, open contracts should be closed to take profits. If not possible, these can be rolled forward to higher strikes expiring later.

Calculating Outcomes: The Complexity of Returns

Whether writing single covered calls or a series, one of the big challenges for every covered call investor is calculating net returns on a consistent basis. The first question that arises is: What price should you use to calculate returns?

> **Key point**
> Return calculations are complex because you first have to decide what stock price to use. There are three choices.

For example, you have two covered call situations. Both yielded about 3% in one month, when returns were calculated based on your original cost. However, one company's stock was bought at $30 and currently value is closer to $55; the other was bought at $40 and currently is valued at $42.

Using your original basis in stock would seem an obvious choice, as this is the normal price for figuring out a net return. However, if your stock has increased substantially since you bought it, the original price will be significantly lower than current value; so original basis can distort returns, especially between two or more situations. In the example, one stock had appreciated $25 points since purchase and the other had grown by only two points. Using original basis is not realistic.

Another choice is to use the current value at the time the covered call expires, is closed, or is exercised. The problem with this is that the outcome is distorted once again if the current price is substantially higher or lower than the strike. Using current value is unreliable as a standard, remembering that the calculation is intended to make reliable and accurate comparisons between two or more different covered call trades.

The third choice is to use the covered call's strike price. This is the most accurate of the three price choices, because this is the price the call will be exercised if that is the outcome. It is also the price used to determine whether the call expires worthless, is rolled forward, or exercised.

The calculation of returns is done at two points: first when you are considering opening a covered call among several choices, and again after the trade has been closed. This brings up a second issue: Should you include potential capital gains or dividends?

Capital gains should not be included in the calculation of covered call returns for the same reason that original basis is not an accurate price for calculating returns. Though capital gains matter and should be calculated, this should be kept separate from the calculation of returns on the option hedge.

Dividends are another matter. These should be added into the calculation of returns, because the dividend yield affects the overall outcome of a covered call trade. Overall returns has to be annualized to make comparisons accurate, but timing of quarterly dividends will change the outcome as well. For example, the following companies offer a similar dividend:

Philip Morris (PM)4.72% (1.18% per quarter)

Consolidated Edison (ED)4.20% (1.05% per quarter)

If dividends were the only consideration in an otherwise equal value for each of these companies, PM is the choice with a higher dividend. However, an in-depth analysis of the outcome for covered calls reveals a more complex outcome.

PM's ex-dividend was timed for September 28, 2015, and due to repeat at the end of December, March, and June quarters. ED's ex-dividend was set for November 16, with quarterly repeats in February, May, and August. A study of options trades reveals that the December option closest to the current price but out of the money yielded a very similar outcome:

Philip Morris (PM), closed Nov. 6 @ $86.37

DEC 87.50 call bid 1.25, net of trading costs = $116

Initial yield: $1.16 ÷ $86.37 = 1.34%

Consolidated Edison (ED), closed Nov. 6 @ $61.95

DEC 62.50 call bid 0.90, net of trading costs = $81

Initial yield: $0.81 ÷ $61.95 = 1.31%

This summary reveals close outcomes: 1.34% versus 1.31%. Based on this, the PM option appears to be a better choice, especially as it yields more cash. However, when dividends are added into this equation, the picture changes. PM's ex-dividend date occurred on September 28 and was due to repeat at the end of December, March, and June. ED's ex-dividend date was set for November 16 with repeats in February, May, and August.

PM did not earn a dividend by expiration of the December contract. The November 20 option expiration date occurred before the December dividend. So calculation of return in the window between November 6 and November 20 does not include a quarterly dividend. Thus, the true annualized return remains at the outcome based on 1.34% over 38 days:

Annualized: 1.34% ÷ 38 days x 365 days = 12.87%

In comparison, ED does earn a dividend in November, so the return here has to be annualized and the quarterly dividend added. The annual yield was 4.230%, representing 1.05% per quarter:

Annualized: 1.31% ÷ 38 days x 365 days = 12.58%

Add dividend: 12.58% + 1.05% = 13.63%

Although the difference here is small, the true overall yield of options and dividends is greater for ED, even with the lower dividend yield, than for PM. This is due to the timing of the quarterly dividend.

If you were to hold either of these stocks in your portfolio, both yield a very attractive annual dividend. However, the point to remember is that once the timing of quarterly dividends is taken into account, the picture is changed.

> **Key Point**
> The level of dividend yield matters, but equally important is the timing of quarterly dividends to be earned between opening a position and expiration of the option.

Writing Calls on Stock Already Owned and Appreciated

If you buy shares of stock at the same time you open a covered call, the relationship between underlying price and strike is straightforward. Ideally, the strike has to be higher than your basis in the stock, meaning the price per share you paid at the time of purchase. In the event of exercise, you end up with capital gains or, at worst, a breakeven in the stock. However, covered calls take on a different meaning and a different hedge profile when you have owned stock for a period of time and it has appreciated in value.

In this situation, your concern goes beyond generating current income and has to include the issue of protecting your net gain, even though you do not want to sell shares. This is an endless problem for even the most conservative investor. Should you sell and take profits, concerned that the stock price will decline? Or should you hold onto high-quality shares and ignore the cyclical price changes?

A third choice is to hedge that paper gain with options. There are many methods for this, including both calls and puts. However, even the covered call can be used to manage the appreciated stock in your portfolio.

In most covered calls, you are motivated to write at-the-money or out-of-the-money options. For appreciated stock, this can make sense; if exercised, these positions yield the option premium and capital gains. But other factors have to be considered as well:

1. **Timing of a covered call.** For appreciated stock, are you willing to risk exercise in less than one year? The long-term capital gains rate is much more attractive than the fully-taxed short-term gain, so if you do write covered calls in this situation, pick expirations that occur after the one-year period. This still contains a degree of risk, especially if ex-dividend occurs before the year has passed. Early exercise could force a short-term gain.

2. **Unintended consequences of exercise.** With appreciated stock, you might consider writing in-the-money calls. This is an attractive scenario. You still get a capital gain, but much higher call premium represents a nice bump in your overall return. However, if you write a ***deep in the money*** call, you face a different risk: An ***unqualified covered call*** might end up with capital gains taxed at short-term rates even if the holding period exceeds a full year.

For example, you bought stock eight months ago at $32 per share. Today the stock is worth $68, more than twice your initial basis. You would be willing to sell at a profit, and you do not want to lose these gains. So you consider selling a covered call with a strike of 45, which is deep in the money. The call expires in five months and, because exercise at the end of the term would mean you held the stock more than a year, it would be a long-term gain. However, under the unqualified covered call rule, the count to full-term status is stopped at the time you open the deep in-the-money call. Exercise at any time would constitute a short-term gain in the stock.

The precise definition of "unqualified" varies by price level, time to expiration, and strike prices. Table 6.4 summarizes then definition of the unqualified covered call.

Table 6.4: Unqualified Covered Calls

Prior day's stock closing price	Time until expiration	Strike price limits
$25 or below	Over 30 days	One strike under close of the prior trading day (however, no call can be qualified if the strike is lower than 85% of stock price)
$25.01 - $60	Over 30 days	One strike under close of the prior trading day
$60.01 - $150	31-90 days	One strike under close of the prior trading day
$60.01 - $150	Over 90 days	Two strikes under close of the prior trading day (but no more than 10 points ITM)
above $150	31-90 days	One strike under close of the prior trading day
above $150	Over 90 days	Two strikes under close of the prior trading day

The in-the-money strategy has its time and place. If you are willing to accept exercise, the in-the-money covered call results in exercise. If times with expiration occur after the next quarterly ex-dividend date, overall income will be higher as well. So as a hedge, the in-the-money covered call is a powerful strategy to generate premium income, capital gains, and dividends. This assumes that you want to sell.

An alternative outcome creates a different kind of hedge. For example, if the current underlying price declines, you will see a point-for-point comparison to intrinsic value in the short call. For each point the stock price declines, a corresponding decline is seen in the option. Because this is a short position, a reduced premium value represents profit; the option can be bought to close for a lower premium than it was sold to open. This is the same level of protection you gain from buying an insurance put (Chapter 2). In that hedge, downside protection caps any loss in the underlying with the long put. With the short call, the same outcome occurs with the difference that you receive the premium instead of paying it. This advantage is offset by exercise risk.

So when you open an in-the-money put, you either accept the risk of exercise or exploit intrinsic value in the case of a price decline. This actually is combined with time value decay, so that the potential profit in the short call contains clear advantages over the long hedge using the put for downside protection. Your primary consideration in this strategy is likely to be whether or not you are willing to risk having shares called away. Remember the basic assumption in hedging with options: This is designed to protect your equity positions against market risk, not to give up shares you prefer to keep.

Rolling to Avoid Exercise

Covered call writers avoid exercise by either closing positions as they approach or move into the money, or by rolling positions forward. Rolling normally creates a net credit if the roll goes to the same strike, as longer-term options contain more time value. But there are risks involved. These include:

1. **Longer time of exposure.** The extended expiration also means your position remains exposed for a longer time, tying up capital, possibly without substantially increasing profit potential. So in evaluating a forward roll of a short call, compare the added credit received to the cost of keeping the position open longer. Rolling to the same strike is not always a wise idea.

2. **The possibility of creating an unqualified covered call.** If the stock price has increased enough so that the current strike is deep in the money, a roll to the same strike could set up an unintentional unqualified covered call. This is a concern only if you have held stock for less than one year; once the 12-month period has passed, the threat has passed as well.

3. **Risk when rolling up.** Some big moves in the stock price justify rolling to a higher strike. This may involve a net debit rather than a credit. The rationale is that the higher strike represents a higher capital gain if the position is

> **Key Point**
> Rolling forward helps avoid exercise, but it should be done only with awareness of time exposure, tax consequences, and added risks.

eventually exercised. However, in this type of roll, keep track of your true net basis. If you end up rolling to a higher strike but losing on the option, the profit potential is reduced.

The forward roll is a smart strategy to avoid exercise. However, if it is possible to close the position at a profit or even at breakeven, it could make sense to take that close and replace it with a later-expiring, higher-strike covered call.

When close to expiration, the roll takes on a different meaning. With time value gone, should you wait out expiration or close the position and replace it? If the call's value is close to zero in the final week, and it is out of the money, there is little chance of a last-minute move in the money; but it can happen. When at the money or even slightly in the money, closing a low-premium short call and replacing it with a new one with higher time value makes sense. When the cost of buying to close is minimal, the risk of a last-minute price move and exercise is not worth the small amount it costs to roll forward.

The Ratio Write

One variation of the covered call will be likely to involve more rolling than the straightforward basic strategy. The *ratio write* involves writing a higher number of calls than you cover with stock. So this can be considered as a partially covered position or a combination of covered and uncovered calls.

The strategy involves more risk than the covered call due to the possibility of exercise. Refer again to Table 6.3 on page 109. To open a ratio write using the December options, ownership of 300 Macy's (M) shares bought at $48.90 could be converted to a ratio write by selling four 55 calls. The December calls were bid at 1.04, and trading fees for selling four options would be about $11 (the first contract costs about $8.75 and additional contracts are priced at about 75 cents each). The net for these four options would be calculated as: 1.04 x 4 = $416, less $11 trading costs = $405.

These options with 55 strikes were 6.1 points out of the money, so they have a comfortable cushion. However, if the underlying prices edged upward toward $55 per share, some or all of these short calls should be closed or rolled to avoid exercise.

Key Point
The ratio write increases premium income but also increases exercise risk.

The ratio write provides additional income, thus a greater hedge. However, the market risk is also increased. So for an additional $104 received for writing the additional ratio position, the risk is minimal but should not be ignored.

To reduce the ratio write market risk, an alternative is the *variable ratio write.* This is the same as the ratio write, but expanded to include two strike prices. For example, returning to the Macy's example with an underlying price of $48.90, owning 300 shares and writing four calls sets up a variable ratio write in the following configuration:

Sell two 52.50 calls @ 1.69 = $338, less $10 trading costs = $328

Sell two 55 calls @ 0.55 = 1.10 less $10 trading costs = $100

The total net of $428 involves two strikes, both out of the money. This is a safer hedge because if and when the stock price moves upward, any of these options can be closed or rolled forward. Because they all are out of the money, this is a reasonable strategy. Relying on time decay gives you a hedging advantage when selling options. The covered call is conservative, and the uncovered call is high-risk. However, the variable ratio write is not as risky as writing uncovered calls without that ratio protection. The variable ratio write has risks, but not as high as the ratio write without the two strikes.

The covered call can be written in all of these varieties. The selection of one level of hedge versus another depends on the volatility of the underlying stock, exercise and lost opportunity risks, and objectives you hold for your portfolio.

An alternative to the covered call is found in the uncovered put. Although this is a much different type of option—short put rather than short call and uncovered versus covered—the market risk of both strategies is the same. The next chapter examines the uncovered put as a form of hedge that offers another form of benefit similar to the covered call.

7 | The Uncovered Put: Alternative to Covered Calls With Less Risk

The uncovered put often is perceived as a high-risk strategy. However, it contains identical market risks to those of the more popular covered call. There are numerous offsets in the comparison; the point, however, is that the uncovered put is just as conservative as the covered call.

This chapter describes hedging strategies using uncovered puts. A true hedge is opened to reduce risks on stock positions owned in the portfolio. So a conservative investor will not be as interested in an option-only strategy. However, some circumstances justify writing a put in place of a covered call or even along with a covered call at the same time.

A Comparison to Covered Calls

The uncovered put and the covered call share the same market value, but the features of each are not the same. Table 7.1 provides an analysis of the differences.

Table 7.1

Covered Calls	Uncovered Puts
100 shares of stock are held in the portfolio.	No stock ownership is required.
No collateral is needed.	Collateral must be held.
When the underlying price rises, the call may be exercised unless closed or rolled.	When the underlying price rises, the uncovered put will expire worthless.
When the underlying price falls, the covered call will expire worthless.	When the underlying price falls, the uncovered put may be exercised unless closed or rolled.
In a price decline, the stock loses value and has to be held until recovery or closed at a loss.	In a price decline, the put can be closed or rolled forward to avoid exercise, using any strike.

119

In a price decline, a new covered call cannot be opened below net basis without risking a capital loss.	Because no stock is associated with the uncovered put as a separate trade, the strike does not affect profitability of stock.
Owners of stock earn dividends as long as shares are held.	Writers of uncovered puts do not earn dividends.

The attributes of each strategy make comparisons difficult, because some of these (dividends, collateral, specific outcomes of stock price changes) make the two strategies appear quite different. So equating them in terms of market risks has to take into account the many variables in attributes.

Key Point

The uncovered put can be rolled with more flexibility than the covered call, because capital gains in the stock are not at issue.

In any short option position, the desire is for the underlying price to remain out of the money. The uncovered put is more flexible than the covered call when the price moves in the money, because it can be rolled without capital gains consequences in an underlying position. The direction of movement is different. With the covered call, a rise in the underlying places the short call in the money. With the uncovered put, a decline in the underlying creates an in-the-money situation.

The dissimilarity in direction is explained by the nature of the covered call. It is also termed a *synthetic short put* because profits accrue in the call as long as the underlying remains at or below the strike.

The technical description of a covered call as synthetic short put explains why market risk is identical. However, the attributes (notably dividends and collateral requirements) make the two positions quite different in many ways. The flexibility of the uncovered put makes this far more flexible than the covered call, even though you have to give up dividend income as part of choosing the put over the call.

A more immediate question for you as an investor seeking hedges against equity position risks is how the uncovered put fits within your program. As a basic standard, a "hedge" should be related directly to the stock positions. So how does this occur? The simplicity and popularity of the covered call is based on ownership of 100 shares per option, so this naturally acts as a hedge by discounting the basis in stock while generating premium income; and in the event of exercise, stock is called away at a profit (as long as the strike is higher than your basis).

The uncovered put does work as a hedge for positions you own, even though it is not tied directly to shares. Just as the covered call hedges the equity position with minimal risks, the uncovered put provides an alternative strategy to accomplish the same end result. You do not want to write covered calls after the stock price has turned volatile, and if the price declines, you end up closing the short call or allowing it to expire. However, if the price decline is below your net basis, you end up with a paper loss. This means you have to wait for the price to rebound.

This "wait and see" timing makes covered calls less desirable as a hedge, especially when compared to the uncovered put. Because the put is not tied to the stock price, a decline in the underlying can be managed by closing the put or rolling it forward. In rolling, it does not matter what strike is selected as long as the roll produces a net credit or a breakeven. This is not possible with the covered call. If you roll to a strike below your basis in stock, exercise would produce a net capital loss; and that outcome is unacceptable in a hedging strategy.

The uncovered put works as a hedge in three specific situations: first, as a replacement strategy after a covered call has expired worthless due to a drop in price; second, as part of a recovery strategy after a large decline in the underlying price; and third, when price is in a consolidation trend.

The Replacement Strategy

The uncovered put, as an alternative to the covered call, has a specific application when stock prices have declined enough for a covered call to expire worthless.

For example, you bought 100 shares of Exxon Mobil on October 28, paying $80 per share. On November 6, the price has risen to more than $84 per share and you sold a November 83.50 call for a bid of 1.53 (net proceeds after trading costs were $144). On Monday, November 9, the price of shares has declined to $83.74 and the November 84 call also fell to an ask price of 0.85. You entered a buy to close order and paid a net of $94. This generated a profit of $50 ($144 – $94).

This chart action is summarized in Figure 7.1.

Figure 7.1: Timing for the Uncovered Put

Based on the decline in stock price, you might hesitate at this point to open another covered call. Given the fact that the next move in this price pattern is uncertain, this would be a good time to open an uncovered put as an alternative with greater flexibility. Like the covered call, the uncovered put brings cash into your account, but closing and rolling are more easily accomplished when you are not concerned about the underlying price. Support appears at about $80 per share, which was your original basis. So selling a put anywhere close to the current value of $83.74 would be one possible way to exploit price behavior. With the price declining over the last three sessions, chances for a short-term price upside reaction are positive. So an 83 put is a good candidate. The bid on the November 83 put was 1.50, so you could sell a contract and net $141.

This short put yields income at close to the premium for the original short call. However, because expiration was only 11 days away, the chances for rapid time decay were excellent. This position could be left to expire worthless as long as the underlying price remained above $83 per share. If price declined, the short put could be closed or rolled forward.

In this example, the switch from covered call to uncovered put makes sense because of the underlying price behavior. After buying to close the original short call, writing another appeared poorly timed, based solely on the risk of a price surge upward and the consequences to the new covered call. With an uncovered put, the outcome is more controllable for a position with the same market risk and greater flexibility.

Recovery Strategy

> **Key Point**
>
> As a recovery strategy after the stock price has fallen, the uncovered put works where the covered call would not.

The replacement strategy is a sensible way to convert from one hedge to another. Normally, an uncovered put would not belong in a hedging strategy; however, in this case, the identical market risk of the two short options made the uncovered put a smart alternative to use while waiting out the underlying price behavior. A different use of the uncovered put occurs when the underlying price has declined below net basis.

The term *net basis* refers to the original cost of stock, discounted for the net premium received when selling a covered call. This basic discount is a primary form of hedging familiar to covered call writers. However, it is also easy to overlook the very real market risk that shows up when the price decline creates a net loss.

For example, at the opening on November 6, you bought 100 shares of Macy's (M) at $50.40 and sold a November 50.50 covered call at the bid of 1.74 (net $165). This reduced your basis to $48.75 ($50.40 – 1.65). By Monday, November 9, the underlying price had declined to $46.30. Your net paper loss at this point was $2.45 per share ($48.75 – $46.30). You bought to close the November 50.50 call at an ask of 1.05, netting $96. Your profit on the call was $69 ($165 – $96). So adjusting your basis after closing the call, the net was changed to $49.71 ($50.50 – $0.69). However, the current value of shares was at $46.30. The revised net paper loss was $341 ($49.71 – $46.30).

Figure 7.2 summarizes this situation.

Figure 7.2: Timing Uncovered Puts in a Recovery Strategy

At this point, the uncovered put offers a potential solution to the $341 net paper loss on Macy's. For example, at this moment, the December 45 put was bid at 3.80 (providing a net of $371 after $9 for trading costs). This turns the net loss of $341 into a $30 profit ($371 – $341).

A potential problem with this is exercise risk, of course; and because expiration for the December contract was 39 days away, the time of exposure was greater as well. However, you would expect time value to fall rapidly as long as the stock price remained at or above the strike

> **Key Point**
> Exercise risk should not be over-looked in the short put position. The put has to be managed and tracked to avoid exercise.

of 45. At the moment of this trade, the stock was 1.30 points out of the money. Any change in that condition could be managed by closing the position and again adjusting the basis, or by rolling it forward. The forward roll is not ideal in this situation, because the purpose is not to keep the short put exposure open, but to offset the loss in net basis.

This provides one example of how the uncovered put is used to manage a paper loss and create a recovery strategy. If the stock price continues to decline, the problem is made worse. Not only would the short put move into an exercise risk status, but the value of shares would also continue to fall. So with this in mind, the uncovered put as a recovery strategy should be employed only when you have faith that the fundamental value of shares remains strong and the likelihood of a price improvement is strong. If this is not the case, additional hedging to limit downside risk would be justified in the form of longer-term long puts or other hedges, such as collars or synthetic stock positions.

The possibility that a loss position could be made worse points out one of the dangers in a recovery strategy. The desire is to absorb the paper loss and return to breakeven or better. However, as far too many options traders have discovered, the outcome does not always yield these results. With this in mind, a recovery strategy should be kept at a modest level. There are instances in which just taking a small loss is preferable to adding greater risks and ending up with greater losses. Every investor has to accept loss as a reality; and the idea of hedging is never to eliminate loss altogether, but to mitigate the effects of losses on the equity side. Just as stock ownership involves taking a loss in some cases, the options hedge can also fail to provide the desired result, meaning losses have to be accepted as a reality in both equity and hedging strategies.

Strategy During a Consolidation Trend

The consolidation trend—in which price is range-bound, often for an extended period of time—is perhaps the most frustrating of all trends. Price is not moving outside of the range, so it is easy to think of this period of time as one between trends, in which neither buyers nor sellers are able to move price in either direction.

In fact, consolidation as a third type of trend (in addition to bullish and bearish) presents exceptional hedging opportunities. The stock you hold in your portfolio is not gaining (or losing) value when prices are fixed in a consolidation, so you have to either wait out the trend or identify actions you can take to hedge the situation. The problem, of course, is that you cannot know whether price will break out to the upside or the downside. Specific signals do exist, and this type of trend is excellent for writing uncovered puts.

Because you own stock during consolidation, the uncovered put acts as a hedge in two ways. First, its market risk (identical to the covered call) is manageable no matter which direction prices move. Upon breakout, a rise in price leads to the put becoming worthless. A downside breakout leads to closing the put and either taking profits or rolling it forward. However, as a *hedge,* the risk in consolidation is inactivity. The uncovered put generates income in the same way as the covered call, but without the risk of exercise (if the underlying prices breaks out above) or paper loss (after a downside move).

Using the uncovered put during consolidation is a safer hedge than the same move during a dynamic trend. Uptrends, especially fast-moving ones, can reverse quickly and pose exercise risk. Downtrends clearly are not the time to write uncovered puts. However, the relatively narrow trading range associated with consolidation presents not only trading opportunities, but clear breakout forecasts.

For example, on the chart of Kellogg (K) shown in Figure 7.3, many signals are present that point to trading opportunities with uncovered puts.

Figure 7.3: Uncovered Puts During Consolidation Trends

The consolidation trend extended for three months, from April to July. During this time, the price remained in a breadth of only three points. Three attempted breakouts below all failed, and formed an inverse head and shoulders pattern. This by itself predicted a breakout in the oppo-

> **Key Point**
> Bollinger Bands uses moving averages to identify price volatility, making this indicator a type of probability monitor.

site direction. This was confirmed in the second half of July when prices narrowed in the top portion of the consolidation range. This also formed a ***Bollinger squeeze***, a pattern seen within Bollinger Bands, a system of three volatility bands (a 20-day moving average, higher band, and lower band, each two standard deviations from the middle).

The Bollinger squeeze is a narrowing of prices close to one of the sides of the consolidation range. It is a period of low volatility, which predicts a coming period of high volatility and potential breakout. On the chart, although the Bollinger Bands are not shown, the squeeze does occur in the second half of July, immediately before the breakout. This squeeze confirms the inverse head and shoulders—and, as expected, price broke out above the consolidation range.

In consolidation, many attempted breakouts fail. So how can you know whether a breakout will succeed? This pattern, combining inverse head and shoulders with a Bollinger squeeze, is a convincing start. Price then formed into an island cluster, described in Chapter 5. This is a period of trading identified by gaps on either side, either above or below the established range. Once price retreated back, the long lower shadow on the first white session revealed that continuation of the consolidation trend was unlikely. In fact, price did begin trending upward at that point. The island cluster was a final confirmation that the consolidation trend was over.

Can signals like the inverse head and shoulders apply during consolidation? Under typical definitions of "reversal," a signal is valid only in a bullish or bearish trend, and there is no clear trend to reverse. However, this concept should be challenged with a new definition of "reversal." A signal can reverse the consolidation trend by setting up a new dynamic trend. This includes any Western or Eastern technical reversal signal located within consolidation, and the Kellogg chart demonstrates how this works.

Key Point
A careful reading of signals effectively forecasts breakout from consolidation. This is especially true of the island cluster following breakout.

So with a series of clear signals, how can this be traded? A hedge consisting of uncovered puts would be effective in this situation. The three declines below support that make up the head and shoulders were likely to reverse and move back into range, as they did. The moment price fell below support, especially in the case of the shoulders, where the move consisted of shadows but not opening or closing range, an uncovered put would have effectively hedged the consolidation of prices. Each of these uncovered puts would have been closed once price returned into range and rose to the point of resistance or to another price peak. The first shoulder touched resistance, marking the point to close. The head peaked at mid-range and then began declining; this decline marked a good price point to close. The second shoulder rose into range and immediately trended into the Bollinger squeeze. At that point, the uncovered put should have been closed, as the squeeze signaled a likely bullish breakout.

The island cluster is always difficult to interpret in the moment. However, once it completes the formation, it clearly identifies a likely price move to follow. The long lower shadow at the first session after the conclusion of the island cluster is bullish (combining the island cluster with the shadow). So it appears that the breakout from consolidation was succeeding, but could this be confirmed? The first two sessions after the conclusion of the island cluster, consisting of the white session with the long shadows and the following black session, formed a thrusting lines signal, a bullish confirming indicator. This would be another excellent spot to open an uncovered out. This put could be closed at the peak with upper shadow occurring in mid-September. Finally, the long white candlestick in late October identified an excellent spot to open a new covered call.

This detailed analysis reveals that consolidation can be a signal-rich period in which option hedges are effective. A covered call writer has to move cautiously, however, because consolidation can end suddenly and move in either direction. So in addition to looking for breakout reversal signals (reversal of consolidation), the use of uncovered puts as a flexible alternative to covered calls continues the hedge even when price is range-bound.

Contingent Purchase Strategy

Most descriptions of selling uncovered puts address risk levels when shares of stock are not owned. So in this context, the uncovered put is seen as a speculative trade. However, it can also be used as a form of hedge when you do own shares, especially if the price of shares has increased.

In this situation, you face a dilemma: Do you sell and take profits, avoiding the possibility that the price could reverse and absorb all of the profit? Or do you hold, hoping for continued profits? A third possibility and a form of hedge is to buy an insurance put. In this strategy, the long put's value increases for every point lost in the stock below intrinsic value. However, because you have to pay for the put, the true cap on loss consists of the strike of the put minus the cost of the put. For example, you buy a 35 strike put and pay 2. Your offset will begin after the breakeven price of $33 per share. So if you paid $30 per share, this locks in at least $300 in profits even if the stock price falls below your original basis of $30.

Another way to hedge appreciated stock is by selling uncovered puts. This is an opposite strategy from the purchase of a long put, but the purpose is also different. With the long put, you want to protect your paper profits. With the short put, you set up a hedge with one of two outcomes: profit in the short put, or purchase or more shares.

For example, you bought 100 shares @ $48 per share. Today, the stock value has grown to $57 and you are concerned that the value could decline. By selling a 55 put for 6, you set up a short position three points in the money. However, the breakeven on this is actually $49 (55 − 6), so that even if the put were exercised, your acquisition cost will be lower than the strike. The net breakeven is $49 per share, compared with your original basis of $48. Exercise increases your position at a price very close to the original. The average basis in stock (original 100 shares plus another 100 shares put to you upon exercise) is $42.50:

$$((\$48 + \$49) \div 2) - \$6 = \$42.50$$

As long as the current price per share at the time of exercise is higher than $42.50, the overall position remains profitable. Even with a large decline from the strike of 55 down to $42.50, or 12.5 points, your original basis remains intact due to the premium from the short put.

Another possible outcome that avoids exercise is closing the short put. At the time it was opened, the premium of 6 included two points of intrinsic value. A drop below the 55 strike eliminates all of the intrinsic value, and in addition time value will decline as well. So the short put can be closed at a profit. It can then be replaced with other short puts, covered calls, or any number of other hedges.

The short put used to hedge against appreciated stock hedges market risk and reduces your overall net basis, adding a safety net to lost paper profits. It provides the same type of hedging value as the covered call, but with one important difference: With the covered call, replacement involves consideration of the strike versus original basis in the stock, but with the uncovered put, this does not matter. Exercise can be avoided by rolling forward to any strike that produces a net credit. Although early exercise is always possible, it is remote as long as time value remains part of the put's premium and as long as the put is at the money or out of the money.

If you are willing to acquire additional shares as the result of this **contingent purchase** strategy, the short put is an excellent hedge. In the event the price of the underlying does not decline enough to move the put in the money, the alternative of closing or rolling provides added income along with the hedge against loss.

Covered Straddles

The covered call and uncovered put can also be combined into an effective and powerful form of hedging. When two short options are opened at the same time, it often indicates a high-risk and speculative move. However, the **covered straddle** is conservative and presents an exception to this general rule by providing income and hedging protection together.

The term *covered* is somewhat inaccurate. The call is covered by the stock, but a short put cannot be covered in the same sense of the word. So although this is a straddle (two offsetting options with the same strike and expiration), it is a combination of two conservative hedges: the covered call and the uncovered put.

The covered straddle can be opened in a consolidation trend, just like the uncovered put. However, this presents a danger for the covered call. A sudden price move out of the fixed range may present a particular form of risk regardless of price direction. So the most sensible point in the price trend for a covered straddle starts at the bottom of a downtrend, assuming that clear reversal signals are present and strongly confirmed. This is a point to open the short put; and once the bullish trend has been established, the second leg, the covered call, can be opened as well, completing the straddle.

For example, the chart of Alleghany (Y) reveals a clear and strong set of signals for reversal, as shown in Figure 7.4.

Figure 7.4: Reversal Point for a Covered Straddle

On this chart, the bottom of the price trend is marked clearly with the unusually long lower shadow. This reveals that sellers tried to move price lower but failed. However, given the signal's proximity to the marketwide decline of August 24, this signal by itself is not enough. However, by

> **Key Point**
> Reversal signals found at the right proximity clearly mark the best points for opening uncovered puts.

the end of the month, two additional signals appeared: a bullish harami and a bullish engulfing. This reveals that the bottom has been reached and prices will begin moving higher. This is the point to open an uncovered put.

The signals for the covered call occurred on October 16, with a strong gravestone doji. This consists of a doji and an unusually long upper shadow. The signal here is that the bullish rally may be weakening or ending. However, price continued moving upward. In this mid- to late-October period, opening a covered call at the 500 or 505 strike would have been well timed, given the strong gravestone doji pointing to weakness in the trend.

In this case, the two legs created the covered straddle. The uncovered put would be left intact for the moment because price rose from the $460 range above $500 per share. So any uncovered put opened with a 460 or 470 strike would have lost most of its value by this point and could be closed; however, given the point spread between strike and current value, there is no urgency to close the put.

A covered straddle also makes sense here because of the lack of clear signals in either direction. The gravestone doji predicted the end of the bullish trend, but price did not react as expected. This indicates a likely consolidation. In fact, in the half-month after this chart, price remained range-bound between $495 and $505. This lack of movement would take both options down to low levels, so they could be bought to close at a profit, or left open to expire worthless.

The range of price movement explains the value of the covered straddle. Opening two uncovered puts does not always make sense and could pose excessive risk in the case of market decline. Opening two covered calls would require buying an additional 100 shares and also poses added risk. With the covered straddle, owning 100 shares allows you to double the hedge value without changing market risk. In addition, opening the position in legs maximizes the potential gains to be earned from this position.

Once the bullish reversal appeared strongly, timing for the uncovered put made sense, but the covered call would not have been well timed. However, once the bullish trend played out and signs of weakness appeared (meaning either a coming bearish move or consolidation), adding the covered call made perfect sense. The subsequent consolidation trend confirmed the wisdom of this position. However, given the price of the stock in the example and the volatility seen in historical price movement, this position has to be monitored closely and one or both sides closed if price begins trending once again.

The uncovered put, by itself or in combination with a covered call, is an effective hedging strategy. The combined use in the form of a covered straddle is a timing hedge, whereas alternating between the covered call and uncovered put can be timed for the peaks and valleys of price movement in swing trends or secondary trend patterns.

The next chapter expands the hedging strategy by explaining the use of spreads to protect equity positions and control market risks.

8 | Hedging With Spreads

The **spread** is any position with two offsetting options, which can be bullish, bearish, or neutral. So as a hedging mechanism, the spread is a flexible and varied form of option trade.

Spreads in their most basic form consist of the same expiration date but different strikes (the **vertical spread**). For example, a short call expiring in October with a 50 strike and a short call expiring the same month with a 45 strike set up a vertical spread.

Another variety is made up of the same strike but different expirations. This **horizontal spread** is intended to exploit the time value differences between the two positions. For example, a long October 50 with a short November 50 put creates a horizontal spread. This is also called a calendar spread or a time spread.

A final version of the basic spread combines different strikes and different expirations. This is called a **diagonal spread**. For example, a long October 50 call and a short November 55 call combine to create a diagonal spread.

Figure 8.1 summarizes the three formations of the basic spread.

Figure 8.1: Types of Basic Spreads

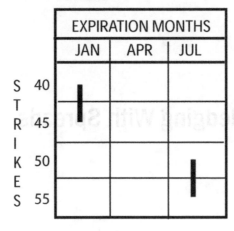

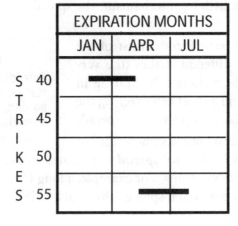

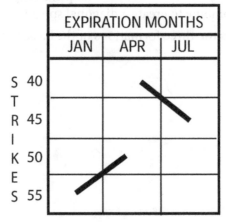

These various formations of the spread work as hedges for your portfolio's equity positions just as they may also represent highly speculative option strategies. An additional variation in this universe of spreads is that positions can consist of either calls or puts, and may also be long or short. When the attributes of a spread are evaluated by themselves (often as speculate trades), it is easy to overlook the true risks. Even a wide distance between strikes in a short position does not protect you from exercise risk, although it does reduce that risk. However, opening such a spread just as a matter of estimating outcomes is purely speculative. However, when spreads are associated with portfolio positions and intended to offset equity-based market risks, the hedging effect of spreads is substantial.

The Selection of a Debit Spread or Credit Spread

A spread may be either a *debit spread* or a *credit spread*. In a debit spread, the net outcome is payment of the difference between a long and short premium. The purchase of the long position costs more than the premium received on the short side.

A *bull spread* is designed to yield a profit when the underlying price rises. It can consist of either calls or puts. A *call bull spread* is one of a debit spread. It combines an in-the-money long call with a higher-strike out-of-the-money short call. In this debit spread, the maximum profit is the net of the short strike value, minus the long strike value.

The profit and loss are both limited in this strategy. The upside profit is maximized when the underlying price moves higher than the highest strike, and will be equal to the difference between the two strikes, less the initial debit:

Maximum profit = Short strike – long strike – net premium paid

Offsetting this limited profit is a limited loss on the downside. A loss occurs when the price moves lower, but it cannot be lower than the initial net debit:

Maximum loss = net debit of the position

The call bull spread's breakeven point is the long side strike plus net premium paid:

Breakeven = long strike + net debit

For example, on November 6, 2015, Exxon Mobil (XOM) closed at $84.47. At that time, the following options could be opened to create a call bull spread:

> **Key Point**
> Understanding the formulas for maximum profit, maximum loss, and breakeven price is an excellent tool for managing risk and identifying the viability of a particular spread.

November 84 long call, ask 1.43	$152
November 85 short call, bid 0.79	70
Net debit	$ 82

Note that in this example, the long position is based on the ask price and the short position employs the bid. The long is also increased by $9 to reflect trading costs, and the short is reduced in the same way to reflect reduced premium income.

In this example, maximum profit is $18 (difference in the two strikes, minus the net debit, or 85 – 84 – 0.82 = $18). Maximum loss is the net debit of $82. Breakeven is $84.82 per share (long strike plus net debit).

When puts are used in a bull spread, the position is opened as a credit. Because puts gain the most when moving against the stock's price direction, the bull spread is also going to be a net credit. For example, a *put bull spread* consists of a long out-of-the-money put with a higher-strike short in-the-money put. This position can be opened on XOM using the following positions:

November 84 long put, ask 1.73	$182
November 85 short put, bid 2.10	201
Net credit	$19

The maximum profit is limited to the net credit received for opening this position, which occurs if and when the underlying price moves above both strikes. Maximum loss is also limited, and is equal to the net difference between strikes, less the net credit:

Maximum loss = short strike – long strike – net credit

Break is equal to the short strike minus net credit:

Breakeven = short strike – net credit

In the example of XOM and a put bull spread, maximum profit is equal to the net credit of $19. Maximum loss is $81, the net of the short strike minus the long strike and net credit ($85 – $84 $0.19). Breakeven is the $182, the difference between short strike and net credit ($201 – $19).

The hedging attribute of a bull spread is a combination of limited profits on one side, versus limited losses on the other. However, with the spread, you have an advantage beyond the profit or loss price ranges. With time decay, the short call or short put can be closed to take profits if price moves down (for the call) or up (for the put). Although buying to close changes the overall net debit or credit, it leaves the long side intact with the possibility of accumulating profits if price continues moving favorably. Eventually (once the net cost has been exceeded) the long option can be closed at a profit. In this respect, both sides offer hedging benefits. In the event that price moves up (for the call) or down (for the put), the short option moves in the money and has to be closed or rolled to avoid exercise. The maximum profit or loss can be altered by closing the short side when time decay makes that side profitable; however, as a hedge, the intention should be to protect the equity position, not only to generate profits. In closing a short side, it is possible to wipe out any net gain while also losing the hedging advantage from the bull spread.

The *bear spread* works in the opposite direction. Profits are maximized when the underlying price declines, so the bear spread works as a hedge against market risk in the equity, as the overall position's growing value offsets declining value in the stock.

Like the bull spread, bear spread profits and losses are both limited. Profit is maximized when the underlying price advances higher than the high strike. The maximum profit is equal to the net credit received. Maximum possible loss occurs if the underlying price moves above the higher strike. This loss is equal to the difference between strikes, less original credit:

Maximum loss = long strike – short strike – credit received

Breakeven in this strategy is equal to the short strike plus credit received:

Breakeven = Short strike + credit received

For example, on November 6, 2015, Exxon Mobil (XOM) closed at $84.47. The following options could be opened to create a call bear spread:

November 85 long call, ask 0.92	$101
November 84 short call, bid 1.25	116
Net credit	$15

The maximum profit is the credit of $15. Maximum loss is the difference between the long and short strike, minus the credit: $85 – $84 – 0.15 = 0.85, or $85. Breakeven is equal to the short strike plus credit received, or 84 + 0.15 = $84.15.

The final version of this basic spread is the *put bear spread*. This combines a long in-the-money put and a lower-strike short out-of-the-money put.

Maximum profit is achieved when the underlying closes below the lower strike. With both options in the money, the higher long strike will have more intrinsic value than the short side. So maximum profit equals the difference between the two strikes, minus the debit:

Maximum profit = long strike – short strike – debit

Maximum loss occurs if the underlying rises higher than the higher strike, and the loss is equal to the net debit received. The breakeven is the long strike minus the debit:

Breakeven = long strike – debit

For example, XOM's options as of November 6, 2015, could be used to set up a put bear spread with the following:

November 85 long put, ask 2.28	$237
November 84 short put, bid 2.10	201
Net debit	$ 36

The maximum profit equals the difference between the two strikes, less the debit: 85 – 84 – 0.36 = 0.66, or $66. Maximum loss is the net debit of $36. Breakeven is calculated as the net of the long strike minus the debit: 85 – 0.36 = $84.64.

Key Point

The various forms of spread enhance your ability to hedge equity, by providing ease of switching from one type to another based on market conditions.

These examples of basic credit and debit spreads using calls and puts, either bullish or bearish, set up the theme of the put: limited profit and loss with great flexibility. Although the dollar values used were small for the purpose of the examples, your imagination can be put to work to devise higher profit and loss levels with wider gaps between strikes, and with the use of farther-out expiration dates and higher time value.

As hedges, the basic vertical hedge is attractive because of the tightly limited profit and loss levels. So this strategy works well during periods of low volatility and especially during consolidation. Like the uncovered put analyzed in the last chapter, the vertical spread creates limited potential income in exchange for limited potential limited loss. Owning stock in your portfolio reduces the short side risk for calls, making the vertical spread desirable when waiting out the low volatility.

Box Spreads

Another type of spread expands the vertical spread by combining both call and put versions. The resulting *box spread* is either long or short, and the selection of one over the other depends on your belief about the price direction. When this is based on chart patterns and confirmed reversal signals, the box spread can work as one form of hedge.

A potential problem with the box spread is that it employs four different positions. As a result, the trading costs will be higher for single options than strategies based on single options or on offsetting two-part positions. For this reason, the box spread is most likely to net the desired result when it is used for multiple positions with a lower average transaction cost. However, in the following examples, single option positions are used to demonstrate how the box spread is constructed and how its maximum profit and loss are calculated.

The box spread sets up a hedge in which profits can be locked in with no risk. This could be viewed as a standalone strategy; however, when the box spread is designed to hedge portfolio positions, it takes on even greater value. For example, if shares of stock are depressed, a paper loss can be absorbed or partially absorbed with a box spread.

The position is established by opening the same number of long in-the-money calls, short out-of-the-money calls, long in-the-money puts, and short out-of-the-money puts. The value of the resulting box at expiration will be equal to

> **Key Point**
> Although the box spread sets up locked-in profits, it can also be viewed as a worthwhile hedge in consolidation periods or as part of a recovery strategy.

the higher strike less the lower strike, and the profit will equal the expiration value minus the net premium paid.

For example, referring once again to Exxon-Mobil as of November 6, 2015, the stock closed at $84.47. The following options could be used to create a box spread (although single options are used, the trading fees make larger sets of options more desirable):

November 83 long call, ask 1.97	$206
November 85 short call, bid 0.79	– 70
November 85 long put, ask 2.28	2.37
November 83 short put, bid 1.16	– 1.07
Net debit	$266

The expiration value is the difference between the spread prices for each side, or $200. Profit will be $200 for the call spread plus $200 for the put spread, for a total of $400. Profit will be $134, or the difference between expiration value and the debit ($400 – $266 = $134). This outcome is summarized for various underlying prices at expiration, in Table 8.1.

Table 8.1

	Calls		Puts		
Expiration Underlying Price	Long Nov. 83	Short Nov. 85	Long Nov. 85	Short Nov. 83	Net Total
$87	$400	$–200	$ 0	$ 0	$200
86	300	–100	0	0	200
85	200	0	0	0	200
84	100	0	100	0	200
83	0	0	200	0	200
82	0	0	300	–100	200
81	0	0	400	–200	200

In practice, the box spread is likely to be closed in increments. When the short side of either the call or put spread loses most of its value, the positions can be closed at a profit, with the long sides left until expiration or shortly before. If the stock moves several points, either the long calls or the long puts will become profitable. However, if you close parts of the box spread, be aware of the maximum net profit and be sure your buy-to-close costs do not exceed that price.

Ratio Calendar Spreads

The calendar spread is another name for the horizontal spread, consisting of a position with the same strike but different expiration dates (also called a time spread). The *ratio calendar spread* combines a short option with two or more long options with the same strike but a later expiration; or it may combine a larger number of short options with a smaller number of later-expiring long options with the same strike.

> **Key Point**
> A ratio calendar spread with more long than short options is not a sensible hedge because it sets up a debit in every case.

When you combine short options with a larger number of long options, the short spread is not at risk of exercise because it is covered by the later-expiring long positions. As a hedge, the ratio calendar spread provides benefits in segments. First, the earlier expiring short position will lose time value more rapidly than the longer-term long positions; second, the long options remaining after the short option has expired or been closed provide potential benefits if the underlying price rises (when calls are used) or falls (when puts are used). The position will create a net debit because longer-term options have more time value.

The second version of the ratio calendar spread is more interesting as a hedge, and it relies on rapid time decay in the shorter-term short options. In this case, you open more of the short options and fewer of the long. As a hedge, this is intended to provide a degree of protection for your long positions, not only in the rapid time decay but also in the longer-term long options that will remain after the short side is closed or expires. Although there is a risk in opening more short options than long, exercise risk is managed by either buying to close some or all of the short options, or rolling them forward. When using calls in this strategy, be aware of the ex-dividend date and avoid keeping short calls open in ex-dividend month. This is the most likely time for early exercise in the event the short calls move in the money.

For example, Exxon Mobil closed November 6, 2015, at $84.47 per share. Ex-dividend date has occurred the same day, November 6, and the next ex-dividend would not be until February. The early exercise risk had passed, because November 5 would have been the last time when this was a possibility. The term *ex-dividend* means "without dividend," so the risk exists up until the day before.

At the close of November 6, the following options were available:

November 85 calls bid 0.79 and ask 0.82

December 85 calls bid 1.62 and ask 1.78

January 85 calls bid 2.16 and ask 2.37

November 85 puts bid 1.84 and ask 1.99

December 85 puts bid 2.94 and ask 3.15

January 85 puts bid 3.55 and ask 3.70

In each case, opening a short position with a higher number of long positions would not make sense, as the overall position would create a large debit. So the focus in the following examples is on the more practical hedge, opening a larger number of soon-to-expire short options with a smaller number of later-expiring long positions. The calls are all slightly out of the money and the puts are all slightly in the money.

> **Key Point**
> The hedge with a higher number of short-term short positions creates a net credit. As long as you can manage that credit, the ratio position is effective and profitable.

A call-based ratio calendar spread could consist of:

Two short November 85 calls (12 days to expiration), @ 0.79,

= $158 minus $10 for trading costs = $148

One long December 85 call (40 days to expiration), @ 1.78,

= $178 plus $9 for trading costs = $187

This sets up a net debit of $39. The hedge in this case applies if you believe the stock price will rise in the longer term. Locking in a close-to-the-money long call with 40 days remaining before expiration at a net cost of only $39 is a great advantage, assuming the two short calls can be managed for the next 12 days. Time decay will be rapid, so as long as the stock price remains at or below $85 per share, the entire short premium of $148 will be profitable. However, if the price trends higher before the November expiration, these can be rolled forward into either the weekly expirations occurring before December expiration, or closed at a net profit. However, closing these positions will increase the basis in the later-expiring long options. The net cost of a buy-to-close of the November calls increases the net $39. Even so, the position still ends up with one December 85 long call; because the underlying price increased, this long position gains intrinsic value.

There is a risk in this bullish use of the ratio calendar spread, in two respects. First, the earlier expiring short positions could move in the money and would have to be managed through rolling or closing. Second, even after the short expiration, if the stock price does not rise, the position ends up with the small $39 net loss. This is a reasonable risk level in exchange for the potential hedge gained if the price did rise.

If you believe the stock price is more likely to decline, a ratio calendar spread can be opened using the 85 puts. For example, a put-based ratio calendar spread could consist of:

Three short November 85 puts (12 days to expiration), @ 1.84,

= $552 minus $11 for trading costs = $541

One long January 85 put (68 days to expiration), @ 3.70,

= $370 plus $9 for trading costs = $379

This alternative sets up a position with a net credit of $162. The three short puts are slightly in the money, so exercise risk exists for the next 12 days. Two factors reduce this risk. First, if the underlying price increases by 0.53 points or more, the November puts will not be in the money. Second, over the next 12 days, the 1.84 points of value (consisting of 1.31 points of non-intrinsic value) are going to evaporate. These short positions can be closed, even if they move in the money. Given the 1.84 points of value, the breakeven price is $86.84 per share.

> **Key Point**
> The net outcome that sets up a free or low-cost insurance put is highly desirable as a hedge and preferable to just buying a long put.

With a net credit of $379, you have flexibility even if you end up having to close the short puts to avoid exercise. They can be closed or rolled forward to one of the weekly options. The roll avoids exercise while increasing the net credit in this overall position. Assuming the short puts are eventually closed or allowed to expire, you end up with one long January 85 put, probably without any net cost and a greater likelihood of realizing a net credit. So this cost-free put provides two months of downside protection, a free insurance put to protect 100 shares in your portfolio.

If you are able to manage the short puts to avoid exercise, this is a "perfect" hedge because the long put is free, while capping maximum losses in the 100 shares of stock at $85 per share. Any price decline in the stock below $85 will be offset by a corresponding increase in the value of the long put; and because the put is "free," it can be closed at any point before expiration to offset losses in the stock.

A further expansion of the ratio calendar spread combines both the call and put positions into a single position. This is called a *ratio combination calendar spread*. This would normally involve the two sides, both slightly out of the money; for example, the XOM 85 calls would be combined with a set of 82.50 puts.

On November 6, the following 82.50-strike puts were available:

November 82.50 puts bid 0.99 and ask 1.14

December 82.50 puts bid 1.83 and ask 2.00

January 82.50 puts bid 2.37 and ask 2.57

The complete ratio calendar combination spread could be set up using:

Three short November 82.50 puts (12 days to expiration), @ 0.99,

= $297 minus $11 for trading costs = $286

> One long January 82.50 put (68 days to expiration), @ 2.57,
>
> = $257 plus $9 for trading costs = $266

This creates a credit of $20. To make the combination complete, add in the call-based ratio side using the 85 strikes:

> Two short November 85 calls (12 days to expiration), @ 0.79,
>
> = $158 minus $10 for trading costs = $148

> One long December 85 call (40 days to expiration), @ 1.78,
>
> = $178 plus $9 for trading costs = $187

With this debit of $39 on the call side and the credit of $20 on the put side, the overall net cost is only $19. This creates a hedge in which the longer-term call and put create profit potential on the upside and the downside. If the ultimate price of the underlying remains between $84 and $85, you lose $19. The risk in this position involves the 123-day short calls and puts. As long as the stock price remains between $84 and $85 per share, all of these short options will expire worthless—but that is a very narrow window. It is more likely that one side or the other will move in the money. Closing these to avoid exercise increases the overall debit; rolling forward to a weekly expiration creates a credit due to more time value, and helps manage the position. However, it is likely that eventually one or more of these positions will expire worthless and the other side will have to be closed. Given the short time remaining for expiration of short calls and short puts, this is not a long-term risk concern, but a short-term management issue. The ultimate hedge is the result, a low-cost or cost-free combination of a long 85 call and a long 84 put, both expiring in January.

Diagonal Spreads

The diagonal spread combines features of the vertical and combination spread, consisting of different expiration dates and strikes. It is an advantageous form of spread that takes advantage of price swings, providing a short-term hedge to equity positions and also managing downside risk.

> **Key Point**
> The diagonal spread is an effective strategy for managing short-term price movement, assuming you have a reasonable sense of price direction.

When you own equity positions in your portfolio, your emphasis is on long-term growth. However, short-term price fluctuations are also of concern, and this is where the diagonal spread works as a worthwhile hedge. In fact, the two sides of this spread can both become profitable if price behaves in a specific manner, moving first in one direction and then back in the other. The use of different strikes means it is possible to use the same number of options on either side, while also creating a net credit. The ability to do this relies on time to expiration and proximity of strikes to the underlying price.

For example, if you expect the underlying to fall in the short term and then rebound, a diagonal call spread will be ideal. For example:

December 85 short call	bid 1.62	less: $9 trading fee	$153
January 87.50 long call	ask 1.37	plus: $9 trading fee	$146

This sets up a position close to breakeven, with a net credit of only $7. However, if the price remains below the short 85 strike for the next 12 days, the short call will expire worthless. It can also be closed, but the cost of the buy to close trade will absorb and surpass the net credit, converting the remaining long option to a net debit. Even so, the new net will be much lower than the cost of just buying the long call. Because the overall cost for the January long call is going to be a small credit or a small debit, it is an inexpensive hedge that exploits any price growth without having to take profits by selling shares. If the rise does not materialize, it is an inexpensive hedge that loses only a small amount in the worst case. The short call can also be rolled forward to a weekly position if the underlying moves in the money during the next 12 days, setting up additional credit.

This diagonal spread can also be varied by adding a ratio feature. For example, combining three short December 85 calls and two long January 87.50 calls sets up a *diagonal ratio spread*:

3 December 85 short call, bid @ 1.62 = $486 – $11 = $475

2 January 87.50 long call, ask @ 1.37 = $274 + $10 = $284

> **Key Point**
>
> The larger the net credit from the diagonal spread, the greater your flexibility in closing the short side without moving into a debit.

In this ratio version, you create a net credit of $191. Two of the three short calls are exposed to exercise risk; however, as in all forms of short positions, these can be closed or rolled if the underlying moves in the money. With a $191 cushion, these can be closed after time decay while keeping a net credit intact. Clearly, the most advantageous outcome would be for a short-term price decline (allowing the short options to expire worthless) followed by a price increase, making the long positions profitable. However, as long as the short options expire worthless, even if the price does not rise, the net credit is the profitable result of this strategy.

If you believe the price will rise in the short term and then decline, the diagonal put spread makes more sense. You can create a net credit even using the same number of options, and the strategy calls for closing or rolling in the event the stock price falls below the short put strike. The ratio version of the put diagonal also works, creating a larger net credit and a cushion in case you want to close the short puts. The outcome is a longer-term long put and a "free" insurance put.

Spreads are effective hedges and can be used in many different combinations and risk levels. The next chapter demonstrates how advanced form of spread, the butterfly and condor, can create a position with limited profits and losses and potential hedging benefits when the underlying moves in either direction.

9 | The Butterfly and Condor

Spread strategies described in the last chapter create strategies with limited profit potential, in exchange for maximum and limited losses. Expanding on this, more advanced hedges can be created in various ways. One of the most popular of these is the butterfly.

A *butterfly* is a spread with three strikes, made up of calls, puts, or both. The high and low strike are both long and the middle strike is short; or high and low are short and the middle strike is long. Normal construction calls for two middle strikes versus one each of a higher and lower strike.

The four varieties of the butterfly follow, with examples based on closing values as of November 6, 2015, for Microsoft (MSFT), which closed at $54.92. December options are used because MSFT's ex-dividend date occurred in late November. Each premium value is adjusted for estimated trading costs: (Note: Margin for each of these was calculated on the Chicago Board Options Exchange (CBOE) free margin calculator [*www.cboe.com/tradtool/mcalc.*].)

Long call—1 long ITM call, 2 short ATM calls, and 1 long OTM call

MSFT 1 DEC 52.50 long call, ask 2.83	$ 292
MSFT 2 Dec 55 short calls bid 1.17	$ –224
MSFT 1 Dec 57.50 long call ask 0.40	$ 49
Net paid (margin $89)	$ 89

Short call—1 short ITM call, 2 long ATM calls, and 1 short OTM call

MSFT 1 DEC 52.50 short call, bid 2.72	$ –263
MSFT 2 Dec 55 long calls, ask 1.21	$ 252
MSFT 1 Dec 57.50 short call, bid 0.29	$ –29
Net received (margin $189)	$ 40

143

Long put—1 long ITM put, 2 short ATM puts, and 1 long OTM put

MSFT 1 DEC 52.50 long put, ask 0.67	$ 76
MSFT 2 Dec 55 short puts, bid 1.59	$ −308
MSFT 1 Dec 57.50 long put, ask 3.45	$ 354
Net paid (margin $94)	$ 122

Short put—1 short ITM put, 2 long ATM puts, and 1 short OTM put

MSFT 1 DEC 52.50 short put, bid 0.64	$ −55
MSFT 2 Dec 55 long puts, ask 1.64	$ 338
MSFT 1 Dec 57.50 short put, bid 3.25	$ −315
Net received (margin $89)	$ 32

The outcomes for profit and loss also vary based on configuration of the butterfly:

Long Call

Maximum profit = short strike – lower long strike – net premium paid

55 – 52.50 – 0.32 = 2.18, or $218

Maximum loss = net premium paid

= $32

Upper breakeven = high strike – net premium paid

57.50 – 0.32 = $57.18

Lower breakeven = low strike + net premium paid

52.50 + 0.32 = $52.82

Short Call

Maximum profit = net premium received

= $40

Maximum loss = long strike – lower strike – net premium received

55 – 52.50 – 0.40 = 2.90, or $290

Upper breakeven = high strike – net premium received

57.50 – 0.40 = $57.10

Lower breakeven = low strike + net premium received

52.50 + 0.40 = $52.90

Long Put

Maximum profit = high strike – short strike – net premium paid

57.50 – 55 – 1.22 = 1.28, or $128

Maximum loss = net premium paid

= $122

Upper breakeven = high strike – net premium paid

57.50 – 1.22 = $56.28

Lower breakeven = low strike + net premium paid

52.50 + 1.22 = $53.72

Short Put

Maximum profit = net premium received

= $32

Maximum loss = high strike – long strike – net premium received

57.50 – 55 – 0.32 = 2.18, or $218

Upper breakeven = high strike – net premium received

57.50 – 0.32 = $57.18

Lower breakeven = low strike + net premium received

52.50 + 0.32 = $52.82

These four variations of the butterfly are straightforward in construction and have predictable outcomes. In practice, traders using butterflies tend to close legs as they become profitable, in the hope of achieving overall profits higher than the maximum if held to expiration. As hedges, the long or short butterfly has limited

> **Key Point**
> The outcomes of butterfly positions assume all are held open to expiration. In practice, it is likely that half of these positions will be closed early to take profits.

value but may generate current income. It is a worthwhile part of recovery strategies for depressed stock prices, or for exploiting volatility. In all of the configurations, one side or the other will become profitable as the stock price moves. The challenge is to time trades to protect against downside risk and to end up with a net profit after a portion of the butterfly has been closed.

The bullish nature of the long call and short put butterfly strategies, and the bearish nature of the short call and long put strategies, are clear. However, a butterfly can also be constructed using a combination of calls and puts.

The Iron Butterfly

The *iron butterfly* is a variation of the basic butterfly, designed to work best for low-volatility stock situations. It combines calls and puts together, using four different option positions and three strikes.

The maximum profit on the iron butterfly is the amount of the net premium received.

Maximum loss is equal to the long call strike minus the short call strike minus the net premium received:

Maximum loss = long call strike – short call strike – net premium received

This loss occurs in two conditions: first, when the underlying price is greater than the long call strike, and second, when the underlying price is lower than the long put strike.

Breakeven occurs in two ways: On the upside, it is the short call strike plus net premium received, and on the downside, it is the short put strike minus the net premium received:

Upper breakeven = short call strike + net premium received

Lower breakeven = short put strike – net premium received

The iron butterfly combines an OTM long put with ATM short call and put and an OTM long call. For example, Microsoft closed on November 6 at $54.92. An iron butterfly could be constructed using the following contracts:

1 December long 52.50 put @ 0.67

1 December short 55 call @ (1.17)

1 December short 55 put @ (1.59)

1 December long 57.50 call @ (0.40)

The net credit from this position is 1.69 before deducting trading costs (estimated $36), for a net total credit of $133.

The changes in value from November 9 through the following five sessions are summarized in Table 9.1.

Table 9.1

Description	11/06	11/09	11/10	11/11	11/12	11/13
1 long 52.50 put	0.67	0.89	1.08	1.00	1.16	1.45
1 short 55 call	(1.17)	(0.86)	(0.62)	(0.64)	(0.60)	(0.49)
1 short 55 put	(1.59)	(1.96)	(2.41)	(2.30)	(2.58)	(2.95)
1 long 57.50 call	0.40	0.28	0.20	0.18	0.18	0.15

Key Point

The hedge from an iron butterfly involves generating profits based on price activity in the underlying.

The maximum profit or loss and breakeven all assume these positions are held open to expiration, which in this example would be December 18. However, in practice, the hedging benefit comes from closing each portion of the iron butterfly as it becomes profitable. The goal in this is to take profits without moving the net below the initial amount received. In this example, the net premium received was $133.

The following reveals what occurred in the week following the opening of the iron butterfly. Several steps could be taken to take advantage of the changing price of the underlying. The closing stock price gradually declined through this week:

December 6	$54.92
December 9	$54.16
December 10	$53.51
December 11	$53.65
December 12	$53.32
December 13	$52.84

In managing this position with a declining stock price, the initial hedge occurs when the lower-strike long call appreciated in value and the short call declined in value. As Table 9.2 shows, both of these became profitable due to the stock's decline:

Table 9.2

Option	Value on Nov. 6	Value on Nov. 13
Long 52.50 put	0.67	1.45
Short 55 call	(1.17)	(0.49)

In closing both of these positions, profits can be taken. Profit on the long put is calculated as:

1.45 – 0.67 – 0.18 fees = 0.60

Profit on the short call is calculated as

1.17 – 0.49 – 0.18 fees = 0.50

The total profit is $110 net of transaction fees on both sides of the trades. However, a net of $96 is spent to close these positions ($145 – $49). This reduces the initial credit from $133 down to $37. The remaining positions left open are the short 55 put and the long 57.50 call. In order for these to become profitable, it will be necessary for the underlying to rise in value.

> **Key Point**
> A danger in any butterfly is closing positions that turn a net credit into a net debit. This is resolved at least partially by closing profitable long and short sides together.

An alternative to taking profits so quickly would be to let the profits ride and eventually take profits after the overall net was smaller. Leaving these open to expiration and then closing all positions would yield a profit of $133, breakeven of either $53.67 or $56.33, or a maximum loss of $117 ($57.50 – $55 – $1.33 = 1.17, or $117). So with the iron butterfly, both profits and losses are limited and you have a choice: let positions ride to expiration, or take profits as they materialize. The position works effectively as a hedge in two ways. First, as long as the underlying continues to exhibit low volatility, the short middle-strike options will decline in value and become profitable, while the relatively cheap OTM lower put and upper call hedge against unexpected underlying price movement in either direction. Second, if the underlying price moves unexpected early on, one-half of the positions will become profitable and the other half (consisting of one long and one short option) will lose value. As the remaining short option moves farther in the money, it can be rolled forward to avoid exercise. However, if you own the underlying, this outcome converts the outstanding short call to a covered call, or the outstanding short put to an uncovered out.

The 1-2-3 Iron Butterfly

An expansion of the butterfly is intended to set up a special type of hedge involving three different sets of expirations for the strike ranges of the strategy. This **hedge matrix** is designed so that one-half of the positions are always moving in a profitable direction; and so that time value of short positions declines as each strike moves closer.

For example, Microsoft options could be applied to create a 1-2-3 iron butterfly, by opening the following positions:

1 November long 52.50 put @ 0.25	$ 25 + $9	$ 34
1 November short 55 call @ (0.61)	$ (61) - $9	$(52)
1 November short 55 put @ (1.00)	$ (100) - $9	$(91)
1 November long 57.50 call @ 0.11	$ 11 + $9	$ 20
Net credit		$ (89)

2 December short 52.50 puts @ (0,64)	$ (128) - $10	$ (118)
2 December long 55 calls @ 1.21	$ 242 + $10	$ 252
2 December long 55 puts @ 1.64	$ 328 + $10	$ 338
2 December short 57.50 calls @ (0.38)	$ 76 - $10	$(66)
Net debit		$406

3 January long 52.50 puts @ 1.10	$ 330 + $11	$ 341
3 January short 55 calls @ (1.63)	$ (489) - $11	$(477)
3 January short 55 puts @ (2.03)	$ (609) - $11	$(598)
3 January long 57.50 calls @ 0.76	$ 228 + $11	$ 239
Net credit		$(495)
Overall net credit		$(178)

The configuration is designed with the attributes of the 1-2-3 position: increasing numbers of options (meaning the trading cost was also adjusted and rounded), with the middle expiration set up as a *reverse iron butterfly.*

> **Key Point**
> A *1-2-3 iron butterfly* is designed to create multiple hedging positions over a series of expirations.

In this strategy, the hedging benefit is derived from the profits to be earned when the stock price moves in either direction. If the stock loses value, the long puts and short calls will become profitable; and if the stock gains value, the short puts and long calls become profitable. In the ideal situation, the stock price will move in one direction and then in the other, so that all of the positions can be closed at a profit. However, the goal is not to always achieve profits in all positions, but to be able to close and take profits without moving the newt credit below the overall $178. With this in mind, closing long and short positions at the same time is the most likely strategy to hedge the underlying.

If the stock price remains range-bound and does not move very much at all, especially within the first and second expiration periods, all of the short positions, both calls and puts, will decline in value due to time decay. This will occur rapidly for each set of expirations as the expiration date approaches. This means that all three of the sets of butterflies (including the reverse iron butterfly) could become profitable from the combined shorts being closed at a profit or expiring worthless, and the long positions either being closed along with the short positions or being closed when they become profitable. Any price movement in the underlying will make one-half of all the positions profitable.

The many varieties of the butterfly present attractive hedging opportunities. The expanded 1-2-3 iron butterfly expands on the basic premise for the butterfly by presenting scenarios of profit when the underlying price moves, regardless of direction. The short-side risk is reduced when you also own shares in your portfolio. The short calls are covered and the uncovered short puts have the same market risk as the covered calls. This combined market risk structure makes the butterfly an exceptional hedge when you also hold shares of the underlying.

The Condor

The butterfly can also be expanded into a strategy that includes four options and four strikes. A *condor* takes the butterfly and its three spreads and adds a fourth spread.

> **Key Point**
> The condor is an expanded version of the butterfly. It uses two middle-level strikes, both out of the money.

Like the butterfly, the condor is likely to be closed in stages rather than keeping all contracts open to expiration. Closing profitable long and short sides together helps maintain a net credit. The condor can be opened in several configurations, using calls, puts, or a combination of both.

The *long condor* consists of a long ITM call, a short ITM call, and two middle-strike calls, both OTM. For example, Boeing closed on November 6, 2015, at $147.94. A long condor could be opened using the following contracts:

Long ITM call: Nov 147 @ 2.67	$267 + $9	$ 276
Short ITM call: Nov 145 @ 3.85	$385 - $9	$(376)
Long OTM call: Nov 149 @ 1.58	$158 + $9	$ 167
Short OTM call: Nov 152.50 @ 0.42	$ 42 - $9	$(33)
Net debit		$ 34

This strategy creates a very small net debit, but also offers a limited profit and loss. One side or the other will always move ITM. If held until close to expiration, some of these positions will be profitable, and others will not. However, the time decay of the short sides makes a difference as well.

In addition to this long strategy, a *short condor* using calls consists of opposite call positions: a long ITM, short ITM, long OTM, and short OTM.

For example, the previous long condor could be converted to the short version with the following contracts:

Short ITM call: Nov 147 @ 2.51	$251 – $9	$(242)
Long ITM call: Nov 145 @ 4.05	$405 + $9	$ 414
Short OTM call: Nov 149 @ 1.47	$147 – $9	$(138)
Long OTM call: Nov 152.50 @ 0.47	$ 47 + $9	$ 56
Net debit		$ 90

Long or short condors can also be constructed using puts. However, with any form of condor, the maximum profit or loss is limited by the offsetting positions. Like the three-strike butterfly, the four-strike condor is a worthy hedge when volatility is low, but if volatility increases while these options remain open, the hedge is not as effective. The maximum gain or loss remains in place in any event, which is what makes the condor an appealing strategy.

The Iron Condor

> **Key Point**
> The iron condor is a further expansion, using both puts and calls.

Opening a condor with calls or puts (either long or short) can be expanded to include both calls and puts. The *iron condor* is very much like the iron butterfly. However, it has four strikes rather than three. The normal construction includes a long OTM put and a lower-strike short OTM put; and a short OTM call with a higher-strike OTM long call.

In the case of Boeing, an example of the iron condor includes the following, based on closing values on November 6, 2015:

110 + $9	$ 119
163 - $9	$(154)
147 - $9	$(138)
115 + $9	$ 124
	$(49)

hen higher volatility is expect-
ondor. For example, the follow-

102 – $9	$(93)
176 + $9	$ 185
158 + $9	$ 167
106 – $9	$(97)
	$ 162

r

ne 1-2-3 iron butterfly, but with
adds another position and the

anded into a 1-2-3 version with

1 Long ITM put: Nov 145 @ 1.10	$110 + $9	$ 119
1 Short OTM put: Nov 147 @ 1.63	$163 – $9	$(154)
1 Short OTM call: Nov 149 @ 1.47	$147 – $9	$(138)
1 Long OTM call: Nov 150 @ 1.15	$115 + $9	$ 124
Net credit		$(49)

2 Short ITM puts: Dec 140 @ 1.32	$264 – $10	$(254)
2 Long OTM puts: Dec 145 @ 2.68	$536 + $10	$ 546
2 Long OTM calls: Dec 150 @ 2.70	$540 + $10	$ 550
2 Short OTM calls: Dec 155 @ 0.97	$194 – $10	$(184)
Net debit		$ 658

3 Long ITM puts: Jan 140 @ 2.24	$ 672 + $11	$ 683
3 Short OTM puts: Jan 145 @ 3.50	$1,050 – $11	$(1,039)
3 Short OTM calls: Jan 150 @ 3.65	$1,095 – $11	$(1,084)
3 Long OTM calls: Jan 155 @ 1.90	$ 570 + $11	$ 581
Net credit		$ (859)
Overall net credit		$ (250)

The butterfly and condor are interesting as hedge strategies because they limit losses, in exchange for also limiting profits. The opportunity based on these strategies is especially worthwhile when the underlying price is depressed; in that case, the butterfly or condor can serve as part of a recovery strategy. It also tends to work effectively during periods of consolidation, when range-bound stock prices do not move outside of the limited range between strongly held resistance and support. Like many hedges, this is an opportunity to generate additional income in exchange for a limited level of risk exposure.

When These Strategies Work as Hedges

For the typical hedge, two elements are required: an equity position requiring protection and the hedge itself, such as options strategies. However, butterfly and condor positions are usually employed by traders who seek profits in the options trade but who do not own stock.

The exception to this occurs when you hold an equity position and you expect price movement, but you are not certain about the direction this will take. Timing could be based on:

1. **Consolidation.** When a stock has been trading in consolidation, the big challenge is determining when or if it will break out. In a typical consolidation, repetitive attempts moving price above or below the limited trading range tend to fail. At some point, a bullish or bearish trend will take over, but it is not always easy to spot this change, or to identify the likely direction of price movement. In this case, the butterfly or condor— especially one designed to produce a small debit or credit—will benefit in either direction. At the same time, if price does not move, the short positions will love time value and become profitable or expire worthless.

2. **Earnings announcements.** You probably have noticed that in the one to two weeks prior to earnings announcements, a stock's price might turn volatile. This is caused by uncertainty about whether revenue and earnings will be in line with expectations or produce an earnings surprise. If a surprise does occur, the nature (positive or negative) cannot be known either, but even a small surprise is likely to have a short-term effect on

price. This is an opportunity to set up profitable hedging outcomes with a butterfly or condor.

3. **Ex-dividend date.** Another time when price is likely to act in an erratic manner is immediately before ex-dividend date and on ex-dividend date itself. At this time, the price is expected to drop due to the recognized dividend earned on the day before ex-dividend. However, this may also create an opposite reaction, anticipating a drop but resulting in a short-term increase in the price. This is the result of investors buying shares before the ex-dividend date, to earn the current dividend, creating increased demand.

4. **Changes in volatility.** When price volatility occurs but the reason is not clearly identified, it could be a sign that investors (most likely institutional traders) are making large buy or sell moves. Mutual funds, for example, might be likely to take profits immediately before the end of a reporting quarter, to bolster the current net earnings for the period. Although this timing is manipulative, it identifies a consequence in price levels expressed as volatility.

5. **Rumors of mergers or acquisitions.** When rumors of M&A activity (or similar fundamentals changes) are floating through the market, price may reflect the expected volatility that results. This identifies good timing for short-term butterfly and condor trades to hedge the equity position in your portfolio.

The butterfly and condor are favored by traders seeking speculative profits with hedged losses. This form of risk hedge may also translate to a longer-term form of risk hedge against equity positions. Even when you favor long-term holdings, awareness of short-term price movement makes trades such as the butterfly and condor attractive, offering alternatives to closing positions or trying to time price movement with swing trades in long or short positions.

The next chapter introduces more spread variations in the form of collars and synthetic stock positions.

10 | Collars and Synthetic Stock

You can bring tremendous flexibility to your hedging program by using several different strategies. Some will be designed to generate income; the covered call, uncovered put, and covered straddle are examples. Others, like the butterfly and condor, are more defensive, representing an exchange of limits—limited profit potential in exchange for limited loss exposure.

The selection of the right strategy relies on the volatility in the stocks you own as well as in the overall market. This chapter describes several hedges consisting of spread positions, all designed to accomplish a hedging advantage and all with effectiveness based on price volatility.

The Collar

One strategy designed to set up conditional exercise of a covered call with an insurance put is the *collar*. This is a combination of a slightly OTM (on-the-money) call and OTM put. However, the collar provides a specific benefit that is appropriate only if you are willing to exchange downside protection for the possibility of profitable exercise.

The collar can be set up at any time. In analyzing it, the position makes no sense if your stock price is at or close to original basis. With this in mind, it works only with appreciated stock. For example, Exxon Mobil (XOM) closed on November 6, 2015, at $84.47. Ex-dividend date was scheduled for November 9,

> **Key Point**
>
> The collar is not practical if set up close to your original basis in the underlying. It is a hedge that works best for appreciated stock.

so entering into a covered call using options on the last day to earn dividends would not make sense. However, the December options presented an appealing condition for setting up a collar. The December 85 call closed with a bid of 1.62 and could be

155

sold after trading costs for $153. The December 80 put closed with an ask of 1.26 and could be bought for $135. The net credit for setting up this collar would be $18.

If you had bought shares of XOM at or close to the November 6 price of $84.47, the collar would not make much sense. If the stock price rose and the call was exercised, stock would be called away at $85, only a few dollars above your basis. If the stock price declined, the 80 put would cap losses at $80 per share, but that is of little practical use if your basis in the stock was several points higher; exercising the put would only be a way to limit losses, not to offset or eliminate them.

However, consider the hedging value of the collar for appreciated stock. If you had bought shares in mid-September when the stock price was ranging between $71 and $74 per share, the appreciated value by November 6 would be worth protecting. In fact, if you sold shares at the November 6 price, you would make a handsome profit in less than two months. At this point, it is worthwhile to protect profits and to set up a contingent sale. The XOM chart in Figure 10.1 shows how this works.

Figure 10.1: Timing of a Collar

The hedging benefits of the collar are of greatest value in a situation like this. You bought stock at a lower price and you would prefer to keep shares in your portfolio. At the same time, you are concerned with the possibility of loss, so you want to hedge your position. In other words, you are willing to risk having shares called away at a profit, in exchange for preventing a loss.

The entire month of September appeared to have settled into a narrow consolidation trend. However, looking back to mid-May, the stock price had been on a downtrend, and this could continue at any time. However, you bought shares at $72 after the market-wide decline of August 24, in the belief that the price had stabilized and could be on the rise. You were correct in your timing. During October and into early November, the price rose about 20%, peaking at $86. However, November 3 and 4 formed a double top that, though moderate, did signal the top of the trend. By

November 6, the condition of this stock was uncertain. This was a sensible time to open a collar.

If the stock price rose above the 85 call strike and shares were called away, your capital gain on stock would be $1,300 (per 100 shares), the difference between basis of $72 and strike price of $85. That would be a desirable outcome based on the call. However, exercise could also be avoided by

> **Key Point**
> A great advantage of positions with offsetting long and short options is that they tend to be low-cost or zero-cost to open.

closing the short call or rolling it forward, good moves if it looked as though the stock had evolved into a bullish trend. If the price declined below $80 per share, you could exercise the put and sell shares to generate an 8-point capital gain ($80 – $72), also an acceptable outcome if it appeared that the downtrend has resumed. Considering that the put had cost nothing (the collar generated a net $18 credit), exercising the put was acceptable. In comparison, just opening an insurance put at a net cost of $135 would mean that the exercise price would not break even with a strike of 80 until price had fallen to $78.65 ($80 – $1.35).

The collar works as a hedge in these conditions. As it turned out, the stock price, as shown on the chart in Figure 10.1, declined to $78 per share before returning to $80 by November 18. Considering that the collar at this point had another full month to run before the December expiration, no action would need to be taken at this point. As time moved forward, the short call would lose time value and could be closed to take profits and rolled forward to a later expiration as a covered call, or just allowed to expire worthless.

Synthetic Stock Positions

The collar, especially if used for appreciated stock, is an effective hedge for protecting paper profits and for setting up a desirable condition: willingness to have stock called away in exchange for limitation of loss. A similar benefit can be gained with the *synthetic stock* strategy. This is a position set up with options and that mirrors price movement in the underlying stock on a point-for-point basis, but for much less cost. This high degree of leverage is effective as a hedge because maximum loss is limited because the net cost of a synthetic stock position is at or near zero; it may also be set up as a small credit.

In comparing synthetic stock as a standalone strategy to stock ownership, the benefits come with short risks. However, when you already own the underlying stock, the synthetic stock position is very low-risk, and it works in many situations, including at the time stock is purchased, when it has appreciated, or when its price has declined.

In a situation when the price has declined, synthetic stock works as a recovery hedge. This is preferable to what some investors prefer to do: buying more shares. When you "double down" on a depreciated stock, further decline accelerates the loss. In comparison, a synthetic stock position combining a long call and a short put limits potential losses to the cost of the options, and price decline can be managed by closing the short put or rolling it forward.

> **Key Point**
> Synthetic stock positions are conservative hedges because the short option is manageable as part of the strategy.

When price has appreciated, the synthetic stock adds a similar version of protection to that of the collar. It combines a short call with a long put. The long put caps potential downside losses, preferably at the current price of the underlying when the synthetic stock position is opened. The short call could be exercised if stock price rises, but this side of the strategy is a covered call, so for appreciated stock, this status is very similar to the collar.

There are two forms of synthetic stock: long and short. In the long version, you combine a long call and a short put, setting up the uncovered put with the same market risk as the covered call. In the short version, you combine a long put with a short call. The short call is covered because you own stock, and the long put provides no-cost or low-cost downside protection.

Because synthetic stock positions of both types do not increase portfolio risks but offer profit potential and loss limitation, they are as close as you can get to a perfect hedge. Under most popular definitions, this "perfect" hedge contains 100% inverse correlation between the risk on one side and profit on the other. This is considered difficult to find; most analysts consider positions like covered calls to be as close as possible to "perfect." Considering the range of risks, this is not an accurate definition; however, for synthetic stock in many situations (appreciated, depreciated, or no-change stock), the synthetic hedge is one way to manage portfolio risks.

The first of two strategies is called the *synthetic long stock* strategy. This combines a long call with a short put. The short put is uncovered, but contains the same market risk as a covered call, so it is considered a conservative method for duplicating underlying price movement.

The synthetic long stock strategy is most effective when the underlying price rises. So after a large price decline in positions held in your portfolio, this strategy is a low-risk method for setting up recovery. Compared to only opening a short put or a long call by itself, the synthetic solves many problems. The short put provides recovery at a maximum equal to its premium value; this does not negate the value of the short put, but it points out a limitation to this strategy. The long call by itself is also limited. If the stock price does rise, it can become profitable; however, time decay is a constant detriment to the potential for profit. So the long call has to exceed not only the number of points it cost to open, it also has to overcome and exceed lost time value premium.

The synthetic long stock strategy combines the best features of the long call with the short put, but without the problems these two sides have by themselves. For example, on November 6, Microsoft closed at $54.92. A synthetic long stock position could have been opened using a December 85 call with an ask of 1.78 and total cost of

$187; and a December 85 short put with a bid of 2.94, netting $285. The net credit for this position is $98. The position benefits the most if the underlying price rises; the combined positions will mirror stock price movement in both directions, as shown in Table 10.1.

Table 10.1

Stock Price	Long Call	Short Put	Net Options	Stock Profit/Loss
$60	$500	$ 0	$500	$508
50	400	0	400	408
58	300	0	300	308
57	200	0	200	208
56	100	0	100	108
55	0	0	0	8
54	0	–100	–100	–92
53	0	–200	–200	–192
52	0	–300	–300	–292
51	0	–400	–400	–392
50	0	–500	–500	–492

The net difference of $8 at each price for the stock represents the difference between the synthetic position's strike and the share price ($55 – $54.92).

The synthetic stock duplicated the movement of the underlying point for point in both directions. This is among the most conservative of strategies. The long call did not cost anything; in fact, the overall position was yielding a net credit of $98. The short put paid for the call. In

> **Key Point**
> When a synthetic stock position yields a net credit, it has an added layer of hedging value.

the event of a price decline in the stock, the short put can be closed or rolled forward to avoid exercise. An interesting alternative would be to accept exercise. Even though the exercise price would be higher than the current value per share, if you believe this company is a worthwhile one to hold in your portfolio, you might be willing to acquire another 100 shares at the higher strike. However, in a majority of instances, it makes more sense to avoid exercise through closing of the put or rolling it forward. Once that is accomplished, if you still want to buy more shares, buy at the current market value, which is lower than the synthetic strike. This reduces the overall basis in shares and presents an opportunity to employ hedges on the new, higher-share position.

In comparison to the synthetic long stock, the opposite *synthetic short stock* combines a long put with a short call. This is another very safe strategy because it combines a low-cost or no-cost long put with a covered call (assuming you own shares in your portfolio and are using the synthetic position as a hedge).

The synthetic short stock is designed to gain maximum benefit if the underlying price falls. As a result, the timing for this position is best when stock has advanced. The hedging benefit here is in the long put, which will gain value as the underlying price declines. If the underlying advances, the covered call will be exercised unless it is closed or rolled forward.

Using Microsoft once again as an example, a synthetic short stock position can be opened with a December 55 long put. On November 6, 2015, ask price was 1.64, total cost $173; and a December 55 short call bid at 1.17, net of $108. This is set up to generate a net debit of $65. In the event of price decline, the short call will expire worthless and the long put will gain 1 point for each point lost in the stock. In the event of a price advance, the short call can be rolled or closed.

Table 10.2 summarizes the synthetic short stock based on the Microsoft 55 strike.

Table 10.2

Stock Price	Long Put	Short Call	Net Options	Stock Profit/Loss
$60	$ 0	$-500	$-500	$508
59	0	-400	-400	408
58	0	-300	-300	308
57	0	-200	-200	208
56	0	-100	-100	108
55	0	0	0	8
54	100	0	100	-92
53	200	0	200	-192
52	300	0	300	-292
51	400	0	400	-392
50	500	0	500	-492

Key Point

Synthetic stock positions combine a certainty of profit in one direction, with manageable offsets in the other.

The profit and loss in this case are opposite that of the synthetic long. As the stock price falls, the loss is offset by gains in the long put. Remembering that the options netted a debit of $65, the overall downside risk is limited to only $65 no matter how far the underlying price falls. If the stock price advances, the profit in the stock is offset by a loss in the covered call. The short call can be closed or rolled to avoid exercise, which is desirable when the stock price is moving upward.

The synthetic long and short stock positions are both advantageous, and short side risks are effectively managed through cover or the ability to roll forward. However, there is more to this strategy. A truly powerful hedge is created to benefit regardless of the direction of underlying price movement. By "boxing" the long and short synthetic stock, you set up a larger net credit. Opening both the long and short at the same time accomplishes this. Based on the two previous examples, a *boxed synthetic stock* would protect the stock position with an overall net effect of zero in both directions. This occurs because long and short positions are completely offset against one another.

The short sides are also easily managed. The short put on the long synthetic can be closed or rolled and has the same market risk as a covered call. The short call on the short synthetic side is a covered call. It can be allowed to exercise, or it can be closed or rolled to avoid exercise when the underlying has moved higher than the strike.

All of these synthetic hedges—long, short, and boxed—will work in protecting portfolio equity positions. Focusing on the use of long synthetics after a price decline and short synthetics after a price advance, is a sensible and conservative hedging method. The alternative of speculating in long options or short options contains much greater risks, either for time decay or exercise. The chart of Microsoft, used in the synthetic examples, is shown in Figure 10.2.

Figure 10.2: Synthetic Stock Timing

If shares had been purchased as indicated, at a price of $44, the large gap into price levels 10 points higher would be troubling. The temptation here would be to sell shares and take profits right after the gap occurred, anticipating a retreat. However, if you want to keep shares as long-term equity positions, selling is not a solution. Buying puts at this level is equally speculative, because the put's value declines as time passes even if the underlying price does not change. A covered call is a reasonable strategy in this situation. However, a synthetic short (long put and short call) gives you the best benefits of the covered call along with the downside protection of the long put. And the cost is close to zero.

Key Point

Timing of the synthetic stock strategy for conditions in the underlying, identifies whether to focus on bullish or bearish movement.

Remembering that the purpose in hedging is not to generate income but to protect portfolio positions, the offset of covered call profits with the cost of a long put should not be an issue. The timing for opening of the synthetic position is based on Figure 10.2 partly on the large price jump in late October, and partly on the level of appreciation since shares were purchased in mid-September.

The next chapter moves into a new form of hedging: the straddle. This is the purchase or sale of calls and puts with the same strike and expiration.

11 | Straddles Hedged

Hedges apply in a vast number of flexible strategies. Among these, some of the most intriguing fall into the realm of the ***straddle***, a strategy most often described as highly speculative. When properly constructed, the straddle provides a conservative hedge for portfolio positions.

This hedge may be long or short, and can also be set up with adjustments in terms of both strike and expiration. The straddle, as a flexible strategy, can be configured as a highly speculative trade or as an appropriately conservative hedge. Just as spreads are intended primarily to manage portfolio risks rather than to take

> **Key Point**
> The straddle can be designed not just as a set of speculative offsetting positions, but as the more effective hedge attained by combining two low-risk positions.

chances on price movement, straddles are also most appropriate when used as part of a long-term plan to reduce market risks in equity positions.

The Long Straddle

The ***long straddle*** (also called a "buy straddle") consists of a long call and a long put, opened at the same strike and expiration. Most investors employing long straddles select strikes as close as possible to the money.

The problem with the long straddle is the same as that for any long position: time value. The closer the expiration date, the more rapidly time value declines. In order to make a profit on the long straddle, the price movement of the underlying has to be greater than the points spent to open the position.

For example, on November 6, 2015, Exxon Mobil's close was $84.47. At the same time, a long straddle using December contracts could be set up using:

1 long December 85 call @ 1.78	$187
1 long December 85 put @ 3.15	$324

The total cost to open this straddle is $511 ($187 + $324). This means the underlying price has to move 5.11 points in either direction just to break even. Price has to move beyond this range to create a profit. This is illustrated in Figure 11.1.

Figure 11.1: Long Straddle Profit and Loss Zones, Exxon Mobil

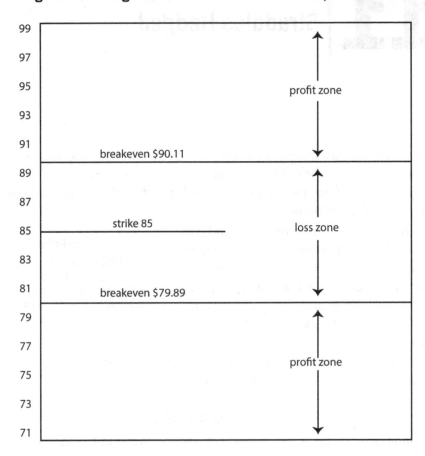

This is a daunting challenge. Assuming time value disappears completely by the time of expiration, the profitability of a long straddle relies solely on intrinsic value. So as a hedge, the long straddle has little or no value. The risks derive from two sources. First, time value is going to decline over the life of the long straddle; this means that even with price movement in the underlying stock, it takes a lot of change just to break even. Second, prices rarely move in one direction for long, but rather tend to move both up and down in turn. So time works against the long straddle in this regard as well.

In looking at the long straddle on paper, these realities are easily overlooked. However, they make the long straddle an unlikely candidate for portfolio management.

You would be better off to buy a long call at the bottom of the price swing, and to buy a long put at the top. This involves two long options, but the danger in the long straddle is that by opening both at the same time, it becomes nearly impossible to end up profitably.

The purpose of a hedge is to reduce risk, not to increase it. The long straddle will not accomplish this because not only is it difficult to create a position profitably, but it does nothing to protect equity positions. The strategy is designed solely as a speculative, income-generating play with high risks. In the example, the need for price to move 5.11 points in either direction sets up a loss zone of 10.22 points.

Is the long straddle ever appropriate in managing a portfolio and hedging its risks? Probably not. It is wise to know about the differences between long and short straddles as a form of comparative analysis, but it is difficult to imagine a scenario that calls for entering a long straddle to hedge a portfolio equity position. The short straddle is a different story. It contains both elements of risk and profit potential, but some forms are conservative and can help manage risks effectively.

The Short Straddle

Compared to the long straddle, the *short straddle* has potential as a hedge. Even so, the risks have to be considered. The short straddle can work as a covered straddle (covered call and uncovered put), making it a conservative strategy. This strategy was introduced in Chapter 7. Used when the underlying price is range-bound in a consolidation trend or when the price has risen significantly in a short time, the short straddle works as an effective hedge.

The long straddle is not going to provide hedging value. In comparison, the short straddle can work as an effective hedge, especially in low-volatility times such as consolidation trends. The range-bound price levels provide opportunities to exploit an otherwise frustrating lack of movement in the underlying.

> **Key Point**
> Long positions like hedges are considered low risk because they do not involve short options. Ironically, they present higher risks and no hedging benefits.

However, because the short straddle is also a covered straddle (assuming the short call is covered with equity positions), it is a very low-risk strategy.

In consolidation, looking for signals of a breakout in the form of Bollinger squeeze or triangle and wedge formations, tells you when to think about closing out the short straddle completely or, at the very least, closing the profitable side, either call or put. In addition to the consolidation-specific breakout signals, reversals (commonly associated with change in direction in either bullish or bearish trends) can also be redefined as "reversing" consolidation into a dynamic trend. In this application of a reversal signal, you require strong confirmation to be convincing. So a breakout without signals is likely to retreat back into the consolidation range and is one form of retracement. In comparison, once a breakout is accompanied by a reversal signal and confirmation, it is time to close the short position.

In thinking about how to manage equity positions in consolidation, the short straddle makes sense. Consolidation is frustrating for investors, who expect to see price movement. The lack of movement outside of a limited range is perhaps even more frustrating than a declining price level. The danger during consolidation is that once the price does break out, it will be likely to enter into a dynamic range, possibly one with strong momentum. Knowing which direction the price will move is essential if you are using a short straddle to generate income in consolidation.

For example, on November 6, 2015, Exxon Mobil's close was $84.47. At the same time, a short straddle using December contracts could be set up using:

1 short December 85 call @ 1.62		$153
1 short December 85 put @ 2.94		$285

This sets up a total credit of $438, meaning that as long as price moves no more than 4.38 points in either direction, this is a profitable hedge. Because it extends in both directions, the total profit zone is 9.76 points wide. This configuration is shown in Figure 11.2.

Figure 11.2: Short Straddle Profit and Loss Zones, Exxon Mobil

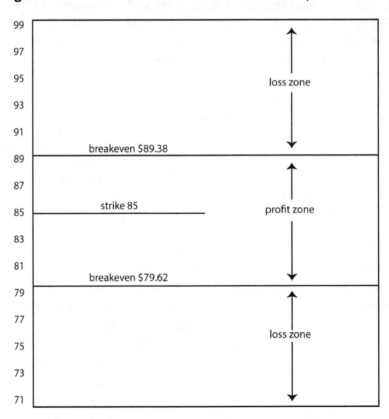

This outcome relies on subsequent price movement in the underlying. There are two elements favoring this as a conservative trade. First is the safety buffer of 4.38 points in either direction; recalling that price tends to move back and forth, first in one direction and then in the other, this buffer provides a considerable level of protection. Second, regardless of interim price movement, time value is continually on the decline. So a short-term option straddle will experience rapid time decay. In the example of XOM entered November 6, the December contracts expire in about six weeks. So time value will fall rapidly during this period.

In the case of Exxon Mobil, the chart reveals the long-term and more immediate price action, shown in Figure 11.3.

Figure 11.3: Short Straddle, Exxon Mobil

On the six-month chart, the long-term consolidation range was identified between $84.25 resistance and $78 support. At the beginning of the period, daily breadth was quite small. This expanded as the price declined below support during August and September. Even though price returned into consolidation range, the daily breadth was broader than in June and July. This higher daily breadth is a signal of growing volatility; so any short position is at increased risk unless price settles into a narrower range. This did occur. The narrower range did not reappear until the middle of November.

The timing of the November 6 short straddle coincided with the first move above resistance since mid-June. Even so, the position works as a conservative hedge and even the in-the-money put can be salvaged. Remembering that time value works in favor of open short positions, it would be very difficult for any option to gain much value before expiration.

Key Point

Rolling short straddles to avoid exercise of one side may require replacing the straddle with a later-expiring short spread.

As of the close of November 20, the December 85 call had declined and could be bought to close for an ask price of 0.54, or $63. This represents a profit of $90 based on the November 6 original bid price. The put is a different matter; it has increased in value to an ask of 5.80, so it will cost $589 to buy to close. Combined, closing both of these positions creates a net purchase price of $499 ($589 – $90).

To close and roll these into positions closer to current value of $79.79 as of November 20, they can be replaced with a January spread. This consists of a January 80 call bid at 2.95, net $286; and a January 82.50 put bid at 4.40, net $441. The total credit would be $727. The overall position's net basis is $666:

$438 original credit – $499 buy to close + $727 net positions = $666

This recovery strategy takes the put's strike down 2.5 points and extends the period of exposure another month. However, based on long-term trends in the stock, it appeared that the consolidation trend had reestablished itself. If this turned out to not be the case, the newly set short spread using an 80 call and 82.50 put can be rolled once again to new strikes, either higher or lower. Does it make sense to roll a short straddle? Given that the idea here is to generate income during consolidation as a form of hedging (in a situation that is not yielding any growth through the underlying), does rolling truly hedge risk? The problem with a forward roll is found in the extension of exposure time. If consolidation ends suddenly and the price begins moving with strong momentum, what happens to the rolled short options? This situation presents risks in place of hedge advantage. With this in mind, it could make more sense to roll forward to a weekly set of options to reduce exposure time while still generating a net credit.

Even in a recovery strategy, there comes a point when closing makes more sense than extending exposure time. A flaw every options trader faces is the temptation to keep positions open until profits develop, even if this means escalating risks. It is more conservative to acknowledge the poor timing of a trade and take the loss.

This recovery strategy is likely to work, however, due to the price buffer and rapidly falling time value. Even conservative strategies can fail; and the short straddle opened during consolidation is certainly more conservative than one opened during a dynamic and volatile trend. This set of events, rolling one side to the same strike and the other side to a different strike, is an example of how a short straddle (later converted to a short spread) can be used to hedge a consolidation trend; and how this can be accomplished with a net credit, even after rolling out of a loss on the uncovered put.

If the price had risen, a similar strategy could be used to take profits on the short out and roll the short call forward to a higher strike. When combined with a new short put, the move creates a net credit in the opposite direction. The same cautionary risk warning applies: If the stock price enters a new and extended bullish trend, the rolled short call has to be rolled yet again to avoid exercise. The strategy makes sense as long as consolidation continues. Once consolidation concludes, it is time to figure out how to escape from the short positions. The forward roll is only one possibility; another is simply taking a loss, hopefully a small one. However, properly managed, the consolidation-based short straddle is likely to yield profits more often than losses, especially when the time to expiration is limited and when you keep an eye on evolving breakout signals.

The hedging value in rolling with a bullish breakout is significant. A covered call cannot be rolled easily as long as the stock's price has declined below the strike. For example, Exxon Mobil's covered call was opened at an 85 strike, but the stock then fell to below $80 per share. In that case, there is little you can do but wait out the price, hoping it will recover; or take the profit on the call and then seek a new strategy, such as a short straddle. However, by starting out with the short straddle, the outcome can be managed profitably whether the underlying price advances or declines.

The Strap

A variation on the straddle is the *strap*. This is a position that adds a ratio weighting to the call side, by opening two calls versus one put. Like the long straddle, the *long strap* has no hedging value and is expensive, involving two calls in the hope of a price advance, versus only one put protecting against a price decline. However, the loss zone is increased by the number of points in the long calls.

Recalling the example of the long straddle, the December 85 Exxon Mobil options could be used to set up a long trap with the following:

2 long December 85 calls @ 1.78	$356 + $10 =	$366
1 long December 85 put @ 3.15	$315 + $ 9 =	$324
Total debit		$690

To become profitable, the underlying price needs to move 6.9 points in either direction, between $91.90 and $78.10. The full loss zone is extended to 13.8 points. Above the higher breakeven of $91.90, the long calls gain 2 points for each point of movement in the underlying; and for each point below $78.10, the long put gains 1 point.

In the Exxon example, even the decline from November 6 down to the November 20 closing price of $79.79 failed to move lower than the breakeven of $78.10. The long strap is very difficult as a speculative strategy, and it offers no hedging value.

In comparison, the *short strap* can work to hedge the underlying, especially in a time of low volatility or during a consolidation trend. For example, using the short options as of November 6, a short strap could be set up with the following positions:

2 short December 85 call @ 1.62	$324 -$10 = $314
1 short December 85 put @ 2.94	$294 - $ 9 = $285
Total credit	$599

Key Point
The short strap represents a low-risk hedge, assuming the higher number of short calls is completely covered with shares of stock.

Given the subsequent decline in the underlying between November 6 and November 20, the profit on the short calls would be substantially higher. The same rolling technique used for the short straddle could then be used for the short strap. To work as a truly conservative move, the short calls should be fully covered, meaning ownership of 200 shares for two short calls.

The Strip

The strap's opposite cousin is called the *strip*. This is a variation of the straddle in which more puts are opened than calls.

The **long strip**, like the long strap, is highly speculative and offers no hedging benefits. Based on the original long straddle, the long strip would consist of:

1 long December 85 call @ 1.78	$178 + $ 9 = $187
2 long December 85 puts @ 3.15	$630 + $10 = $640
Total debit	$827

In order to become profitable, the underlying price would need to move 8.27 points in either direction. So the loss zone extends from $93.27 down to $76.43, a total loss zone of 16.54 points.

The long strip does not present a favorable outcome based on the high cost and required movement required just to break even. In comparison, the **short strip** does have hedging benefits.

Based on the original short straddle for Exxon Mobil, the short strip could be constructed with the following positions:

1 short December 85 call @ 1.62	$162 - $ 9 = $153
2 short December 85 puts @ 2.94	$588 - $10 = $578
Total credit	$731

In this example, the profit zone extends 7.31 points above and below the strike of 85, between $92.31 and $77.69, a zone of 14.62 points. In the Exxon example, a problem arises because the stock price fell from the $85 range down below $80. To roll this forward, you would need to create a new straddle, spread, or strip designed to replace the appreciated short puts with new ones at a net credit.

The short call could be closed on November 20 at a net profit of $90. However, the short puts would have grown to 5.80 each, so a buy to close requires $1,169

($580 + $580 + $9). These positions could be replaced with a single 80 call bid at 2.95 and *two* 82.50 short puts bid at 4.40 each. The total credit would be:

One 80 call @ $295	$295 – $ 9 = $ 286
Two 82.50 puts @ $440	$880 – $10 = $ 870
Total credit	$1,156

The buy to close came out to $1,169 and the two extended short strip yielded $1,156, a net reduction of $13. This by itself is not a problem, because for a cost of $13 net, the in-the-money puts are replaced with new short puts and a lower strike. This means all of the new positions will benefit from time decay until the January expiration.

> **Key Point**
> The roll that creates a net debit is potentially a problem for short option positions. It makes sense when an ITM strike is replaced with a later one that is closer to the money. However, this type of roll has to be entered cautiously.

The recovery of the original short strip points out a problem in hedging with short options. This position is recovered and, at the very least, expiration is deferred. This process of rolling forward can be continued indefinitely, but it points out the potential risks of this type of hedge. Because of the added shorts options on one side or the other, when the underlying price moves against the higher ratio (two options versus one), the replacement and recovery are made more difficult. This is due to the higher premium value for twice as many options. Given the case of Exxon Mobil and its long-term consolidation trend, this hedge is not out of the question, but it does contain greater risk than the more basic short straddle.

Calendar Straddles

Another variety of the straddle is the ***calendar straddle***. This involves opening two straddles on the same underlying: a short straddle expiring first and a long straddle expiring later. Like the long straddle, this position has only limited hedging value. The short position provides short-term hedging value, but once this is expired, the long-term long straddle position is strictly speculative and requires substantial price movement.

The overall speculative nature of the calendar straddle is made more troubling by the fact that the overall position will yield a net debit. The later-expiring long straddle contains more time value, so this position is a speculative one, making it difficult to produce a profit. For that to occur, you rely on short-term low volatility followed by longer-term high volatility. This is impossible to predict.

As an expanded trade, the short-term short calendar straddle can be combined with a long-term long spread with a higher call strike and a lower put strike. For example, the December 85 short straddle could be followed by a January long spread using a 90 long call and an 80 long put. However, these provide no hedging value.

The long call and put provide some limited protection against exercise of the earlier short positions; however, if you own shares, the short call is covered and the short put is easily managed. So the calendar combined straddle and spread makes no sense compared to the short spread by itself.

The more elaborate forms of straddle may present greater risk and less hedging benefit. One risk of all options strategies is in the attraction of what appears to be an elegant strategy. In fact, the simple and more basic hedges are invariably more effective in managing risk than the more complex ones. In either case, the need to roll forward as an exercise avoidance technique is unavoidable. The next chapter explores methods of rolling and loss recovery.

12 | Rolling and Recovery Strategies

No matter how cautiously you set up options strategies to hedge equities, some portion are going to lose rather than gain. In these instances, you will need to figure out how to manage the paper loss. This can involve just taking the loss, waiting out the market, or applying a series of rolling and recovery strategies.

A danger in any form of recovery is the potential increased risk. Most forms of recovery involve replacement strategies, and this can easily be translated into an exchange of a low risk for a high one, or an exchange between a conservative strategy and a risky one. Because the purpose of the option hedge is to *reduce* risks, one of your primary considerations should be **risk awareness** as a basic requirement for portfolio management and for hedging.

With risk awareness as a first requisite for managing equity positions, especially when they have declined in value, you are better positioned to maintain a conservative risk profile while still devising strategies to continue hedging against loss. When options are involved, the first form of management over paper losses is the forward roll.

Rolling Strategies

Previous chapters have explained rolling forward in various ways, but the context of the forward roll with risk levels in mind has not been explored previously. As a form of recovery from a position that has worked against you, the **forward roll** contains three key attributes:

1. **Exercise avoidance.** The most apparent reason for rolling forward is to avoid exercise. This is also the most legitimate reason for rolling. Assuming your purpose is to maintain your equity portfolio, exercise presents a problem: A called-away position has to be replaced. If you prefer keeping well-selected equities, exercise avoidance makes sense.

> **Key Point**
>
> Avoiding exercise is a sound reason to roll forward. However, the outcome has to be analyzed to ensure that the overall benefits outweigh added exposure.

Even so, a few observations have to be made as well. Exercise avoidance is not itself a hedge against market risk, but a hedge against exercise. There may come a point where accepting exercise makes more sense than rolling forward. For example, if the call has moved far in the money, rolling will yield a small credit and it only delays inevitable exercise. A covered call may also be opened with exercise in mind. It is one way to set up an excellent hedging choice. Either the short call expires worthless (or is rolled), or shares are called away at a profit (and that profit consists of a capital gain as well as option premium).

> **Key Point**
>
> The roll creates a net credit due to higher time value. However, the added premium is justified only when the added time of exposure also makes sense.

2. **Creation of a net credit.** The forward roll will invariably create a net credit as long as the new short position has the same strike. This occurs due to a later-expiring short position containing more time value. As a hedge against exercise, a forward roll or even a series of forward rolls generates net income. If enough credit is available to increase the roll to a higher strike (for short calls) or a lower strike (for short puts), the forward roll gains hedging value. In the case of a short call, it makes exercise less likely, or, if exercise does occur, it will be at a higher price per share. The short put rolling down avoids exercise or sets up a lower cost per share if the put ends up exercised against you.

> **Key Point**
>
> Increasing exposure to loss with the forward roll is ill-advised, because the potential for recapturing lost value is offset by an equal risk of doubling the amount of the loss.

3. **Potentially higher risks.** Finally, the aspect of forward rolls often ignored or overlooked is the potential for higher market risks. This occurs especially when you replace a one-to-one covered call or short put with a greater number of new contracts, setting up a ratio write or just more market exposure. This is likely to occur when the option has moved in the money and you want to set up a net credit while also changing the strike. So for example, a covered call has moved in the money. So it is bought to close and replaced with a greater number of higher-strike, later-expiring calls. The rationale is that with a greater number of contracts, the net is likely to remain a credit, while eventual exercise is avoided or set to occur at a higher price per share. However, by converting a covered call to a ratio write, the risk level is also increased.

This can be mitigated to a degree by setting up a variable ratio write. For example, with 300 shares and three current covered calls with 40 strikes, you buy to close and replace with later-expiring sets of two 41 and two 42 strike calls. This creates higher risk, but remains manageable. However, if your primary purpose in originally opening the covered calls was to hedge market risks while earning premium income, what happens with the forward roll and conversion? The hedge is replaced with a more speculative position because a portion of the new set of short calls is uncovered. The variable ratio write is a worthwhile strategy, but moves such as this are most effective when used for situations with one-point increments between strikes. If the increments are 2.5, 5, or 10 points, the roll forward and conversion is less practical.

The same observation applies to uncovered puts. The market risk of the short put is the same as that of the covered call. However, if the desire is to roll forward to a lower strike, it is tempting to also increase the number of contracts. This also increases the risk that becomes real if and when the short puts are exercised. This will occur only when the current price per share is lower than the put strike; so with a greater number of short puts open, the risk is higher as well. Like the roll of a covered call, the roll of an uncovered put that also includes increasing the number of contracts replaces the initial hedge with a higher-risk position.

Is the Forward Roll Worthwhile?

The initial trade that sets up a hedge may effectively avoid losses on the equity side of your portfolio. However, the forward roll is not part of that hedge, but a defensive strategy to avoid exercise of a short option. Although exercise avoidance is desirable, is the forward roll worth the effort? There may be times when exercise is acceptable and even desirable.

For example, if your basis in stock is far below the current market value, opening a covered call may produce two desirable results. First, it expires worthless and yields current income, allowing you to repeat the trade. This hedges the current value of stock to the extent of option premium. A second outcome is exercise, which combines three sources of profits: capital gain on the stock, option premium, and dividends.

> **Key Point**
> When your basis in stock is far below current market value, you gain greater hedging potential and profits.

The forward roll might not have a part in one form of trade: the deep in the money covered call. For example, you buy 100 shares of stock at $30 per share and the price has risen to $42. With the possibility of a $1,200 profit, you would be content to sell but you also see value in keeping those shares. One way to use these shares to generate income and capital gains is to write an in-the-money call. For example, a 35 strike yields immediate intrinsic value of $700, a 23% profit on the original $30 per share investment. If the stock price declines, the short call hedges market risk. It can be bought to close at a lower priced than the original sale, so that the profit in the covered call offsets the loss in the stock. As an alternative, you can wait out the expiration cycle with one of two possible outcomes. First is exercise and having stock called away at a profit (capital gain and option premium). Second, if the option premium has declined by the time of expiration, the short call can be closed at a profit.

A third alternative in this situation would be to roll forward. Even though this was not part of the original plan, this situation sets up a powerful hedge. The original deep in-the-money call protects against downside moves in the stock (acting much like a long put), and the potential of profits from significantly reduced time value provide added current income. By rolling forward, this experience can be repeated.

A fourth alternative occurs if and when the stock price falls below the call's strike. In this case, the stock loses market value but it is offset by the short call. It is conceivable in this scenario to alter the hedge by rolling forward and down to a lower strike (but a strike that is higher than original basis in stock). Or if expiration is close, the call will expire worthless. In this case, you created a hedge while earning a rich option premium.

The point here is that appreciated stock contains great potential for hedging. The covered call, employed as a contingent sale transaction, sets up current income in double digits, and all outcomes will be profitable while hedging market risk in the stock.

Types of Forward Rolls

> **Key Point**
>
> The forward roll is not a risk hedge, but an exercise hedge.

The roll forward to the sale strike is the best-known type of roll, and the one that is likely to be employed in a majority of instances. However, all forms of forward roll have to be considered as defensive adjustments, in order to avoid exercise.

Beyond the strictly horizontal forward roll, a *diagonal roll* is also possible. When a covered call is involved, avoiding exercise may also involve rolling to a higher strike. By *rolling up*, the current in-the-money or at-the-money strike is increased. This reduces the chance of exercise, and, if exercise does occur in the future, you will receive a higher capital gain based on the higher strike.

When rolling an uncovered put, the opposite diagonal direction is possible. The advantage of the short put over the covered call is flexibility. Based on premium values, you can roll forward to any strike you wish, without concern for having shares of stock called away. The most desirable roll moves to a lower strike, *rolling down*, while still creating a net credit.

This usually involves extending the position out further than desired in order to set up a net credit. Greater flexibility is going to be found in stock with 1-point increments between strikes. As a strategy to avoid exercise, any roll that also changes the strike in a profitable direction is a sensible combination of a recovery strategy with an *exercise hedge*.

Rolling may become necessary whenever profitable hedge positions have been partially closed, but remaining open positions are in paper loss status. These "orphan" positions should be rolled forward to strikes closer to the money, creating an overall credit. In rolling, the new position's basis has to be adjusted to absorb the loss on the original position.

Other Recovery Strategies

Any *recovery strategy* should be designed to recapture a paper loss, preferably without increasing risks. Whenever such a strategy replaces a conservative hedge with a higher-risk speculative trade, it violates this concept.

The range of strategies is vast, and recovery itself is part of portfolio management. However, it often is wiser to accept losses and move to the next trade. The quest for a perfect record of profits invariably leads to greater losses. So a well-designed recovery trade should be made with hedging in mind. Because the idea is to hedge risk, a recovery trade may consist of a new current trade or of a *reconstituted hedge*, which employs later-expiring positions to exploit time value without adding market risk.

Some examples of recovery strategies that conform to the hedging standard without added risk are:

1. **Replacement strategy.** In this trade, a current loss is replaced with the same strategy or a similar strategy but with later expirations. This may constitute a forward roll or replacement of one type

   > **Key Point**
   > Replacement strategies should be made carefully to ensure that risk levels are not increased.

   of trade with another. When using this method, the relative levels of risk should be kept in mind. The most desirable outcome is to not increase market risks.

   An example of a replacement strategy is to accept a loss on a covered call by closing the position. This avoids exercise. It is then replaced with an uncovered put with an adjusted strike. The advantage in this is two-fold. First, it offsets the loss on the covered call. Second, it can be set up using any strike regardless of your basis in stock, but with the same risk levels as those of the covered call.

2. **Alternative strategy with higher credit premium.** This involves accepting a loss on an initial strategy and replacing it with a different strategy whose market risk is the same or lower. This allows you

   > **Key Point**
   > Losses on an initial hedge may create opportunities for stronger hedges and higher net income.

   to keep portfolio management intact without loss.

   An example: You opened a covered call and the stock price has moved above the strike. With exercise approaching, you want to avoid exercise so you close the short call at a loss. You then open a later-expiring, higher-strike covered call that is out of the money and at the same time sell an uncovered put with the same strike. This creates a covered straddle. The risk is no higher than a covered call, and creation of higher premium income further discounts your basis. At the same time, by using a higher strike, you offset the loss on the original covered call while creating a higher capital gain in the event of exercise.

3. **Increased equity with new hedge.** This involves increasing the position in stock after a decline in market value. This discounts your basis in all shares and is also called averaging down. It is not advisable when the company's value is declining, meaning the drop in the stock price reflects a fundamental problem. However, when the downward swing is cyclical, this is an effective recovery strategy that also introduces added hedging opportunities.

> **Key Point**
> Adding more equity positions as part of a recovery strategy has to be done cautiously, and only when your view of the company justifies adding to your equity holdings.

For example, you purchased 100 shares at $38 and sold a covered call at a 40 strike. The stock price has declined to $35 per share. Your covered call expires worthless. However, the paper loss of $300 creates a problem. Analysis of the company reveals continued fundamental strength, so you do not want to dispose of shares. You decide to increase your equity position by purchasing an additional 200 shares @ $35. This changes your average basis to $36 per share. You next sell three 35-strike covered calls @ 3 ($300). Even though the strike is one point below your adjusted net basis of $36 per share, the covered call premium exceeds this. The one point in the money is acceptable under these conditions, as the original 3-point paper loss is entirely absorbed by this trade.

Some trades intended as recovery strategies actually increase your risks and should be avoided. In the interest of maintaining a conservative profile, increasing risks is not a wise move. By "doubling down" on a loss, you could break even or just make that loss much worse. This is a *speculative hedge* and is not a conservative trade. Too often, options traders with equity positions are not willing to take relatively small losses. This is an error, and realistically, you will have losses some of the time. The purpose in hedging and recovery is to minimize losses without adding risks.

For example, after opening a covered call for 4 ($400), the underlying price rises substantially and the call moves in the money, increasing to a valuation of 9 ($900). You buy to close and take a loss of $500. Your rationale is that the underlying price has risen so the loss on call premium is justified or, at the very least, offset. However, you want to replace the lost value in the short call. Believing that the underlying will continue to rise, you buy two at-the-money calls expiring in two months, paying premium of 4 on each, or a total of $800. This increases your overall net loss to $1,300. Contrary to your belief (and speculative hope), the underlying price remains below the strike of the new calls, and you end up losing. In this case, the loss was made far worse. A more prudent move would have been to accept the $500 loss and sell a later-expiring, higher-strike covered call. This would generate immediate income and set up a higher strike, meaning you would earn a higher capital gain if the new short call were exercised.

The lesson in this situation is that speculative hedging is a high-risk move. It can work out, but more often it only ends up making losses worse. Hedging does not guarantee net profits in every case. However, accepting losses and figuring out how to offset them with more hedging is a mature and sensible method for portfolio management. In the example, the attempt to offset losses did not work out; but by duplicating the conservative hedge (covered call), the loss would have represented only one part of the overall experience, with a likely increase in profits from later decisions.

In addition to working as a way to reduce portfolio risks, well-designed hedges accomplish a second benefit: reducing the degree of losses in the portfolio. When hedges are timed to coincide with the cyclical moves in equity positions, they are also more likely to succeed. So timing a covered call when the underlying is at or near the top of its trading range is one hedging method relying on proximity of price to resistance. Timing an uncovered put to coincide with price at or near the bottom of the trading range sets up an identical market risk but with support proximity ruling the decision.

The covered straddle also works well with proximity in mind, as a form of hedging. As a recovery strategy, the covered straddle increases current income without increasing market risk. For many investors, when stock prices move into consolidation, it is considered a form of "loss" if only because the stock price is not moving in a dynamic fashion. In this case, consolidation could last several weeks or months. To recover from this inactivity in the equity value, hedges like the covered straddle exploit the lack of movement by generating option premium income. As long as you monitor the position to identify likely breakout points, a short-term covered straddle can generate attractive levels of income.

Anticipating Price Decline With No-cost Hedging

A second benefit to using short options to hedge equity: This enables you to keep shares in your portfolio. Assuming you want to keep your equity positions intact, a dilemma arises when the stock price rises: Do you sell shares and take profits, or do you wait out the cycles? Another alternative is to anticipate potential price decline and hedge against it. In this way, you recover a possible loss of equity value in advance. Positions like the synthetic short stock set up insurance for little net cost, and the short call pays for the long put. The risk is minimal in this position because the call is covered and can be closed or rolled to avoid exercise if the equity price moves that call in the money. If the stock price does fall, the long put side of the synthetic position offsets losses in the stock with gains in the put.

> **Key Point**
>
> Synthetic stock positions create hedges not in response to a price move, but in anticipation of it.

If you just buy an insurance put, you have to consider the cost of the put as part of the hedge. This means a breakeven does not occur until the stock price declines a number of points equal to the cost of the put. However, with the synthetic short stock trade, the net cost of the long put and short call is at or close to zero; so the insurance benefits of the put are based on a zero cost; the offset begins as soon as the underlying falls below the strike.

Recovery With Multiple Share Increments

The process of loss recovery is more flexible when an equity position is higher than 100 shares. With only 100 shares, you are limited to single contracts for one-to-one positions such as covered calls or covered straddles.

The limitation does not apply to some hedges such as synthetic stock. For example, a synthetic long stock position combines long calls with short puts. Net cost is at or close to zero. This eliminates the market risk of the long calls, which consists of time decay risk. The short put risk is identical to the risk of covered calls; so in theory, a hedge could consist of any number of offsetting calls and puts in this synthetic position. However, realistically, the hedging properties are more important than the theory. A synthetic long stock position duplicates movement in the underlying even if you do not own stock. This means that the synthetic is not a hedge, because there is no equity position to offset. However, when you own shares and the price has declined, the synthetic long stock is an effective hedging device that exploits expected price swings.

> **Key Point**
>
> When you own several increments of shares, hedging is more flexible and many opportunities are presented.

This benefit is augmented when you own multiple increments of the underlying. For example, if you own 500 shares, how do you hedge the position when the underlying price has dropped? For example, your basis was $47 per share and today you sold five covered calls with 50 strikes, gaining 2 ($200) for each, or a total of $1,000. Today, the price has dropped to $44 per share. The five covered calls expired worthless, and the net outcome is an adjusted net basis of $45 per share ($47 paid minus 2 points for covered calls). The profit of $1,000 on covered calls is desirable, and current value is only one point below your net basis.

One way to hedge this relatively small net paper loss would be to sell more covered calls. However, the timing does not make this ideal, and you believe the stock price has a good chance to recover. So in place of covered calls, uncovered puts are more attractive. However, concern about the management of this hedge if the underlying price continues to fall makes the short put questionable as a safe hedge.

An alternative to both of these is to identify additional strategies you can use to create hedges while recovering the loss as well. For example, a covered straddle with a strike above current value (at $46 or $47, for example) generates income while offsetting the entire loss. A synthetic long stock consisting of a long call and a short put will create net income if the stock price rises, while presenting manageable short put risks (which can be closed or rolled). These are manageable because the strike is higher than current market value of stock, so time decay should absorb enough of the current premium to make it possible to close at a profit.

Even so, the exposure of five short puts can be daunting. With this in mind, ownership of 500 shares presents an opportunity to combine hedges in a variety of combined strategies. For example, you may want to sell two covered calls, two covered straddles, and one synthetic long stock. This creates a combination overall of four short calls, three short puts, and one long call:

2 covered calls = 2 short calls

2 covered straddles = 2 short calls and 2 short puts

1 synthetic long stock – 1 long call and 1 short put

Although this is a complex series of positions, it does present profit opportunities no matter which direction the stock price moves. Out of the eight positions, seven are short. This also means time decay provides exceptional opportunity for profit.

Why would anyone want to set up such a complex series of trades against 500 shares? It does diversify the short risk, but for many, the alternative of staying with a single strategy might be seen as more desirable. It is a matter of personal choice. For example, you could just sell five uncovered puts with a strike above current price per share. The risks of the short put are identical to covered calls; however, a drop in share price translates to a risk of having an additional 500 shares put to you upon exercise. So a set of five uncovered puts, opened as a hedge against an equity position of 500 shares, would have to be monitored with this is mind. They can be closed to take profits, or rolled forward if the puts move in the money. Otherwise, as long as the underlying price remains at or above the strike, they will expire worthless.

With multiple increments of shares, the hedging potential is more flexible than for sets of only 100 shares. In setting up a recovery strategy, this flexibility also translates to more effective forms of hedging than for only 100 shares. In one definition, the market risk of hedges against 100 shares is lower than the equivalent risk for multiple increments. However, the risk is identical for any number of shares and hedged options, with a notable difference: The income from short positions is greater, but the dollar value of a loss is also greater, even with identical risks.

This risk can be further diversified with calendar positions. This means opening positions with several different expiration dates as a means for avoiding the singular risk of several options expiring at the same time. For example, with 500 shares in your portfolio, you could sell uncovered puts in the following combination:

2 puts slightly out of the money, expiring in under 30 days

2 puts one strikes higher, expiring in 60 days

1 put two strikes higher, expiring in 90 days

Key Point
The potential for varying hedges against multiple increments of stock adds flexibility, but might not improve the overall hedge.

The higher strikes are further out of the money for uncovered puts, but the longer expiration timing increases time value. The earliest expirations will have rapid time decay, and the later ones will decline more slowly. However, the extended period allows you to manage these positions effectively through closing or rolling if and when the underlying price takes these puts in the money. The most important question with this strategy is whether or not the varying of hedge positions improves the hedging effectively, or not.

The same calendar position method can be used for any hedge, including covered calls, covered straddles, or combinations of several different hedging strategies. You could also set up a series of hedges to benefit whether the underlying moves up or down. Consider the following set of five trades to hedge 500 shares:

1 uncovered put slightly in the money, expiring in under 30 days

1 covered call slightly out of the money, expiring in under 30 days

1 covered straddle one strikes higher, expiring in 60 days

1 synthetic long stock one strike higher, expiring in 90 days

1 synthetic long stock one strike lower, expiring in 90 days

In this set of five hedges over three upcoming expiration cycles, you combine uncovered puts, covered calls, covered straddle, and synthetic long and synthetic short stock. Because the two synthetic positions benefit with stock movement in opposite direction, they both represent low-cost or no-cost hedges with protection on the upside and on the downside. However, a related concern with these combined hedges is timing of dividends. When ex-dividend date occurs, it presents a potential time when short options will be exercised early. So a prudent hedging policy is to avoid having short calls open during ex-dividend month.

As a matter of practical limits, extending hedges—especially with short options—for such an extended period of time presents higher risks than those expiring within 30 days. However, this diversification of hedges also presents attractive variation to the selection of option hedges against equity positions in your portfolio.

The next chapter extends the idea of recovery to a different topic, avoiding early exercise on short positions. One of the problems of the varied hedge is the potential for exercise of short positions. This is a management issue for the portfolio as well as for the hedges you design to mitigate risk.

13 | Avoiding Early Exercise of Short Options

A general rule of thumb for anyone opening short positions regards the possibility of exercise: You should be willing to accept exercise as one of several possible outcomes.

This does not mean that exercise is the best outcome, but it is a possibility. When using options to hedge equity positions, exercise is not desirable. It contradicts the basic reason for the hedge, which is to minimize or eliminate equity market risk. For example, if a covered call leads to having shares called away, it disrupts the portfolio and presents a problem: Do you get back into the stock position or find a suitable replacement? It would be more in line with the hedging goal to avoid exercise as long as that does not mean adding risks to the hedge.

The Events Leading to Short Call Exercise

Most options traders are aware that exercise is automatic on the last trading day, as long as an option is in the money, even minimally. *Automatic exercise* occurs for all options that are one penny or more in the money by expiration.

For anyone with an in-the-money option by the third Friday of the month, the most rational action is buy to close, and either take the profit or loss, or roll forward. If these actions are not taken, the option will be exercised. For a call, 100 shares of stock are automatically taken from you for each option; and for an exercised put, 100 shares of the underlying stock are put to you at the strike.

> **Key Point**
> Automatic exercise is worth avoiding in most hedging strategies, and exercise at the end of the cycle is the most common timing for this outcome.

Some covered call positions are designed as a form of contingent sale, meaning exercise is acceptable and even expected. However, this is not a typical hedge but a process for selling shares of the underlying at a profit. For the more typical hedging position, avoiding last-day exercise is desirable. It should also be profitable to close the short call or put, because time value has evaporated by this point in the cycle. However, if intrinsic value has increased so that the position would create a net loss, two choices remain: buy to close and accept the loss, or roll the position forward to a later-expiring option to avoid exercise.

Beyond the last trading day, early exercise is also a possibility. An option can be exercised at any time as long as it is in the money. Realistically, the chances of early exercise are remote with one exception: the few days right before ex-dividend date. *Ex-dividend* means "without dividend," representing the end of the period in which a dividend can be earned. So as long as you are a stockholder of record by close of business the day before ex-dividend date, you are entitled to the current dividend even if you sell stock on the following day. The details of this event were described in Chapter 6.

As a short call seller, this timing is a likely period when early exercise will occur. But what are the chances of this? Not every short call is exercised right before ex-dividend date, because long option holders did not all pay the same amount for the call. So in order for a call owner to put early exercise into effect, three values are in play: the original cost of the long call, the current price of the underlying, and the amount of the dividend.

It makes sense to exercise when the long call owner will be able to make a net profit by calling away shares. For example, if the strike is 50 and current value of stock is $53 per share, the owner can buy 100 shares from you at $50 and realize a $300 profit (because the current price is $53). If the dividend is $35, the total initial profit will be $335. This makes sense as an early exercise candidate as long as the initial cost of the call was lower than $335. However, if that long call owner paid 4.50 ($450) for the call, early exercise would not make any sense.

Key Point

Early exercise is most likely to occur immediately before ex-dividend date. However, not all in-the-money calls will be exercised in this situation.

This means that for in-the-money calls, not all will be exercised right before ex-dividend date. Only those that yield an overall net profit are likely to be exercised only. Even then, not every long call owner will decide to exercise. Some will prefer to sell the call at a profit and not want to earn the dividend as well. If they are uncertain about the investment value of shares, or simply don't want to take an equity position, they will not exercise the short call. The decision will also rely on how many points in the money the call has moved.

The percentage of calls exercised early is not easy to determine. It depends largely on the amount of capital gain and on the dividend. Because the capital gain is different for every strike, the portion likely to be exercised early will vary. The often-cited 75% of all options expiring worthless is wrong. In fact, 75% of all options held until expiration will expire worthless. Most are exercised beforehand or closed before expiration occurs. Overall, only 17% of all options are exercised according to the Options Clearing Corporation. Figure 13.1 shows a breakdown of outcomes.

Figure 13.1: Option Outcomes

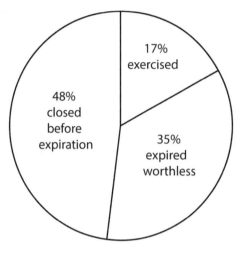

Source: Options Clearing Corporation (OCC)

The portion of all options that is exercised, 17%, represent activity occurring mostly on the last trading day. Some of these exercised options were early, but only a small portion of all options suffer this fate, even for in-the-money short calls right before ex-dividend date.

Even so, as a short call seller, you should be aware that some options traders use the early exercise provision as an intentional strategy. The idea is to buy at-the-money options immediately before ex-dividend date and exercise them immediately. This allows them to earn the current dividend. On or after ex-dividend date, the shares received through early exercise are closed. So the quarterly dividend is earned for a very short holding period of only a few days.

Early exercise of your short calls can be avoided in three days. First, focus only on stocks that do not pay dividends (this strategy makes little sense because dividends represent attractive forms of income). Second, avoid selling calls expiring in ex-dividend month, which for most stocks occurs only in four months per year. Third, monitor the situation closely and roll forward when calls go in the money, to avoid early exercise.

When time value and extrinsic value (implied volatility) are relatively high right before ex-dividend date, the chances of early exercise are reduced. However, if the option's premium is predominately intrinsic value, this greatly increases your exposure to early exercise. One way to look at early exercise of a covered call is that, even with the loss of the dividend, it is a positive outcome. This is true as long as the option's strike is higher than the basis in stock. Even so, a hedging strategy should be based on the desirability of keeping portfolio positions and benefitting from share price growth and dividend income.

Early Exercise and Short Puts

For short put sellers, early exercise related to ex-dividend date is not an issue. A put is not vulnerable to early exercise in the same way as a covered call. This brings up an interesting hedging advantage.

> **Key Point**
>
> The risk of early exercise applies to covered calls. For uncovered short puts, this is not a problem because no dividends are in play.

The uncovered short put has the same market risk profile as a covered call, with the exception of dividends. First, because you do not have to own shares in a short put strategy, a standalone short put does not earn dividends. However, as a hedge, the basic assumption is that you do own shares in your portfolio and want to use a variety of strategies (including uncovered puts) to hedge market risk. So you can combine covered calls and uncovered puts to continue this hedging device each and every month.

In two out of three months, no ex-dividend date is involved, assuming dividends are paid quarterly. So writing one-month covered calls is a sensible and advantageous strategy at these times, because time decay is rapid. In ex-dividend month, when you will want to avoid exposure of short calls to the possibility of early exercise, leave shares intact but write uncovered puts. This provides a similar income stream without being at risk of early exercise. The hedge continues without the exposure.

The covered call is further at risk in months when earnings are announced. This could be a month entirely different than ex-dividend month. The risk here is that any earnings surprise, either positive or negative, creates a momentary overreaction in the underlying price. Because it is most likely to self-correct quickly, the price reaction to an earnings surprise can be ignored; however, this may also present another potential timing for early exercise.

For example, in the case of either a covered call or uncovered put, a negative earnings surprise may cause the underlying price to fall many points. In this case, the call loses value and can be closed at a profit, but it could end up with a paper loss in the stock. The put gains value and could be exercised, so it could become necessary to roll forward to avoid exercise. A positive earnings surprise causes the stock price to rise temporarily. However, at that price spike, the uncovered put can be closed at a profit, but a covered call could be exercised to take advantage of the difference between current market value and a much lower strike.

With the potential risk related to earnings surprises, it could make sense to avoid earnings month or to close out of positions before the date of announcement. It does not matter whether a short option is in the money or not before earnings are announced. The earnings surprise will change status very quickly. So if a surprise does occur, a previously safe and buffered short position could become an exposed one in a single session. Because you cannot know in advance whether earnings will meet expectations, or end up above or below, this risk is potentially severe. To hedge against this risk, it makes sense to be out of short positions ahead of time.

After the earnings have been announced, you can take action to move into long or short hedges. Knowing that price reaction to earnings surprises is invariably exaggerated, this moment presents an excellent opportunity. When the earnings surprise is negative and the underlying price declines, the paper loss is not likely to last. This presents an opportunity to sell as put or even to buy a call or other form of hedge. If the earnings surprise is positive, timing is excellent for selling a covered call or buying a long put.

Even for the most conservative investor focused on the long term, hedges that are timed for price spikes following earnings surprises can be very profitable short-term moves. They will not always work out as expected, but they usually will, so like all hedges, the timing of this move based on likely price behavior is easily spotted and has a better than average chance of resulting in a profitable outcome.

> **Key Point**
> Although price behavior after earnings surprises typically reverses very quickly, the price spike presents a risk of early exercise.

When traders do not use options to hedge against price movement, events like earnings surprises are likely to lead to ill-advised action. When price falls drastically after a negative earnings report, some equity investors panic and sell, only to see the price rise in following sessions. When the price jumps after a positive report, some will buy shares in the belief that a strong bull market has commenced. They are likely to see a price decline shortly after. This gut reaction to earnings surprises is typical of market behavior, in which so many people buy high and sell low instead of following the simple advice to buy low and sell high.

Another consideration about early exercise is the tax consequence. If you have greatly appreciated stock, exercise does not appear to present a great problem; in fact, it yields a profit. However, tax consequences could change this picture. For example, if your stock has appreciated rapidly but you have only owned it for 11 months or less, that capital gain is treated as short-term. You need to exceed a full year before getting the favorable long-term tax rate. So when ex-dividend date occurs prior to the full-year holding period, rolling forward makes sense, and when the capital gain is substantial, it makes even more sense to extend your holding period.

Options: American Style vs. European Style

Most options on stock treaded in U.S. markets are called *American style*. This means that exercise is allowed at any time during the option's life. For a trader of long options, this is an advantage; for the short seller, it presents a range of risks related to timing of dividends and earnings.

In comparison, a *European style* option can be exercised only at the end of the life of the option. This is most commonly seen for options on stock index funds, where physical exercise would not be practical. In these forms of European options, settlement is done on a cash basis, meaning any settlement involves equivalent cash payments versus exchange of shares.

Early Exercise and Multiple Option Contracts

Some hedges consist of more than single options, and may be set up in a calendar spread or straddle. These complex hedge positions, designed in some cases to protect against downside market risk while creating short-term profits, may also set up cost-free or low-cost situations that also improve your ability to hedge against the risk of early exercise.

Key Point

The use of multiple options adds flexibility to many hedges, and this raises potential for added profits in the hedging strategy.

This is most likely in multiple option positions when current in-the-money or at-the-money options are rolled forward. If this is done only to avoid in-the-money status or specifically to escape ex-dividend or earnings month, the flexibility of multiple contracts becomes a hedging advantage to you as well. This type of complex option rolling demands monitoring, and can provide you with low-risk hedging advantages. For example, rolling a short option forward to a higher strike (for calls) or a lower strike (for puts) avoids being at or in the money, and may also create a breakeven or small credit outcome. These diagonal moves gain added flexibility when you are able to roll forward and increase the number of outstanding option contracts. For covered calls, maintaining complete coverage may involve buying more shares or initially opening positions on only part of your total portfolio position.

For uncovered puts, the situation is even more flexible. As a first step, the put will hedge your portfolio position with the same market risk as covered calls. However, if the put moves closer to the money, it can be rolled forward and down, with a larger number of outstanding contracts. For example, if you have 200 shares and you sold two uncovered puts, these can be rolled forward and down to three new uncovered puts.

Unlike the call, for which a full coverage relationship between stock and short call is desirable, the short put has no such restrictions. The danger in this diagonal roll is that the stock price could continue to fall. This demonstrates why selection of companies for your portfolio demands low volatility and strong fundamentals as a starting point. There is no danger in adding more puts, but if the stock price continues to decline, this can get out of hand and potentially lead to losses and a greater demand for higher-risk recovery strategies.

The most conservative version of increased contracts with a diagonal roll is the purchase of additional shares. This does not always make sense for covered calls, for which a diagonal forward roll is likely when the underlying price has increased; so buying more shares means increasing average basis and a higher risk in the case when the underlying price retreats. For short puts, however, rolling forward and selling a higher number of contracts does not require buying more shares. But doing so is a recovery move, because the price per share in this situation will be lower than the original strikes, so buying additional shares averages your basis down.

If You Own Long Calls

Within a hedging strategy, there will be instances in which you own long calls. For example, as part of a spread or straddle, or a synthetic long stock strategy, one side of the overall trade could involve a long call. One likely outcome is that a short side loses value and you enter a buy to close to take profits and remove market risk. What happens to the long call?

The same arguments presented earlier about the risks to sellers may also translate to advantages to long call owners. There are several instances in which owning calls present opportunities for hedging. These include:

1. **The desire to buy more shares.** The contingent purchase is one type of hedge based on ownership of a long call. Whether this is bought by itself and represents an orphan position in a more complex hedge, it is the application of the call to fix the price per share in a future purchase of stock.

2. **Creation of future hedges with other options.** The orphan long call can be combined with other positions, usually short, to set up future hedges. This outcome is likely to occur with a calendar spread, in which a short call with earlier

> **Key Point**
> Once the short side of a spread or straddle is closed, the remaining long option can be used to set up additional hedges.

   expiration is covered by the long call with later expiration. After the short side has expired, the long side can be used to create new hedges on the same underlying.

3. **Buying stock to earn dividends.** Just as your short option places you at risk of early exercise, your long option sets up an opportunity to exercise right before ex-dividend date, and earn the current dividend. This is an excellent return on investment. Although the current divi-

> **Key Point**
> Risks to sellers often are offsetting profit possibilities for buyers. With long options outstanding, you can take advantage the dividend timing.

   dend is based on a three-month period, you can earn it with ownership of stock over only a few days. This enhances the current position in the same equity within your portfolio.

If You Own Long Puts

The opposite side of this analysis applies equally well and presents hedging opportunities. When a long put is left over from an earlier hedge (when the short side has been closed to take profits, for example), the long put is not a disadvantage but a potential benefit. For example:

1. **The desire to sell shares.** The contingent sale is a hedge based on ownership of a long put. You might desire to sell shares in the future, and the long put fixes the sales price well in advance in case you decide that selling shares makes sense.

2. **Creation of future hedges with other options.** The orphan long put works like the long call; it can be combined with other positions, usually short, to set up future hedges. This outcome is likely to occur with a calendar spread, in which a short put with earlier expiration is covered by the long put with later expiration. After the short side has expired, the long side can be used to create new hedges on the same underlying.

> **Key Point**
>
> The insurance put is one happy consequence of closing a short side before a long side. The outcome is fixing maximum loss at the net basis in the overall position.

3. **Insurance put.** The remaining long put serves another hedging purpose, which is to set up an insurance put. This fixes the maximum loss at the strike, adjusted for the profit or loss on the original position. If the stock price declines below that adjusted basis in stock, the put gains intrinsic value of one point for each point of decline in the stock's price.

Early exercise is generally a problem within a hedging strategy—unless part of the hedge accepts a contingent purchase or sale as part of the overall strategy. When you want to keep equity positions intact, the techniques for avoiding exercise can be applied. These include avoiding being in a risk situation—avoiding ex-dividend month for short calls and avoiding earnings month for all short options.

The next chapter includes a summary of option collateral and tax rules. Although these do not relate specifically to hedging, the possible advantages or disadvantages of the tax and collateral rules can affect your selection of one hedge over another.

14 | Collateral and Tax Rules for Options Trading

The strategies used to set up hedges involve a rich variety of option-based positions. These are not necessarily complicated, and can be put into action assuming a few basic requirements:

1. **You understand option rules and risks.** The first rule for options (and all types of investments) is that you know the trading rules and the risks involved. When you first look at the terminology and variety of options, the whole idea seems exotic and risky. And in fact, if you do not

> **Key Point**
> Knowing your limitations is essential for successful investing. With options, knowing the rules of trading and the risks is a wise first step.

first master the basics, you should not use options, either as a conservative hedge or for speculation.

2. **You are qualified by your broker.** When you apply for approval to trade options, your broker requires that you complete an option application. On this document, you explain your experience and knowledge about options. Your broker then assigns a "level of approval" for trading. This defines how much risk your broker will allow you to take. Every broker defines a series of levels and the types of options trades allowed. The lower level is the most conservative strategies, and as the levels advance, the allowed trades become more complex.

3. **Your risk profile is conservative.** If you are a speculator willing to assume high risks, you probably are not at all interested in setting up a long-term portfolio of equities or in hedging against risks. Speculators are interested in very short-term profits and tend to favor using high-risk options strategies. However, conservative investors understand the importance of setting up a permanent portfolio and protecting it against market risk.

4. **When losses occur, you are able to accept them.** In order to succeed in any investing program, especially one involving hedges, you also need to be able to accept losses. While the purpose of hedging is to reduce loss exposure, you will have losses in some percentage of your trades. An important element of hedging is to know when to walk away and focus on the next trade. Anyone who "doubles down" and tries to offset yesterday's loss with total's higher-risk trade is only inviting problems.

5. **You know your breakeven rate.** In Chapter 2, the concept of a breakeven rate was explained. This is the rate of return you need in order to break even after accounting for inflation and taxes. Most investors who calculate this are surprised and disturbed at what they discover: that they need to exceed the typical net return from investing. In fact, to make a breakeven rate consistently, you have only two choices. First, you have to increase the risk levels you are able to tolerate (which also adds the possibility of higher losses). Second, you need to use options to set up conservative trades and hedges, not only to increase your typical rate of return but also to *reduce* market risks.

> **Key Point**
> Many investors are not aware of what they need to break even after inflation and taxes. This is a troubling fact of life.

Once you meet these initial requirements, entering into a hedging program is both sensible and profitable. Options are being used more and more as hedging devices, versus emphasis in the past on speculation. However, two aspects of options trading add complication to this process: margin rules and taxes.

Margin Rules for Options

When you buy stock, the margin rules allow you to finance 50% of your purchase in the margin account. This is an attractive feature for stock trading, but it also adds significant risk. Some traders assume that the same margin rules apply to options trading, but they do not. In options trading, "margin" is not a reference to leverage alone, but also defines required collateral that has to be placed on deposit. The rules are complex, but they can be studied free by getting a copy of the *CBOE Margin Manual*. (The link was included in Chapter 1.)

The basic collateral rules are easily mastered. Long calls and puts have to be paid in full at the time of the trade. Short option trades at least 20% of the underlying value based on the strike. This is adjusted for the moneyness of the option and for the proceeds received. For advanced strategies like spreads and straddles, the calculation is more complex. Use the CBOE Margin Calculator to determine the amount required to be placed on deposit for each type of trade. (See Chapter 1 for a link to the Margin Calculator.)

Tax Rules for Options Trading

The federal tax rules for trading options are perplexing and complex. In Chapter 6, the essentials of a "qualified" and "unqualified" covered call were explained. The important point to remember is this: If you open a deep in-the-money covered call before you have reached the one-year holding period to qualify for long-term gains on stock, the count is tolled as long as the call is open. This means the period of time required is stopped as long as the unqualified call remains open. Although this affects only a small portion of trades, it can become an issue.

For example, if you have owned stock for less than one year and the value has increased substantially, the loss of long-term capital gains rates can add to your tax liability. An unqualified covered call can also be created unintentionally if you roll a short call forward to avoid exercise after the underlying price has risen. The two trades—the initial call and the new call—are treated as separate transactions, and this could result in an unseen tax burden.

> **Key Point**
> The term unqualified doesn't mean you cannot open such a trade. It does mean you risk losing favorable long-term capital gains rates.

To fully understand the tax rules, refer to the free booklet provided by the CBOE entitled "Taxes and Investing." This runs down the essential rules you need to know. However, for any level of complex options trades, you should also consult with your tax advisor and make sure he or she fully understands how options taxation works.

> **Resource**
> To get a free download of "Taxes and Investing," link to *http://bit.ly/1WHnCsn*.

Capital gains are well understood by most investors. However, with options a few qualifiers have to be added into the mix. Here are a few of the options-based rules:

1. **The constructive sale rule could apply.** This occurs when you are taxed as if you closed a position even though you did not. When you open offsetting long and short options on the same underlying, you could create a constructive sale. For example, you own 100 shares of stock and you open a long and a short position involving a straddle or spread. This might or might not set up a constructive sale. This is defined in IRC Section 1259, which explains that offsetting positions against positions already owned are constructive sales, such as a short sale of stock when you also own shares of the same stock. An exception arises when the trade is closed at least 30 days before the end of the year.

2. **Wash sales prevent loss deductions.** A *wash sale* occurs when a position is closed and then reopened within 30 days. Some traders have attempted to set up tax

> **Key Point**
> You cannot move in and out of trades timed for taking losses at the year ends, unless you wait more than 30 days.

deductible losses by selling close to the end of the year and then moving back in right after the beginning of the new year. A wash sale also applies when shares of stock are sold and replaced with an in-the-money out.

3. **Exercised long options are treated as part of basis in stock.** When you exercise a long position, it is not treated as a separate trade, but adjusts your basis in the shares of stock bought or sold.

4. **Short option premium is not taxed at the time the trade is opened.** When you sell an option, you receive proceeds. However, this trade is not taxed until it is closed, expires, or gets exercised.

5. **Some losses are not deductible in the year of the loss. A straddle is treated as an *offsetting position*.** This means that deductions could be deferred until the so-called "successor position" (the other side of the straddle) has been closed or expires. In this situation, a loss in the initial closed position might not be deductible until both sides are closed.

6. **Married puts may be treated as adjustments to stock basis.** A married put (an insurance put) is treated as an adjustment to the basis in stock when the put is purchased on the same day as shares of stock. However, if the put is sold before expiration, the outcome is treated as a short-term capital gain or loss.

The many tax rules make options more complex than most forms of investing. As a hedge against equity positions, the option can provide safety and risk elimination in many forms; and the best of these is the hedge that also creates added income. Considering the desirability of capital gains and dividends, options add another form of income as well as hedging benefits.

Considering the difficulty of balancing a conservative risk profile with breakeven returns (based on inflation and taxes), the options hedge is one of the few varieties of investing that enables you to beat the averages without needing to accept higher risks.

15 | **The Final Twist: Proximity**

In the overall analysis of options as hedges, the biggest question of all involves when and *where* the trade should be entered. In Chapter 5, the discussion of timing for options trades was based on the study of Western and Eastern reversal signals. However, there is one final point to study: the proximity of signals.

The "proximity" of the signal to the trading range determines more than anything else when a specific trade is likely to be profitable. This is a reference to the location of price in comparison to two important lines: *resistance* and *support*.

These terms are well understood by most investors; however, for the purpose of hedging, the

> **Key Point**
> Hedges are most effective when they are timed to coincide with price proximity to resistance and support, where the greatest uncertainty enters the picture.

range in between resistance and support is the area of agreement between the two sides, the range of prices agreed upon by the forces of supply and demand. The widely accepted significance of resistance and support define the proximity issue for hedging purposes.

Investors understand that if and when price moves above resistance, it can indicate a coming reversal back into range, or a breakout to a new, higher range; and that when price moves below support, it may represent a coming upward reversal or the beginning of a new, lower trading range. However, this widely accepted view of the trading range and its borders is applied mainly to determine whether a new trade should be entered. So equity holders will either buy or sell based on how they perceived the movement of price above resistance or below support. Ironically, this decision-making process turns buy-and-hold, conservative equity investors into speculators. If an investor makes a trade based solely on the movement of price outside of the current trading range but without understanding what happens next, then the buy-and-hold standard is being abandoned.

> **Key Point**
> Decisions investor make based on price behavior at or near resistance and support can easily turn conservatives into speculators.

This is one of the many flaws in how many investors operate. However, when focused not on exploiting what might be a momentary price movement, but on how to hedge the move, the process of portfolio management becomes more stable. Assuming that the equity positions in your portfolio are ones you prefer to keep, the proximity of price to the edges of the trading range are a concern, but that move should raise hedging questions rather than the question of changing the equity position.

The Zone of Resistance or Support

When price is in proximity to resistance or support, reversal signals take on greater meaning. A reversal signal occurring at midrange is less likely to lead to actual reversal, especially when compared to the proximity at or moving through resistance or support. This is true whether using a specific price level or a *zone of resistance or support*.

For example, the one-year chart of Atmos Energy (ATO) includes more than nine months of a consolidation trend, ending with a breakout above resistance near the end of September. The levels of resistance and support varied during consolidation, but only by a single point. This is typical of the zone approach to resistance or support. The zone itself tends to be quite small compared to typical trading price movement, as shown in Figure 15.1.

Figure 15.1

The use of zones helps identify resistance and support in situations such as this, as well as clearly identifying the nature of a breakout. This was signaled in late August with a single session displaying an unusually long lower shadow. Although the shadow remained within range, it

> **Key Point**
> Identifying resistance or support zones may make it easier to decide where price range actually exists.

revealed a weakness among sellers, anticipating a breakout to the upside, which did occur one month later.

The many instances of interim reversal make the point about proximity. The consolidation range was characterized by offsetting tests of resistance and support, versus periods of reversal comfortably within range. The period of mid-March through the end of April, for example, saw reversals of 2.5 points numerous times. However, the price level remained in midrange and more than 2 points from either zone. In this chart, the interim range reversals were weak because the price proximity was also weak.

In every instance where price reached resistance or support zones, daily trading range increased to as much as 3 points. However, because price failed in each case to break through either zone border, consolidation held. This is a demonstration of one form of strength and weakness in reversal signals based on proximity.

Dynamic Trading Range Patterns

The typical trading range is strong. This means that reversal signals at or near resistance and support carry greater weight. At the same time, once price does break through, a reversal back into range is the most likely outcome. Eventually, all trading ranges give way to new dynamic trading either above or below; however, in the short term, the range tends to rule and gives order to the price pattern.

This means that hedges can be timed to protect equity positions against sudden moves in price. When support holds strongly, the hedge against downside market risk is of less concern. When resistance holds over time, it indicates a stronger likelihood of a coming price decline. In a sense, the failure of price to move outside of the established range indicates more likely movement in the opposite direction. So strong support indicates a bullish tendency, and strong resistance points to a bearish move in the future.

For example, on the chart of Church & Dwight in Figure 15.2, support held over the entire period as resistance gradually rose. However, on two occasions, price levels moved above resistance and then retreated. These failed breakouts confirm the strength of resistance.

Figure 15.2

It is noteworthy that volume spikes accompanied the larger movements in price, especially during and preceding the breakout periods. Volume spikes can identify either opportunity or danger, depending on price behavior at the same time, and on what types of signals emerge.

Proximity as a Measurement of Strength

Key Point

Reversal and confirmation normally are stronger when in close proximity to resistance and support, and tend to be weaker at mid-range.

The likelihood of breakout relies on the strength of a reversal signal followed by strong confirmation. A mid-range reversal signal is weak, meaning less likelihood (but no certainty) of a change in the range. However, when reversal leads to immediate breakout, it is likely to succeed if strongly confirmed by other signals. This further indicates the timing and placement of effective hedging strategies.

For example, the four-month chart of Canadian Imperial Bank (CM) shown in Figure 15.3 begins with a narrow trading range and a bullish reversal that occurs with a breakout below support. This is one of the strongest forms of proximity for a bullish move. The failure of price to hold below support points the way to strong moves to higher levels. The bullish piercing lines is the initial reversal, and this is immediately confirmed with a series of price gaps, moving above resistance.

Figure 15.3

The move sets up a new consolidation trend lasting nearly two months. This concludes in a similar pattern with proximity to support. The bearish harami cross leads to a move of price strongly below support and characterized by repetitive gaps.

Both of these patterns, the same type of breakout, located in proximity to the edges of the trading range, lead to strong breakout. Recognizing this pattern also identifies the timing for effective hedges. Once the first and second gaps appeared in late September, it looked like a bullish trend was starting above resistance. This would be a good point to close any short calls or to open long calls, anticipating a new bullish trend. By mid-October, the daily range narrowed, pointing to an end to the price move.

When the bearish harami appeared, it pointed to a possible bearish breakout. However, this was not confirmed until the second gap, which moved below support. This would have been a good point for a long put to hedge the equity price, or even to open a covered call in anticipation of the price decline.

Applying Hedges to Recognized Patterns

The entire concept of hedging, you may recall, is based on applying one set of strategies (options) to reduce or eliminate risk on portfolio positions. Without this hedge, every investor is at the mercy of unknown market forces. No one anticipates big corrections, and no one knows how far they go or which stocks will be affected.

Hedging for its own sake is no better than just buying shares of stock and hoping for the best. A hedge is effective only if and when it is based on recognized patterns

> **Key Point**
> Awareness of proximity helps decide which hedge works best, based on the most likely price behavior to follow.

seen in the price of the underlying stock. This applies to even the most basic hedge. For example, opening a covered call when a stock's price is at a bottom is ill-advised. When the stock price rises, the call goes in the money and is at risk of being exercised. Proponents of the strategy argue that as long as the strike is higher than the basis, this is an acceptable outcome. Even if this is true, why open the covered call at the *wrong* proximity?

It makes more sense to open the covered call at the top of the price swing. If and when the underlying price declines, the call is closed at a profit or allowed to expire. Meanwhile, the shares of stock cover the risk and you continue earning dividends. Then, at the bottom of the swing, different strategies are employed, such as short puts. This version of hedging is timed to exploit the cyclical price swings, but it relies on pattern recognition and reversal signals.

Another example is the frustrating but common consolidation pattern. Investors tend to be impatient. They want action, and they want to see profits accumulate quickly. (Losses also accumulate quickly with high volatility, of course.) However, in consolidation, prices are range-bound, often for several months. So impatient investors are likely to sell shares during consolidation, even at a loss, and look for more volatility elsewhere. This occurs even when the underlying stock remains a sound investment with strong fundamentals. There is a solution to this inactivity, and it does not include selling positions. Specific hedges work in this situation.

> **Key Point**
> Strategies (like short straddles) often labeled as high risk may in fact be the most conservative. It all depends on how and where they are used.

The covered straddle is one of the most effective hedges. It combines a covered call with an uncovered put. Some will point to a short straddle as high risk, but this position is one of the lowest-risk hedges possible. The covered call is conservative and the uncovered put has the same market risk; in consolidation, whether price trends upward or downward, one of the two sides will lose value and can be closed at a profit or allowed to expire worthless. Recognized breakout patterns point to the best timing for closing one or both sides of the straddle, or rolling forward to avoid exercise. It is, once again, all a matter of proximity. Recognizing how price behavior changes when it is close to resistance or support, and then acting on discovered reversal and confirmation signals, ensures that the timing will work for you. In this situation, the hedge not only protects equity positions, but uses them to generate added income with very little added risk. This is the best possible form of hedge.

The hedge takes many forms, and each contains its own element of risk. However, in order to accept the premise that hedging improves profits while reducing risks, several popular assumptions have to be examined. These include:

1. **Long-term investors should not make short-term trades.** To the contrary, short-term hedge trades are effective at reducing and controlling market risk. The idea that conservative investors should just buy value stocks and forget about them is a reckless and dangerous form of advice. The once-popular blue chip stocks that have fallen out of favor and even gone into bankruptcy cannot be ignored. Companies like General Motors and Eastman Kodak once were considered the best investments available; but nothing is a certainty.

   A wiser and safer method is to find high-quality investments based on strong and long-lasting fundamentals; buy shares and monitor the fundamentals continuously; and hedge market risk with conservative option-based strategies.

2. **Contrarian investing is high risk. The majority is usually right.** In spite of evidence against this belief, it persists. The majority is wrong more often than it is right, and when investors follow majority thinking (the "crowd mentality") it is a dangerous decision. Because emotions such as greed and panic rule market thinking, far too many investors buy high and sell low, instead of doing the opposite.

   Contrarian investing is not a reference to only doing the opposite of the majority. It is a method for determining *why* to buy or sell, based on cold analysis rather than on gut reaction, emotion, or wishful thinking.

3. **Consolidation is a pause between trends, a period when no one knows what to do.** This is another popular belief, and investors not yet in positions tend to wait until consolidation ends before putting cash into positions. This means many opportunities are lost. By failing to recognize consolidation as a third type of trend (sideways rather than up or down), those opportunities are lost.

   A related belief is that no reversals can be found because there is no trend to reverse. However, if you change the definition of reversal to movement away from consolidation and into a dynamic trend, it is easy to spot signals and confirmation for timely trades.

4. **An entry point is "zero."** Although few people say it out loud, some investors view their entry price as a zero point. They expect equity values to rise from that price forward. So if price falls, they are taken by surprise. Everyone knows that any price is part of an unending series of movements every day. However, with the unstated belief that stock prices will rise, too many people are taken by surprise when things don't work out as they assumed.

   This reality points to the essential nature of proximity. By recognizing price behavior at mid-range compared to how it changes as it moves into proximity with resistance or support, better-timed decisions are possible in all types of trends. Reversal and confirmation also are more reliable at close proximity to the resistance and support levels, improving timing of equity trades as well as hedges.

5. **Diversification is a smart management method.** This basic idea makes some sense, but excessive diversification is a mistake. It is an admission that risk cannot be avoided, which is not true. Using hedging strategies is more effective at mitigating market risk than just spreading risks among many different products. Excessive diversification through mutual funds or ETFs makes the point: When you rely too heavily on diversification, you cannot expect a better return than the average of the portfolio, including the best and the worst. The same argument applies to asset allocation, which is simply a different name for the same idea but based on industry sectors rather than on individual stocks.

   Most investors can create effective net returns in a less-diversified portfolio of well-chosen value investments, especially if those positions are protected with conservative hedges. Options used in this manner are not high risk, but actually are more conservative than trying to beat the averages by relying too much on diversification.

6. **Options are too risky for conservative investors.** A thoughtful analysis of options strategies reveals the truth: Some strategies are designed as speculative plays, intended to time the markets to exploit price movement—even when there is no equity portfolio involved. Speculators often rely on options to leverage capital, and they often are less concerned with risk, believing that a few good trades (or lucky trades?) make up for high risks.

Other strategies, which have been described in this book, are designed for the most conservative purpose, protecting a portfolio of equity positions against market risk. So creating current income or setting up low-cost or no-cost hedges creates the effective safety net that every stock market investor wants. The solution is not based on wise stock selection or broad diversification, but on timing and proximity, emphasis on the fundamentals for long-term growth, focus on high-dividend companies, and faithful application of options strategies based on the specific conditions and the current proximity of price to resistance and support.

• • • • •

Key Point

An effective hedging strategy begins and ends with stock selection. The fundamentals determine the health of your equity portfolio

The selection of a company for your portfolio is a starting point. The desirability of holding positions for the long term does not mean applying a "get and forget" strategy, but demands constant monitoring. If strong fundamentals turn weak, it is time to close out equity positions and look elsewhere. Option hedging works most effectively when used for equity positions in companies with strong long-term fundamentals. At the very least, this should include analysis and comparison of dividends, P/E ratio, revenue and earnings, and long-term debt trends.

Once you have created a strong portfolio of exceptional companies and their stocks, the option hedge is the effective measure of risk reduction and elimination. The same hedge positions are also used effectively to time trades after exaggerated short-term price movement, or to enter a safe and thoughtful recovery strategy. There are no certainties in the market, but the combination of high-quality investments and well-designed hedges reduces the uncertainty that every investor faces.

Glossary

1-2-3 iron butterfly: A strategy employing three strikes for a series of butterflies, with an increasing number of options positions at each strike.

1-2-3 iron condor: A condor with three strikes, with the middle expiration a reverse iron condor; and with each subsequent expiration, the number of contracts is increased.

American style: The type of option most common for underlying stock in the U.S. markets. An American option can be exercised at any time.

Annualize: A process of restating a net return as if the position were open for one full year; this is necessary to make valid comparisons between two or more options trades with dissimilar periods.

Ask: The price a buyer pays for buying an option.

Asset allocation: A strategy intended to balance risks among several different products, such as equities (stocks), debt (bonds), and commodities.

Automatic exercise: A procedure by which all options in the money are exercised at expiration.

Basis: The price used to calculate a return, which for options trades may be the cost of stock, current market value of stock, or the strike of the option.

Bear spread: A spread designed to increase in value when the underlying price falls.

Beta: A measurement of how closely a stock's price follows or responds to the overall market. A beta of 1.0 is held by a stock that moves the same as the market. Higher beta indicates higher volatility.

Bid: The price a seller receives for selling an option.

Bollinger squeeze: Within a range of Bollinger Bands, the tendency for prices to move close to either upper or lower band and to narrow considerably, which often occurs just before a period of increased volatility.

Box spread: A combination of call and put vertical spreads to create a bullish or a bearish combination.

Boxed synthetic stock: A hedge combining a synthetic long and synthetic short stock, opened at the same time. It offsets price movement in both directions.

Bull spread: A spread designed to increase in value when the underlying price rises.

Butterfly: A spread strategy using calls, puts, or both, with three strikes; the butterfly can also be either long or short, depending on selection of options at each strike.

Calendar straddle: A variation of the straddle in which an earlier-expiring short straddle is combined with a later-expiring long straddle.

Call: An option granting its owner the right to buy 100 shares of stock at a fixed price or a specific stock, by or before expiration date.

Call bear spread: A credit spread combining a long out-of-the-money call with a lower-strike in-the-money call.

Call bull spread: A debit spread combining a long in-the-money call with a higher-strike short out-of-the-money short call.

Collar: A three-part strategy combining long stock, a short call, and a long put. Both options are out of the money. The collar is designed to limit profit and loss without cost.

Condor: A strategy with four options and four strikes, offering limited profit and limited loss, working as an effective hedge for low-volatility stocks.

Confirmation bias: A tendency to find confirmation of a previously set assumption, even when opposite signals are plentiful.

Conformity risk: The risk associated with following the majority of the market, and of making decisions with the majority rather than based on logic and analysis.

Conservative: An investor who bases investment decisions on analysis of risk and with the idea of reducing risk while maximizing return.

Consolidation trend: A trend moving sideways within a narrow price range, with neither buyers nor sellers able to move price beyond its current range.

Constructive sale: A tax rule defining some offsetting positions as taxable even though there was no sale. This applies to some options positions.

Contingent purchase: The use of a long call to fix the price for a future purchase at the strike, which may or may not come to pass depending on price behavior.

Contingent sale: The use of a long put to fix the price for a future sale at the strike.

Continuation: A tendency for a trend to continue in the same direction until a reversal signal appears. This tendency is confirmed through continuation signals.

Contrarian: An investor who times trades based on logic and analysis rather than emotion, acting unlike the majority in the market.

Contrarian investing: The practice of making investment decisions based on logic rather than on emotion, and acting contrary to the prevailing market tendency to trade based on emotions.

Covered call: A basic option hedge in which a call is sold against 100 shares of stock. In exchange for receiving a premium, the call writer may be required to sell stock at the fixed strike.

Covered straddle: A bullish conservative strategy combining 100 shares of stock, a covered call, and an uncovered put, using the same strike and expiration.

Credit spread: A spread yielding more income from the short side than the cost for the long side.

Debit spread: Any spread with the long side costing more than the premium received for the offsetting short side.

Debt capitalization ratio: A fundamental indicator identifying the percentage of total capitalization represented by long-term debt, versus stockholders' equity.

Deep in the money: An option far from current value of the underlying stock, usually 5 points or more.

Delta: A measurement of changes in an option's premium in relation to changes in the underlying stock.

Diagonal ratio spread: A diagonal spread employing different numbers of short and long options.

Diagonal roll: A forward roll to a higher or lower strike, intended to decrease exercise risk or to improve capital gains in the event of exercise.

Diagonal spread: A spread with different expirations and different strikes.

Diversification: Spreading investment capital among several dissimilar products in order to manage risks, on the theory that the overall return will be greater than the return on any one investment.

Dividend yield: The percentage of a dividend per share, calculated by dividing the annual dollar amount of the declared dividend, by the current price per share.

Dow Theory: A set of beliefs concerning price behavior, based on the writings of Charles Dow, co-founder of the Dow Jones Company.

Early exercise: The action of exercising a long call or put before the last trading day.

Earnings surprise: An earnings outcome that is not the same as analysts' expectations. This surprise often results in short-term exaggerated price reaction.

Eastern technical signals: Broad description of reversal and continuation signals based on price patterns found in candlesticks indicators.

Efficient market hypothesis (EMH): A belief that stock prices reflect all known information at all times.

European style: An option for which exercise can occur only at the end of the option's life, on a predetermined date or range of dates.

Exchange-traded fund (ETF): A mutual fund with a predetermined basket of securities, which trades like a stock and may also offer options trading. An inverse ETF becomes profitable when the basket of securities declines in value; a leveraged ETF multiplies the effect of profit or loss based on the basket of securities.

Exercise: The act by an owner of an option to call 100 shares from a call seller, or to put 100 shares to the put seller. This action is controlled by the option's owner, who will choose to exercise when that is profitable.

Exercise hedge: A trade that hedges against exercise rather than against market risk.

Expiration date: The fixed month and date on which every option expires. Expiration date is the third Saturday in expiration month, and the last trading day is the third Friday.

Extrinsic value: Alternative term for implied volatility (IV).

Forward roll: Closing to buy an existing short position and replacing it with a later-expiring one, with the same strike or a higher strike.

Fundamental volatility: The degree of reliability in fundamental trends over time, used to determine fundamental risk levels for a company.

Gamma: A Greek that measures the degree of change in Delta, useful in spotting responsiveness of option pricing to underlying stock movement.

Greeks: A set of calculations defining option price and volatility levels in relation to the underlying stock.

Hedge matrix: An arrangement of multiple legs to a single strategy, designed to take advantage of price movement so that profits are realized in either price direction.

Hedging: Any form of investment made to offset or reduce the risk of loss in another position. For example, an option may hedge a stock position so that a loss in the stock is offset by a profit in the option.

Historical volatility: The level of volatility based on price movement over time and within a range of trading; a basic test of risk.

Horizontal spread: A spread consisting of two options with the same strike but different expiration months.

Implied volatility (IV): The portion of option premium that changes based on the historical volatility of the underlying stock and is also affected by time remaining until expiration.

Informationally efficient: An attribute in EMH reflecting efficient pricing, but not always accurate interpretation of information.

Intrinsic value: The portion of an option's premium equal to the number of points in the money.

Iron butterfly: A butterfly employing both calls and puts, consisting of four different options and three strikes.

Iron condor: A condor employing both calls and puts with four strikes.

Island cluster: A series of trades occurring after a gap out of range and concluding with a new gap back into range.

Leverage: A method for duplicating opportunity or risk with a reduced amount of capital. For example, every option controls 100 shares of stock for a small percentage of the cost of stock.

Long: Status for an investor who has bought an option, following the sequence "buy-hold-sell."

Long condor: A condor consisting of calls, a long ITM, a long ITM, a long OTM, and a short OTM.

Long straddle: A straddle consisting of the same number of long calls and long puts, with the same strike and expiration.

Long strap: A strap using long calls in greater numbers than long puts; a speculative expansion of the long straddle.

Long strip: A strip using long puts in greater numbers than long calls; a speculative expansion of the long straddle.

Lost opportunity risk: In a covered call position, the risk that the underlying stock's price will rise above the call's strike, and potential added profits will be lost due to exercise of the in-the-money position.

Magical thinking: A set of beliefs that adhering to some form of ritual leads to positive outcomes, even when the outcomes are not related to the rituals.

Market risk: The risk faced by investors that a position will lose value rather than gaining, resulting in either paper losses or realized losses.

Married put: A position involving a long put opened as insurance for 100 shares of stock held in the portfolio. The put protects against losses below its strike price.

Moneyness: The relationship between the underlying stock price and the strike price of an option.

Net basis: In a covered call, the net cost of stock, discounted by premium received for selling the call.

Net return: The percentage derived when dividing net earnings by revenue.

Offsetting position: Description in tax law of straddle legs, in which a loss on one may not be deductible until the other side has also been closed.

Payout ratio: The percentage of earnings used to pay dividends, best analyzed over a period of time to determine whether the use of earnings for dividends is rising or falling.

Perfect hedge: A hedge in which the cost of one side is exactly the same as the benefit on the other side, so that the net outcome is no gain and no loss.

Pinning the strike: A tendency for underlying stock prices to move toward the closest option strike in the last few days prior to option expiration.

Premium: The price of an option that a buyer pays or a seller receives; expressed at price per share without dollar signs, premium translates to dollar value at 100 times higher (for example, a premium of 1.25 is equal to $125).

Price spread: The difference between bid and ask of an option.

Put: An option granting its owner the right to sell 100 shares of stock at a fixed price or a specific stock, by or before expiration date.

Put bear spread: A two-part position consisting of a long put with a lower-strike short put, with the combination creating a net credit.

Put bull spread: A credit spread combining a long out-of-the-money put with a higher-strike short in-the-money put.

Random walk hypothesis (RWH): A belief that price movement is random and that it is not possible to beat market averages consistently.

Ratio calendar spread: A horizontal spread consisting of dissimilar numbers of short options and later-expiring long options sharing the same strike.

Ratio combination calendar spread: A single strategy combining the call-based and put-based ratio calendar spreads, opened at the same time, and usually involving out-of-the money strikes on both sides.

Ratio write: A variation of the covered call combining a greater number of calls than are covered by long stock.

Reconstituted hedge: A form of recovery strategy that consists of extended expirations and modified strikes, to offset current losses.

Recovery strategy: A trade intended to offset a prior loss by recapturing value through a subsequent trade.

Resistance: The highest price level in the trading range, identifying the price at which buyers are willing to buy.

Reversal: The tendency of all trends to eventually end and move in a different direction, either dynamic (bullish or bearish) or consolidation (sideways).

Reverse iron butterfly: A butterfly employing both calls and puts, but with out of the money short and middle-range long options.

Reverse iron condor: A condor with the long and short sides of the condor opened in reverse.

Risk: Exposure to loss, a threat, or a possible negative outcome, which may be reduced or eliminated with specific options hedging strategies.

Risk awareness: Knowledge about a range of risk involved with initial and recovery strategies, and the levels of risk involved with a series of decisions.

Rolling down: A forward roll on a diagonal, replacing a current strike with a later-expiring lower strike.

Rolling up: A forward roll on a diagonal pattern, replacing a current strike with a later-expiring higher strike.

Round trip cost: The cost to complete both sides of an options trade, entering and then exiting a position.

Short: Status for an investor who has sold an option, following the sequence "sell-hold-buy."

Short condor: A condor reversing the positions of the long condor.

Short straddle: A straddle consisting of an equal number of short calls and short puts, opened with the same strike and expiration.

Short strap: A strap using short calls in greater numbers than short puts; an expansion of the long straddle hedge.

Short strip: A strap using short puts in greater numbers than short calls; an expansion of the long straddle hedge.

Speculative hedge: A form of hedge that increases market risk in the hope that a loss can be offset with a higher-risk position.

Speculator: A trader willing to take high risks in the desire to out-perform typical net returns.

Spread: A position combining two options that offset one another in one of several configurations.

Standardized terms: The four terms defining an option by its characteristics, which apply to every listed option and cannot be altered or exchanged.

Straddle: An option position combining call and puts with the same strike and expiration, both either long or short.

Strap: A variation of the straddle combining more calls with fewer puts.

Strike price: The fixed price at which every option can be exercised, regardless of price movement in the underlying stock.

Strip: A variation of the straddle combining more puts with fewer calls.

Support: The lowest price level in the trading range, identifying the price at which sellers are willing to sell.

Synthetic long stock: A hedge combining a long call with a short call at the same strike; it duplicates price movement in the underlying and performs best when the underlying price advances.

Synthetic short put: Alternate name for the covered call. Combining 100 shares of stock and one short call creates a position that behaves exactly like an uncovered put.

Synthetic short stock: A hedge combining a long put with a short call, with the same strike; it duplicates price movement in the underlying and performs best when the underlying price declines.

Synthetic stock: A position set up using options that duplicates price movement in the underlying stock, point for point—but with less market risk.

Theta: A Greek that measures the rate of time decay for specific options.

Time decay: The decline in time value as expiration approaches, which is accelerates toward the end of the option's life.

Time value: The portion of an option's premium related directly to the time remaining until expiration.

Total capitalization: The combination of long-term debt and stockholders' equity, the overall capital valuation of a company.

Total return: A calculation of net returns combining option yield with dividend yield. The rationalize is that stocks may be selected for option trades based at least in part on dividend yield.

Trend: A tendency for change over time to continue in one direction until it concludes; this is applicable to fundamental as well as to technical outcomes.

Underlying security: The stock or other security to which every option is tied, which cannot be changed.

Unqualified covered call: A call whose deep in-the-money status tolls the period leading to qualification for long-term tax rates.

Variable ratio write: An expansion of the covered call in which more calls are written than can be covered with stock, but using two different strikes.

Vega: A measurement of changes in an option's premium caused by implied volatility (IV). It may be used to measure the speed of volatility collapse during the final month of the option's life.

Vertical spread: A spread made up of two options with the same expiration date and different strikes.

Volatility: The degree of uncertainty in pricing of an asset, as a reflection of price and market risk. Stock volatility affects an option's volatility, because greater uncertainty equals greater potential profit or loss.

Volatility collapse: The tendency for volatility tracking to become unreliable during the final month of the option's life. During this month, the tracking mechanisms such as Delta cannot be used to spot changes in volatility.

Wash sale: The rule preventing deduction of a loss when a sale and replacement occur within 30 days.

Western technical signals: A set of technical price-based indicators used to identify reversal or confirmation.

Zone of resistance or support: A price range identifying resistance or support, rather than a single price level.

Bibliography

Augen, Jeff. *Trading Options at Expiration* (Upper Saddle River, N.J.: FT Press, 2009).

———. *Day Trading Options* (Upper Saddle River, N.J.: FT Press, 2010).

Bittman, James B. *Trading Index Options* (New York: McGraw-Hill, 1998).

Cohen, Guy. *The Insider Edge* (Hoboken, N.J.: John Wiley & Sons, 2012).

Gidel, Susan Abbott. *Stock Index & Futures Options* (Hoboken, N.J.: John Wiley & Sons, 2000).

Hull, John C. *Options, Futures and Other Derivatives*, 8th edition (Boston, Mass.: Prentice Hall, 2012).

Kobayashi-Solomon, Erik. *The Intelligent Option Investor* (New York: McGraw-Hill, 2014).

Kolb, Robert W., and James A. Overdahl. *Financial Derivatives*, 3rd edition (Hoboken, N.J.: John Wiley & Sons, 2003).

McMillan, Lawrence G. *Options as a Strategic Investment*, 4th edition (New York: New York Institute of Finance, 2002).

Natenberg, Sheldon. *Option Volatility & Pricing* (New York: McGraw-Hill, 1994).

Overby, Brian. *The Options Playbook*, 2nd edition (Charlotte, N.C.: TradeKing, 2009).

Rhoads, Russell. *Trading VIX Derivatives* (Hoboken, N.J.: John Wiley & Sons, 2011).

Sincere, Michael. *Understanding Options*, 2nd edition (New York: McGraw-Hill, 2014).

Index

About the Author

Michael C. Thomsett is author of 12 options books. He has been trading options since 1978 and has worked as a full-time author since 1984. He has also written extensively on the topics of technical analysis and candlestick charting. Thomsett is a frequent speaker at The Money Show, Trader's Expo, and other investment seminars. He also teaches options courses with Moody's and other institutions. The author lives near Nashville, Tennessee.